FIRESIDE
PARKSIDE

FIRESIDE PARKSIDE BOOKS

Addictionary: A Primer of Recovery Terms and Concepts from Abstinence to Withdrawal, by Jan R. Wilson, C.E.D.C., C.A.P., and Judith A. Wilson, C.A.P.

Anatomy of a Food Addiction: The Brain Chemistry of Overeating, by Anne Katherine, M.A.

Behind the 8-Ball: A Guide for Families of Gamblers, by Linda Berman, M.S.W., and Mary-Ellen Siegel, M.S.W.

Believing in Myself: Daily Meditations for Healing and Building Self-Esteem, by Earnie Larsen and Carol Hegarty

Blues Ain't Nothing But a Good Soul Feeling Bad: Daily Steps to Spiritual Growth, by Sheldon Kopp with Bonnie B. Hesse

Codependents' Guide to the Twelve Steps, by Melody Beattie

Compassionate Touch: The Role of Human Touch in Healing and Recovery, by Dr. Clyde W. Ford

Freedom from Food: The Secret Lives of Dieters and Compulsive Eaters, by Elizabeth Hampshire

From Love That Hurts to Love That's Real: A Recovery Workbook, by Sylvia Ogden Peterson

Growing Through the Pain: The Incest Survivor's Companion, by Catherine Bronson

Growing Up Gay in a Dysfunctional Family: A Guide for Gay Men Reclaiming Their Lives, by Rik Isensee

Help for Helpers: Daily Meditations for Those Who Care

Hooked on Exercise: How to Understand and Manage Exercise Addiction, by Rebecca Prussin, M.D., Philip Harvey, Ph.D., and Theresa Foy DiGeronimo

Meditations for Men Who Do Too Much, by Jonathon Lazear

Meditations for Parents Who Do Too Much, by Jonathon and Wendy Lazear

Reclaiming Our Days: Meditations for Incest Survivors, by Helena See

Repressed Memories: A Journey to Recovery from Sexual Abuse, by Renee Frederickson, Ph.D.

Sex and Sobriety: Facing the Fear and Building a New Sexual Life, by Jack Mumey

Soul Survivors: A New Beginning for Adults Abused as Children, by J. Patrick Gannon, Ph.D.

Understanding the Twelve Steps: An Interpretation and Guide for Recovering People, by Terence T. Gorski

GETTING
LOVE
RIGHT

Learning the
Choices
of Healthy
Intimacy

TERENCE T. GORSKI

A FIRESIDE BOOK/PARKSIDE BOOK
Published by Simon & Schuster
New York London Toronto Sydney
Tokyo Singapore

FIRESIDE/PARKSIDE
SIMON & SCHUSTER BUILDING
ROCKEFELLER CENTER
1230 AVENUE OF THE AMERICAS
NEW YORK, NEW YORK 10020

COPYRIGHT © 1993 TERENCE T. GORSKI

DESIGNED BY SONGHEE KIM
MANUFACTURED IN THE UNITED STATES OF AMERICA

1 3 5 7 9 10 8 6 4 2

LIBRARY OF CONGRESS CATALOGING-IN-PUBLICATION
DATA IS AVAILABLE

ISBN: 0-671-86415-7

PARKSIDE MEDICAL SERVICES CORPORATION IS A FULL-SERVICE
PROVIDER OF TREATMENT FOR ALCOHOLISM, OTHER DRUG
ADDICTION, EATING DISORDERS, AND PSYCHIATRIC ILLNESS.

PARKSIDE MEDICAL SERVICES CORPORATION
205 WEST TOUHY AVENUE
PARK RIDGE, IL 60068
1-800-PARKSIDE

ACKNOWLEDGMENTS

This book would not have been possible without the help and support of a number of key people in my life. My lifelong friend, Joe Trioani, provided invaluable support during the writing process.

Janet Voss, Executive Director of Cenaps Corporation, kept my business running while I was preoccupied with writing. Her support in maintaining day-to-day operations was invaluable. Karen Plath helped extensively by dedicating literally weeks of her life to typing and retyping revisions of this book.

There are four special people I wish to thank. My literary agents, Candace Fuhrman and Theo Gund, made it all possible. They listened to a tape of a lecture on intimacy and recovery, became excited about the concept, and aggressively sought me out. Without their vision, encouragement, and at times outright pressure, this book would never have been written.

Two editors, Carol Ranalli and Barbara S. Brauer, provided invaluable assistance and rescued me from one of the worst cases of writer's block I have ever experienced. With their help, the manuscript was radically revised and reorganized into the form that you now see.

Most of all, I would like to acknowledge the thousands of people in this nation who have decided to break the cycle of dysfunctional intimacy. It is only through the widespread support of twelve-step recovery programs and other self-help groups that this book is possible. Without the interest and excitement generated by my initial lectures, I would never have written *Getting Love Right*.

CONTENTS

III. Learning to Change

INTRODUCTION

On January 17, 1987, more than 600 people crowded a convention center in San Diego, California to hear me speak. The group was different from any I had addressed before. Many sat clutching Teddy bears. Some appeared alone and lost in their thoughts, while others talked openly and enthusiastically with one another. What they shared in common was an inability to make their love relationships work. They had come to this lecture for one reason: to learn how to get love right.

As I stood behind the podium looking out at the audience, I asked myself, "How can I reach them? How can I say something that can make a difference?"

I was uncomfortable because I felt I was essentially there by accident. Counseling and lecturing on intimacy and relationship building was not my chosen profession. I received my formal training as a counselor in chemical addiction and specialized in the treatment of relapse-prone people—chemically dependent individuals who, no matter how hard they try, just can't stay sober. My work in relapse prevention had led me to the discovery that a lot of people who relapse do so because of problems with relationship and intimacy issues. As I worked with these clients and their spouses or partners, I developed techniques to help them understand and overcome the unique relationship style that recovering chemically dependent people seem to have.

I worked with this model over a number of years both as a supervisor of other therapists and as a therapist in my own private practice. I didn't think the skills and concepts I had developed were anything very special or unique. I was simply working with what patients were telling me about their relationships and the problem solving they did in therapy.

In 1984, I was traveling around the country lecturing about relapse prevention as well as talking a little about relationships, but relationships were not my major focus. Then Fate intervened in the person of Donna Marie Swain. I was scheduled to speak at a conference at Scripps Hospital in San Diego. Donna Marie, in charge of the conference schedule, called and asked me to do a keynote talk on intimacy.

I explained that I worked on chemical dependency and on relapse; I didn't do intimacy. I didn't have any interest in doing intimacy because I didn't think I had anything to contribute in that area.

The next thing I knew, Donna Marie had mailed out 35,000 brochures announcing that I was doing a luncheon keynote address on intimacy. Caught in what seemed to be a no-win situation, I brought out my old notes, went to San Diego, stood up, and did a forty-five-minute keynote speech on intimacy. I said, "This is dysfunctional intimacy, this is healthy intimacy. Here's how you get from here to there." I sat down and I forgot about it.

Unknown to me, that lecture was audio-taped by a professional company and was offered for sale. Overnight that tape was duplicated and spread throughout southern California.

Two years later, I was home in Chicago continuing my work in relapse prevention, completely unaware of the tape. I received a call from the San Diego Chapter of Adult Children of Alcoholics. They were planning their first annual ACA conference. The woman said, "We'd really like you to speak at our conference."

I said, "Thank you very much, but I'm not recovering in ACA. I think you've got the wrong Terry Gorski."

"Well, we don't want you to do a recovery talk. We want you to do your lecture on intimacy.'"

I said, "You don't understand. I don't do intimacy."

She said, "Well, we've got this wonderful tape. We want you to do that presentation."

I said, "What tape? I don't know that I have tape out. It's probably not me."

She sent me a copy of the tape and then I remembered the lecture. I said, "Of course I'll come and talk to the conference. I'd be honored to do that."

So there I was, in San Diego in January 1987, speaking at the first ACA conference. It, too, was recorded and, since that time, the tape has spread throughout the world. In a few short years, to my amazement, the concepts and original model I presented then have become widely recognized and well received. The irony is that I spent years working to get relapse prevention installed in the consciousness of the chemical dependency field and, twenty years later, it's finally starting to happen. I do one keynote on intimacy and it reaches thousands and thousands of people in a few years.

RELATIONSHIPS 101

What is it about intimacy that people so desperately want to know? As I began to consider what I saw around me, I realized that people everywhere are starving for information on how to get love right. I began to understand that, as much as we may want and need healthy intimate relationships, many of us have never learned the skills necessary to develop them. Most of us received more training in how to drive a car than in how to select a partner and build a healthy relationship.

Our fundamental knowledge of intimacy is formed in our family of origin from our earliest years. Parents can teach children only what they know, however, and show them how to do what they do. If our parents were practitioners of destructive love, that's all they were able to teach us. Men and women raised in a dysfunctional family by parents who never learned how to get love right conduct their relationships in the same manner their parents did.

This is the sad reality for many people. The collective legacy of a dysfunctional upbringing is reflected in the nation's skyrocketing divorce rate and an epidemic of failed love relationships. The individual victims of this epidemic can be found everywhere. Singles bars teem with these men and women every night. Recovery centers and psychotherapy clinics rush to meet their needs. Each and every sufferer, and they number in the millions, is battling the same demon, loneliness. These people are actively seeking the information they need to win this battle, transform their dysfunctional relationships into healthy, satisfying ones, and acquire the skills they need to get love right.

Other people were more fortunate. They grew up in households in which healthy intimacy was demonstrated on a daily basis. As a result, they naturally learned basic skills of communication, caring, and commitment. They, too, attend my workshops and lectures. They know that love relationships can be more than good or just satisfactory. They come to learn how to deepen and enhance their existing relationship or to build more fulfilling relationships in the future.

Many of these men and women are discovering that what their parents taught them about relationships and healthy choices doesn't work satisfactorily in today's society. In the last thirty years, we have seen tremendous changes in our social environment and the ways in which individuals choose to build their relationships. The sexual revolution and the advent of AIDS have altered forever the way men and women conduct their sexual relationships. In our parents' time, a single, lifelong monogamous relationship was the norm against which people measured their relationships. Today many people find themselves in a series of committed relationships; some are forgoing marriage and/or choosing alternative family units. As a result, many of the choices and relationship goals our parents passed on to us are insufficient to guide us in our relationships today.

This book is designed to teach you what you need to know to get love right; it's what your parents should have taught you but probably never did. Whether you never experienced healthy intimacy in your family of origin and have never been able to build a healthy, satisfying relationship, or whether you have had some success in your relationships but want to make them better, the principles and skills presented in this book will help you build the relationship you want. I have written it to be a comprehensive course on intimacy, including the models and guidelines that have worked so well for so many people over the last ten years and more.

This book answers the questions I am frequently asked as I travel around the country lecturing and leading workshops: Where do I find a partner? Are my standards realistic? How do I know when to make a commitment? How do I know if I should settle for what I have or look for something better? How do I go about meeting my sexual needs in a time when AIDS is a risk?

This book begins with a Background and Overview to help you understand the nature and source of dysfunctional patterns and behaviors that may be keeping you in cycles of painful relationships. It will also help you understand answers to the questions: What is healthy intimacy? What is dysfunctional intimacy? Part II, Building a Healthy Relationship, takes you through the practical sequences of relationship building. Learning to Change discusses how to transform your relationship and how to evaluate whether your relationship is meeting your needs.

Perhaps one of the most important questions I'm asked comes from the many gay and lesbian couples and individuals attending my lectures and workshops. They ask if the skills for building healthy intimacy are the same for homosexual, or gay/lesbian, couples as they are for heterosexual, or straight, couples. The answer is yes. Relationship choices, the selection of an appropriate partner, how to initiate, maintain, and renegotiate a relationship are all relevant to any sexual relationship.

Gay and lesbian readers should be aware, however, that there are issues beyond the scope of this book that may interfere with their ability to be intimate. It is my hope that gay/lesbian readers will read and benefit from this book and it will help them to work through the issues that affect all human love relationships, and sexual love relationships in particular. Then, I hope they will seek additional information that can help them work on other issues unique to their needs and life-style.

HOW TO CHANGE

This book is not about relationship theory but about relationship change. When you choose to invest the time and energy in your relationship to do what is necessary to abstain from dysfunctional patterns and replace them with healthy patterns, your relationships will change. They will get better. The self-assessments and questionnaires at the end of each chapter can help you make those changes.

As a lecturer and instructor, I've found that you can learn important information and gain a solid theoretical understanding of a subject and yet still be unable to make practical use of it. You need a way to personalize this information and bring it to bear on your own experience.

If you want to see positive changes in your relationships as a result of what you read in this book, you will find that the self-assessments can serve as a practical way to apply this information to your own situation. These assessments are not meant to provide quick answers to complex problems but rather to identify some of the issues you may need to address as you work to improve your relationship skills. They will help you see what you are doing in your relationships so that you can begin choosing how you want to do things differently.

These assessments serve another important purpose. I have found that most relationship self-help books do not significantly improve relationships between partners because one partner reads the information but does not communicate about it with his or her partner. The techniques and principles are not brought into the relationship in a practical way that can make a difference.

If you are in a relationship, you need to talk over what you learn with your partner, using the assessments as a practical device to initiate discussion. Complete the questionnaires yourself and ask your partner to fill them out. Then go over your answers together.

THE CHOICE IS YOURS

No matter what your relationship goals, you can choose to start a program of relationship growth and change by making a commitment to yourself to practice healthy intimacy. Relationships skills can be learned. By learning those skills, practicing them while abstaining from the old patterns you may have learned as a child, you can begin to enjoy healthy intimacy.

First, you will need reliable information. Start with this book. I know this information is reliable—I have seen it used with success by many, many people. I have seen the transformation as people make the commitment to themselves to improve their relationships. You, too, can use it to realize your full potential in the context of a healthy and productive relationship with a partner who can meet your needs.

I
BACKGROUND
AND
OVERVIEW

Chapter 1

GETTING LOVE RIGHT

According to ancient Greek mythology, human beings were originally created with both sexes, male and female, combined in one person. They were whole and complete within themselves and lived in a fulfilled state of perfect union.

Then, as human beings have a tendency to do, they angered the gods. The gods punished humanity by cutting each person in half. One half became male and the other half became female. Then the gods cursed human beings for the rest of their existence to try and become whole again by reassembling themselves.

On a fundamental level, relationships represent a search for that wholeness, a search for completeness and the ability to feel as one with another human being. In many ways, this striving for unity with another person is a fool's game. Ultimately, it is impossible to merge and stay merged with another human being. At best, we can find moments of completion, moments of closeness and oneness. But then what happens? We always come back to the reality that we are two separate individuals.

Yet, like all myths, there is a measure of truth to this one, too. When we get love right, two individuals become *us*, an entity that makes the two of us together stronger than we ever could be alone. The *me* and the *you* still remain as separate entities, however, in conjunction with *us*.

So the question becomes, How can we come together and build a relationship that creates this better us? How do we go about developing relationships that can meet our needs for wholeness and fulfillment? It is not simple, but it can be done. We can learn to share our life with another person in a way that enhances rather than diminishes who we are.

This book will demonstrate the step-by-step process involved in building and maintaining a healthy relationship. It will enable you to understand the origins of your relationship patterns, show you how to analyze them, and identify alternative behaviors so you can replace dysfunctional patterns with healthy patterns.

If you are single, *Getting Love Right* will help you learn how to develop into the kind of person who is capable of a healthy relationship; how to select an appropriate partner who can meet your needs; and how to guide your relationship through different levels and stages.

If you are currently in a relationship, *Getting Love Right* will teach you how to transform that relationship. It will provide information and assessment tools that will enable you to evaluate your present relationship and identify areas for growth. It will give you the techniques to problem-solve in a productive way and undertake a fundamental relationship renegotiation with your partner.

DECIDING ON HEALTHY LOVE

Many people experience problems in relationships because they hold mistaken beliefs about the fundamental nature of love. We have been taught since childhood to believe that love is a mysterious phenomenon beyond our control. Just look at the way we talk about it. We "fall" in love, sometimes "head over heels." We say she "stole his heart," or "she lost her heart" to him. Cupid shoots his arrow and we are powerless to resist. These myths tell us that love comes into our lives suddenly through little or no choice of our own. No wonder we are confused about how to achieve a lasting, fulfilling relationship.

Healthy love is not an accident. Nor is it a temporary feeling that comes and goes. Love is a decision we make based on essential choices about ourselves, our partner, and our relationship. While healthy love is often profound and passionate, we can build it into our lives step by step, one choice at a time.

To get love right, therefore, we need to revise our concept of love as some romanticized ideal and understand a relationship for what it is: an agreement between two people to meet each other's needs and to have their own needs met in return.

There are three common relationship errors:
1. Expecting too much from a relationship
2. Expecting too little from a relationship
3. Expecting a relationship to remain unchanged

Some people expect too much from a relationship. They hold onto the belief that the right partner or the right relationship can magically fix them and free them from taking responsibility for their lives. They expect a partner to have the ability to make them feel better on demand. As a result, they are constantly disappointed. They experience cycles of intense highs, when the relationship seems to be going well, and intense lows, when it fails to meet their unrealistic expectations.

Other people expect too little from a relationship. They are so sure they can never feel whole and complete with another human being that they never give themselves the chance to have their needs for love and intimacy met. They equate intimacy with pain and do everything they can to insulate and protect themselves from it. They do not know that there are two kinds of pain: pathological pain that comes from dysfunctional, unsafe relationships and the healthy pain of growth in normal intimate relationships.

Still others may have found a satisfying relationship, but then make the mistake of expecting it to stay the same year after year. They don't realize that relationships are not a one-time event but an ongoing process. As time goes on, both partners need to continue to talk and problem-solve together, and, when necessary, renegotiate the terms of the relationship so that it stays current with their needs.

HEALTHY RELATIONSHIPS:
PASSION AND SAFETY

Healthy relationships meet our needs for both passion and safety. Dysfunctional relationships, by contrast, represent extremes in which only one or the other exists. People who expect too much from relationships seek passion. Unfortunately, they almost always give up safety in the process and end up being hurt. People who expect too little from relationships choose safety over passion. They often lose the chance to have their needs for intimacy and passion met.

Healthy partners know that passion and safety can coexist in healthy relationships because these relationships are rational, flexible, and safe.

Healthy relationships are *rational* because you choose them. You choose the type of relationship you're ready for. Then you choose to become a person capable of being in a healthy relationship. You select your partner on the basis of a variety of characteristics and choose the rate at which the relationship develops. Ultimately, you and your partner choose whether to continue the relationship or to end it.

Built in this way, a relationship becomes a series of choices, all of which have logical consequences. If you choose as a partner someone who is incapable of meeting your needs, the logical consequence is that your partner and the relationship will not give you what you want. If you choose a dangerous partner, you can expect to have a dangerous relationship. If you choose a healthy, compatible partner who is capable and willing to meet your needs, it is logical to expect that you will have a compatible relationship in which your needs are met.

Healthy relationships are also *flexible*. They operate on a variety of levels, depending upon the needs of the partners. Sometimes they may be very exciting and intense. Other times they will be very relaxed and comfortable, even boring. Such relationships allow each partner to be flexible: You can be together as a couple or alone as individuals, according to the situation and your preference. You are not forced to be strong all the time; you are not forbidden to be strong. The flow of give and take enables you to be both strong and weak, to be yourself. This flexibility means you can be accepted as a fallible person who will make mistakes and who, in turn, is willing to accept the mistakes of your partner.

Finally, healthy relationships are *safe*. No matter how committed you are to the relationship, no matter how much you love your partner, you do not abandon who you are and your partner does not abandon who he/she is. You don't lose yourself in your partner or in the relationship. To stay in the relationship, you may make compromises if necessary, but not at the expense of your own safety or well-being. Healthy partners do not tolerate abuse and will do whatever is necessary for their own safety, even at the expense of the relationship.

Many people prize spontaneity in their relationships. They fear that by becoming conscious of the choices they make, going through a rational decision-making process, they will lose the spontaneity and passion that make love exciting. Fortunately, that is not true. Choosing safety and making sound choices allow you even greater freedom in your relationships. Once you know your partner is safe, you are free to give in to your passion and spontaneous desires. When you are able to communicate openly and honestly about who you are without fear of guilt or retribution, you don't have to hide from your partner or pretend to be something you are not. You are free to be yourself and know deep down that your partner will love and accept you.

BECOMING A CHOICE MAKER

Once you understand what healthy relationships are, you can work to create them in your life by becoming a choice maker. If you come from a dysfunctional family, you may have been taught that choices are all or nothing, yes or no, black or white. As a result, you may not have learned basic decision-making skills, which include thinking through a number of options and selecting the best one on the basis of what you want. You may find it useful to think of decision making as a three-step process, outlined by the following questions.

1. **What choices do I have?** First, you need to identify your options and the likely consequences of each choice. This will help

you see that, in most cases, your choices are not black and white but include a range of options. In examining the likely consequences of a particular option, you may discover that what feels good now may not, in the long run, be in your best interest.

2. What do I need/want? You need to know yourself well enough to assess your particular needs and wants. This includes knowing what you're thinking, what you're feeling, and what is motivating you to think, feel, and act that way.

3. Which option is best for me right now? On the basis of your answers to the first two questions, you can select the option that promises to best meet your unique needs and wants at the present time, with the realization that these needs and wants may change over time.

The more you practice this three-step process, the more experience you will gain as a choice maker. The more you apply it to your relationship choices, the better your chances to get love right.

As you consider the options available to you, keep in mind the following:

Most choices are not perfect. We can rarely get 100 percent of what we want. Many times we are afraid to make a decision because we fear making the wrong choice or having to give up one thing for another. It is important to remember that choices typically involve a trade-off. All we can do is strive to make the best choice among the options we have, based on what we know or believe to be true.

Mistakes are unavoidable. As fallible human beings, we can't always choose the best option. Once you accept the fact that you will make mistakes, you can choose to learn from them to make better and better decisions in the future.

Choices are not forever. Choice making is an ongoing process. The best option one day may be very different the next. We change, and our needs and wants change, too. We need to be prepared to reevalute and, when necessary, renegotiate and alter our decisions.

If you have had relationship problems in the past, healthy change is possible. It may be, however, that before you can begin to make healthy choices, you need to alter some fundamental aspects of the way in which you go about your relationships. Change is not easy, especially when it requires us to alter deeply ingrained patterns learned in childhood from our parents.

This book is designed to help you make those changes by giving you the tools you need to alter the way you conduct your relationships and to become a person capable of healthy love. The chapters in this book are designed to give you the concepts and models you need to answer the question, "What are my choices?"

In understanding what this book can do to help you get love right, it is important to discuss what it will not do. This book will not teach you how to have a perfect relationship. It will not teach you how to find Mr. or Ms. Right who is going to magically fix you and make all your pain and problems go away. It is not going to teach you how to transform your present relationship into some romanticized soap-opera ideal of love—because ideal love does not exist. This book is not going to give you an effective relationship overnight—because healthy love is achieved by slow stages.

Another thing this book will not do is to save you from the responsibility of thinking for yourself or making up your own mind. You need to decide what kind of relationship you should have to be happy. There are many choices available. All this book can do is to show you the skills involved in becoming a healthy choice maker and point out some of the options available, along with the logical consequences that some of those options may have.

This book will not teach you how to have a problem-free relationship, because relationships have problems. Partners are fallible human beings, and, no matter how much they love one another, they will encounter problems. What this book can do is to demonstrate concrete skills so that you can effectively practice problem solving with your partner.

Finally, this book will not save you from the pain of loving another human being. Being in love means you're going to be hurt. If you don't want to get bruised, you don't want to play football; if you don't want to fall down, you don't want to ski. The same is true for relationships: If you don't want to get emotionally hurt, you don't want to be in love. Why? Because you're going to love another fallible human being who is going to make mistakes, who is going to have faults, and who is going to inadvertently hurt you.

You, too, are a fallible human being and you're going to make mistakes. You are going to do things that hurt your partner, even if you don't want or mean to.

What this book can do is to show you how to build a relationship in which pain and disappointment are the exception, not the rule. It can show you how you can build relationships in which support, love, and mutual respect are the everyday reality, not just the dream.

Healthy relationships are possible. Through knowing the processes and steps involved in relationship building, learning to make choices, solving problems with your partner, you can replace painful, dysfunctional relationships with healthy relationships in which both passion and safety coexist. You can learn how to get love right.

Chapter 2

THE ROOTS OF
DYSFUNCTIONAL LOVE

PRINCIPAL CHOICES
• To identify the areas of dysfunction in your family of origin, if any.
• To live out the programming established in your family of origin or to break free and become a choice maker.
• To understand how the legacy of your childhood affects your adult relationships.

If you are among the millions of Americans struggling to get love right, the odds are you came from a dysfunctional family. In fact, in the United States today, more people come from dysfunctional families than healthy families. It is estimated that approximately 70 to 80 percent come from dysfunctional families. Consequently, being normal in the United States today has very little to do with being emotionally healthy.

How can these figures be right? As we become more aware of how families work and how healthy behavior patterns are set, we recognize that child abuse, substance abuse, and other destructive behaviors affect far more people than was realized even a generation ago.

Of course, the perfect family or childhood does not exist. Despite the idealized portrayals of American family life in movies and television, real parents aren't perfect and most childhoods will have been disrupted by problems of one sort of another.

To say that a family is dysfunctional is to say that it *doesn't work:* It doesn't provide to a minimum degree what its members need for mental, physical, and emotional well-being. By contrast, a functional family is one that teaches children how to think clearly and act responsibly, to understand their feelings, and relate to others in a healthy way. It equips them with the mental, emotional, and living skills to deal with life as an adult. To the extent that your family failed to teach you these important skills it was dysfunctional.

TWO DIFFERENT WORLDS

Children raised in dysfunctional families develop a way of thinking about and viewing the world that is not shared by others. As a result, they have a hard time understanding people from functional families and vice versa. It is as if they come from different worlds.

One of the strangest things about growing up in a dysfunctional family is that you don't know the difference between what is healthy and what is not. You may have thought that your family was fairly normal. Consequently you were not prepared for the shock of sharing your family experiences with others. John, who was raised in a dysfunctional family, joined a support group that began its first meeting by having everyone introduce themselves by telling the stories of their childhoods. As they went around the circle, John listened in disbelief. He thought some of these people were lying, because their stories were so completely different from the childhood he had experienced. He could not believe that they really received that kind of love and attention, that they were actually able to identify and talk about feelings, think clearly about reality, and express opinions. It seemed impossible to him that they actually learned how to relate productively to other people. These are the skills a functional family teaches its children day by day, and that a dysfunctional family doesn't teach in the course of an entire childhood.

The effects of being raised in a dysfunctional family are lifelong, because we never truly outgrow them. Even though what occurred in our childhood may have lasted only a relatively short time compared to the rest of our lives, our early training establishes our primary understanding of life and the way people act in the world. It constitutes our blueprint for adult behavior and the patterns we will re-create in our adult lives. The deeper our involvement with another person, the more strongly these patterns emerge. The more dysfunctional the patterns, the more difficulty we have in our relationships and our lives in general.

If you came from a dysfunctional family, it is important that you recognize this and the ways in which it may be affecting your choices and your ability to build healthy adult relationships. Without this awareness, it is far more difficult to address problem areas accurately and overcome the difficulties you may experience as a result.

Many people do not realize the extent to which their families were dysfunctional. Recognizing unhealthy patterns in your family of origin is difficult for two reasons. First, like many people, you may never have thought your family was dysfunctional because your family's ways of thinking, feeling, and behaving are the norm against which you measure the rest of the world. Second, it is sometimes difficult to detect dysfunction in a family because the dysfunction is often subtle. While some children suffer from obvious neglect and abuse, other children from dysfunctional families appear perfectly normal.

There are eight basic areas of potential dysfunction in families. The more these problem behaviors were present in your family of origin, the more dysfunctional your family was (see also page 45).

Family rules. Without learning healthy rules, we cannot create them as partners in adult relationships or as parents to our own children.

Role expectations define who we are and the parts we play in all our relationships: as child, friend, sibling, lover, spouse, parent. When our role expectations are dysfunctional, we do not know how to fulfill our responsibilities in a healthy way, what others expect of us, or what to expect of others.

Rituals. These are important to our understanding of ourselves and what is of importance to us. Without healthy rituals, we cannot celebrate what we value or our commonalty with others. Our sense of belonging may be compromised.

Social or physical neglect. When neglected as children we will not know how to conduct ourselves in appropriate ways as adults. We may find we lack the social skills to create healthy friendships, hold down a job, or develop relationships. We may neglect our physical needs, and our well-being may suffer.

Psychological, physical, or sexual abuse. Abuse causes very serious problems in adult relationships in one of two ways. Victims

Areas of Dysfunction in Families

1. **Rules**
   - inadequate rules
   - inconsistent rules
   - excessive rules

2. **Role expectations**
   - poorly defined roles
   - inflexible roles
   - culturally inappropriate roles

3. **Rituals**
   - absence of rituals
   - disrupted rituals
   - rigid, empty rituals

4. **Social neglect**

5. **Physical neglect**

6. **Psychological abuse**
   - age inappropriate expectations
   - inconsistent and contradictory messages
   - discounting and criticism

7. **Physical abuse (first, second, third degree)**

8. **Sexual abuse or incest**
   - covert sexual abuse
   - seductive abuse
   - abusive incest

may continue to allow themselves to be victimized by abusive partners, or may become the victimizers of their partners in a reenactment of their own abuse. Some people alternate between the roles of victim and victimizer.

DYSFUNCTIONAL INTIMACY

Perhaps the most important consequence of coming from a dysfunctional family is that we don't experience healthy intimacy in our homes. Many of us had parents who never talked to each other. Some of us had parents who always argued and fought. Many of us had chemically dependent parents whose addiction prevented them from being intimate, with us or with anyone else. In many families, one parent made all the decisions, and the other always gave in and did what he or she was told.

If you came from a dysfunctional family, there are two very good reasons you may have trouble getting love right. The first is that dysfunctional relationships are contagious: Children catch them from their parents because they learn by doing what their parents do. If your parents were practitioners of destructive intimacy, that is all they were able to teach you.

As a child, John learned that intimacy was when his mother sobbed on his shoulder after his drunken father wrecked the car.

Intimacy for Karen was when her father came into her bedroom at two in the morning and told her he loved her after he forgot to show up at her school play.

Intimacy for Lou meant sex, because the only time his mother and father weren't fighting was when they were making love.

To many people, intimacy was secret. It was not to be shared or discussed. Intimacy meant something mysterious that happened in the dark. Others saw intimacy as a loss of control. For them, losing control was something very frightening yet very exciting, and the danger of that sparked in them a feeling that they confused with intimacy.

Brenda said intimacy meant sharing, really opening up to people. And then she asked me, "How can you do that when it's really not okay to talk honestly? How can you open up to somebody when you don't know what you feel? How can you be honest with someone when a part of you deep inside believes you are crazy or defective?"

These are all misperceptions of what intimacy is, and these misperceptions (and those like them) set us up for dysfunctional relationships. In dysfunctional homes, we don't have the chance to learn that healthy intimacy involves the ability to communicate in an honest, open way about our most important experiences, feelings, and thoughts without fear of pain or abandonment. As adults without knowledge of healthy intimacy, we conduct our relationships in the same way our parents did. We may not like it, and we may try not to, but we don't know what else to do. We fall in love and find that old family patterns start to appear in our relationships. We don't plan it, it just seems to happen all by itself.

It is hard to overestimate the strength of this early teaching about intimacy. As a therapist, I counsel couples. My favorite couples to work with are other therapists. These sane, rational, intelligent people come into my office, sit down, and we begin. When they try to communicate with each other, out comes a dysfunctional harangue of blaming and miscommunication.

Then I say, "All right, we're going to role-play." I turn to one. "You'll become the therapist and get into a therapist mode. Now try to communicate to your partner." Instantly, they click into healthy communication.

Then I ask them, "Why don't you do that with each other all the time?"

"That would be phony," they reply.

"What's phony about it? You're listening to each other, you're understanding each other, you're paraphrasing your responses, you're looking each other in the eye, you're treating each other with dignity and respect. What's phony about that?"

"Well, it doesn't feel natural."

What they're really saying is "That's not how I learned to do it in my family of origin. 'Natural' behavior is acting out the way my parents trained me to act. To be in love means to be dysfunctional, like Mom and Dad. If I don't act like Mom and Dad, it's not love."

Think about the models for relationship you've had. Can you see where you learned your style of intimacy?

The second reason you are liable to have relationship problems is that dysfunctional families fail to provide their children with the emotional, intellectual, and communication skills necessary to conduct healthy relationships. How can you drive a car safely without learning driving skills? You can't. You can't drive a car by relying on instinct. You can't control a car by wishful thinking. Safe driving requires going through the process of learning driving skills and practicing them in a safe environment until you get them right. In order to have rational, flexible, and safe relationships, you need to learn to think rationally, respond adaptively, and know how to protect yourself from abusive people and situations. You need to be a choice maker who can evaluate the risks and benefits of a given relationship. You need to be given the opportunity to practice these skills in a safe environment until you can get them right. Unfortunately, these are precisely the skills dysfunctional families fail to teach, and so the cycle of destructive intimacy repeats itself again and again and again.

CHILDREN FROM FUNCTIONAL FAMILIES

Susan was raised in a functional family. From infancy on, Susan's parents taught her how to manage her feelings and emotions. Since Susan's parents knew what they felt and could talk about a wide range of feelings without shame or guilt, they encouraged Susan to express herself as well. They taught her to look within herself to recognize her inner experiences. They were patient with her as she learned to describe those experiences with words. Since everyone in Susan's family regularly used the language of feelings, Susan learned how to communicate her feelings effectively to others.

Susan enjoyed the company of each of her parents and learned to communicate with them comfortably. She learned she could talk over problems and even confide secrets without censure or ridicule. She learned that she could rely on others for help and support.

Susan's parents cared about her. They listened to her and tried to understand what she was saying. They took her seriously and affirmed that her personal experiences were important. As a result, Susan learned to care about and love herself.

Susan's parents cared about each other, too. They made time to be together as a family and alone as a couple. When problems arose in their relationship, they sought counseling and resolved the conflict.

Since Susan's parents cared about themselves, they insisted that Susan treat them with dignity and respect. When Susan misbehaved, there were consequences, but the consequences made sense. When she didn't put away her father's carpentry tools after she had borrowed them, Susan wasn't allowed to borrow them the next time she asked. Susan learned that the world operates by the laws of consequence and that she has the power to determine the consequences that she receives in life.

Susan also learned to care about other people. She was taught to be concerned about what others were thinking and feeling. She was taught to listen to other people and to respond in a genuine way. She learned how to be intimate.

The result of her upbringing was that Susan developed the ability to get love right. As she dated in high school and college she was attracted to men who could balance their thoughts and feelings and take responsibility for their behavior.

In college, Susan was very attracted to Jim. He was intensely passionate and had the habit of turning off his mind whenever a problem developed. Susan enjoyed his intensity and passion, but his irrational nature was unacceptable to her. Because she had learned to balance her feelings and thoughts, Susan was able to handle this conflict in their relationship responsibly. She didn't try to control Jim or try to trick him into changing. She explained to Jim how important it was to her that he become more thoughtful and responsible. She told him that she expected him to think about and work with her at solving problems instead of avoiding or overreacting to them. She also told Jim that she wanted him to take responsibility for his behavior and stop doing things that repeatedly caused problems. When Jim refused to change, Susan didn't hang on, hoping that things would get better between them. Instead, she ended the relationship.

Susan eventually fell in love with Arthur and they married. They are strongly attracted to one another and have an active and exciting sex life. They also are able to plan and solve problems together. They help each other learn and grow. They are consciously moving together in life toward common goals based upon common values. In raising their children, Susan and Arthur both found themselves following their parents' patterns of discipline, love, and communication.

A healthy family teaches its members
- to relate in a responsible, loving, and caring way with others.
- to protect themselves physically and emotionally while in relationships.
- to be realistic about relationships.

Susan's education in healthy intimacy began when her family taught her three primary skills: how to think, how to feel, and how to act responsibly. I call it the TFA Triangle. If a person isn't capable in all three of these skills, his/her chances of having a healthy, intimate relationship decrease. Susan learned that different rules apply to each of these areas: that thinking is governed by the rules of logic; feeling is governed by the rules of emotion; and action is governed by the rules of skill acquisition.

People raised in functional families learn to understand the difference between thinking, feeling, and acting. They learn that they can think about something without acting it out. They learn to separate their feelings from their behavior. They learn that they can feel strongly about something, but they do not have to act out their feelings. They learn that they control their thoughts and their feelings.

Susan put it this way: "I know that I am not my thoughts. I am the person who *thinks* my thoughts. I also know that I am not my feelings, I am the person who *experiences* my feelings. I know that I am not my behavior, I am the person who chooses to act or not to act."

Parents in functional families teach their children to balance their thoughts and their feelings, to use thinking to deal with intellectual problems, and feelings to deal with emotional problems. They are available to model effective problem solving and help their children learn problem-solving skills. They demonstrate how thoughts and feelings work in harmony to provide checks and balances, so that when they get a feeling or a hunch, they don't act on it right away, on impulse. They think about it and decide what to do. Or they get a new idea and check out how they feel about it before putting it into action. When their head says one thing and their gut says another, they recognize it as a warning sign that they need to take more time to make a decision.

People raised in families such as Susan's learn to resist the urge to feel good now when they know it will create long-term pain or problems. They learn to make decisions that take into consideration both the immediate and the long-term consequences. They are willing to do things that may be painful or frightening, or require a sacrifice of their time or resources in order to get a payoff in the future. They may return to school to get a college or graduate degree, sacrificing the time and expense in exchange for something that will enhance their lives in the future. In other situations, people are willing to defer gratification if it is in their best interest in the long run.

When Charlie and his wife developed marital problems, they separated. Charlie wanted to make their marriage work. One day Donna, an attractive woman Charlie worked with, asked him out to dinner. He accepted the invitation.

During dinner, it became obvious that there was a powerful sexual chemistry between Charlie and Donna. After dinner, Donna asked Charlie if he wanted to come back to her apartment. Charlie thought about it and declined.

Donna became embarrassed and apologized. "I must have misread the feelings between us," she said. "I thought you were as attracted to me as I am to you."

"You haven't misread the situation," Charlie replied. "But even though I'm separated from my wife, I really want her back. If I went to bed with you tonight, it would lessen my chances of getting her back. I have a lot of strong feelings for you. But what I feel and what I do about my feelings are two different things."

Parents in functional families teach children that behavior follows the law of consequence through their own example and through effective limit setting: When Susan was home late for dinner, her parents chose to limit her after-school activities for a time. Behavior is what we do. Consequences are what happen as a result of our actions.

Healthy families teach their children that they can decide what they do and don't do, regardless of what they think or feel. Susan may be angry at her sister Toni for breaking her watch, but Susan knows she is not justified in breaking Toni's watch in retribution, no matter how angry she is. Because she broke Susan's watch as a result of her carelessness, Toni must replace it out of her own money. Children from functional families learn to accept responsibility for what they do and for the consequences of their actions, even unintended consequences.

CHILDREN FROM DYSFUNCTIONAL FAMILIES

Janet was raised in an upper-middle-class home and had many advantages in life. She always had food, clothes, and a warm bed to sleep in. She was rarely spanked. Everything about Janet looked good on the outside, but Janet was never allowed to be a child. No matter what developmental stage Janet reached, she was never advanced enough to satisfy her mother. She was constantly pushed to attain the impossible. Janet is typical of children who grow up in families where everything appears fine on the outside, but where subtle psychological and emotional abuse cause lifelong problems.

Janet's mother tried to potty train her early. "I just couldn't stand the mess!" her mother confided to her therapist. To train her, Janet's mother made her sit on the toilet for several hours each day. When Janet would wet her pants, her mother would make her stand in front of her brothers and sisters and tell them what a bad girl she was.

Janet grew up with the deep-seated belief that she wasn't and never could be good enough. A's on her report card were never mentioned, but every B was criticized.

Janet became desperate for affirmation. She needed someone to tell her that she was worthwhile. She developed an emotional hunger that constantly gnawed at her. At first she tried to satisfy this hunger by being a good little girl. She would fantasize about her mother being pleased with her and praising her for her accomplishments. When her fantasy failed to materialize and she was repeatedly criticized and humiliated, Janet became discouraged. "Why bother?" she thought, "I can never be good enough anyway." She learned that her behavior did not earn her the result she wanted, and she stopped trying.

She also stopped talking to her parents about what was important to her. Her father dismissed her problems as "kid's stuff" while her mother told her to stop fussing and behave. "What's your problem?" she would yell at Janet. "You don't know how good you have it!"

A lot of her mother's energy went into keeping everything in order for Janet's father, who traveled a great deal on business. When he was home, the entire household revolved around him. He was often tired after long trips, and Janet and her siblings quickly learned to stay away or risk his anger.

As she entered adolescence, Janet's anger toward her mother grew. "Since I couldn't do anything right anyway," she told her therapy group, "I decided to drop out and do things my way." Janet joined a group of rebellious kids at school. She began smoking cigarettes, drinking alcoholic beverages, and eventually began smoking marijuana.

She met Michael at a party and instantly fell in love with him. Michael was rebellious. Janet's parents called him a delinquent and a loser, but Janet loved him anyway. Why? Because Michael liked Janet for what she was. When Janet was with Michael, her feeling of emotional hunger disappeared. For the first time in her life, Janet felt as if she were good enough. When she was with Michael, she felt complete.

In her relationship with Michael, Janet went about following the rules of intimacy she had learned from her parents. Like her parents, Janet and Michael seldom argued. In fact, they never really talked at all. Janet did everything she could to make Michael happy. She tried to anticipate his every wish. Yet because Michael never told Janet what he wanted or expected of her, she was wrong most of the time. Janet tried harder and harder in vain to guess what it was that would make him happy.

Michael like to drink a lot on Saturday nights and he would come home drunk and start a fight with Janet. Sometimes when he was drunk, he was physically and verbally abusive. Janet never learned to value herself and was unable to set limits on Michael's behavior. Janet dreaded the weekends, but rationalized Michael's behavior by reminding herself how sorry he was on Sunday and how little he drank the rest of the week.

Eventually Michael became involved with someone else. Janet was devastated. "Never again!" she vowed. "I'll find someone safe. No more sacrificing myself to a relationship."

True to her words, her relationship with Alan was very different. Alan never hit her and never drank. Yet somehow Janet never felt the same excitement as she had with Michael.

Children from dysfunctional families are "survivors" who have learned how to cope with abuse and neglect. They have never learned to feel good about themselves or how to cope with life effectively. They were never taught to think clearly, to manage their feelings and emotions, or to take responsibility for what they do or for the consequences of what they do. As a result, they lack the basic building blocks necessary to develop healthy interpersonal relationships.

People from dysfunctional families have problems thinking clearly because they were taught to turn off their minds and not think. The message was that something awful would happen if they did. In Janet's family, everything needed to look good. Janet was never allowed to talk about her problems and so never learned how to analyze them or find solutions to them. As a result, when she tried to think something through, she often became confused and contradicted herself. When she would finally hit upon a solution, she often found that it didn't work. Why? Because the "logic" she used, the way she believed the world to be, was different from the way the world really is.

Like Janet, other people from dysfunctional families are often cut off from their feelings and emotions. Since they don't know what they feel, they can't tell other processes. Since they experience intimacy only on an emotional level, this alienation from feelings blocks their ability to be intimate.

People from dysfunctional families have never learned how to balance thinking and feeling. Some people get the two processes confused. They try to "feel" their way into the solution of an equation, or put together a bookcase by intuition rather than by reading the instructions. Others try to "think" their way into an orgasm or have a good time through meticulous planning. When they don't succeed, they can't figure out why.

As individuals, we may identify with thinking, feeling, or acting to the exclusion of the others. People who are more comfortable with thinking tend to block out and repress their feelings and to have trouble acting on their thinking. People who are more comfortable with feelings tend to block out or repress their ability to think and act.

This natural preference becomes a problem when we allow it to become the only way we respond to problems or situations in our lives. Healthy people may have a preference for thinking, feeling, or acting, but have also developed the ability to use thinking and feeling in balance, and to act on their thoughts and feelings when necessary.

Dysfunctional parents often teach their children that there are "good" feelings and "bad" feelings. In essence, they say, "Good feelings are those that I approve of. Bad feelings are those that make me feel uncomfortable." These children learn to judge their feelings as good or bad, and to judge themselves for having them.

In reality, there are no good or bad feelings, only pleasant and unpleasant feelings. Pleasant feelings tell us that things are going well. Unpleasant feelings tell us that things are not going well. Both are necessary to successful living, just as physical pain warns us of disease and injury, and pleasure, such as satisfying appetite or thirst, guides us to what we need.

Finally, dysfunctional families teach children that they don't have to be responsible for the consequences of what they do. Punishment is often handed out based upon the mood of the parent, not the behavior of the child. Sometimes the children are punished when they are good and not punished when they are bad, so they learn to believe that their behavior has no real consequences. They learn to believe that somehow things will get better without their doing anything to make them better. They fall into the trap of expecting different consequences from the same behavior and repeating unproductive behavior again and again, hoping each time it will be different. This magical thinking keeps them from learning how to get what they want by changing their behavior. Despite Michael's unwillingness and inability to stop drinking on Saturday nights, Janet continued to hope their situation would improve.

Unlike functional families, who teach children that to feel better they first have to think better and act better, dysfunctional families teach children to believe that they must feel better before they can start thinking or acting better. They believe that feeling bad justifies acting bad and there is no responsibility to start acting good until after they start feeling good. They are taught that certain feelings are linked with certain behaviors. "If I feel mad, I must yell! If I am hurt, I must cry! If I am disappointed, I must blame others!" As a result, what they feel dictates what they do and their emotions run their behavior. This becomes a justification for acting out in ways that can result in emotionally and/or physically abusive behavior.

THE LEGACY OF
THE DYSFUNCTIONAL FAMILY

Without the ability to balance our thoughts, feelings, and actions, we experience life as chaotic and painful. When we don't learn to feel our feelings or think clearly about ourselves and others, we can't make healthy choices about our needs and how to meet them. We eventually become alienated from ourselves and our sense of emotional pain grows.

The legacy of a dysfunctional upbringing is a feeling of deep emotional hunger that we carry with us into adulthood and which governs the ways in which we create our intimate relationships. In his book *The Fantasy Bond,* Robert W. Firestone defines emotional hunger as "a strong need caused by emotional deprivation. It is a primitive condition of pain and longing which people often act out in a vain and desperate attempt to fill a void or emptiness." This emptiness is related to the pain of aloneness and separateness and can never be realistically satisfied in an adult relationship. Emotional hunger begins in our family of origin where we learn to relate to others in one of two ways: apathetically or compulsively.

One way in which people respond to emotional hunger is based on the belief that intimate involvement with other people is over-whelmingly painful. They believe the only way to escape the inev-itable pain of relating to others is to protect themselves by remaining detached. So these people shut themselves off and re-fuse to let others close to them. They learn to turn off their feelings. Their ultimate goal in relationships is to choose partners who are undemanding and who are safe because they won't hurt them. They expect little or nothing in the way of gratification from their partners. They establish *apathetic* relationships.

The second way people respond to emotional hunger is based on a belief that they themselves are responsible for their pain because they are inadequate or defective. Like Janet, they believe that the only way they can relieve the pain of their emotional hunger is to latch on to another human being who can make them feel whole and complete. They establish compulsive relationships in which they cling to their partner with the desperation of a drown-ing person.

Like their apathetic counterparts, people with a compulsive style of relating have learned from their family of origin that love is painful, but they respond in a very different way. They conclude: "My parents love me, but my parents hurt me. Therefore pain is an expression of love." Instead of running away from the pain, as those in apathetic relationships will, these people seek intense relationships that hold out the promise of making them whole and complete. They accept pain as an unavoidable part of relationships, believing that unless they are hurting, they are not loved. As a result, their ultimate goal in relationships is to find people who will allow them to experience intense emotions: soaring highs and crashing lows.

April could not believe her luck when she and Roger started dating. He was so sophisticated and he knew so many interesting people. Roger was often condescending, insulting her tastes and opinions, but April could stand that. He couldn't help but think that she was inferior; after all, she felt that way herself. She just felt honored to be with him and to be able to share his world. It took her mind away from the drab life she lived alone.

Because of their emotional hunger, people from dysfunctional families experience intimacy in extremes: relationships are all or nothing. People who have learned only dysfunctional intimacy either desperately seek to merge with another through intense involvement in compulsive relationships or close themselves off from others in apathetic relationships.

Healthy love exists between these two extremes. Love is different from emotional hunger because it is based upon a feeling of strength, capability, and fulfillment rather than emptiness and desperation. The feeling of love reflects itself in a sense of having something to give and a genuine desire to care for someone else in an undemanding way. The need to give and receive love is realistic in a healthy intimate relationship. While an emotionally hungry person drains his or her partner with demands, or abandons the partner through detachment, an emotionally loving person nurtures the partner with support, encouragement, and affirmation.

I. Self-assessment: Eight Areas of Dysfunction in Families

As you read through the following descriptions of the eight areas of potential dysfunction in families, think back to the experiences you had or the lessons you learned as a child in your family of origin. Then consider how your adult relationships may have been affected by these early experiences.

1. Family rules. We learn how to set limits on our own and others' behavior by the rules we were taught to follow as children. If your family had *inadequate rules,* it didn't provide enough rules to give you proper structure and guidance in your behaviors. As a result, you will not have an adequate understanding of the rules that govern an effective love relationship. If your family had *inconsistent rules,* rules which were changed constantly without warning, you will have trouble being consistent in your own limit setting as an adult. If your family had *excessive rules,* you are liable to become more rigid, inflexible, and demanding as your adult relationships develop.

A. The rules in my family were
    ____**a.** nonexistent   ____**b.** inconsistent
    ____**c.** excessive   ____**d.** healthy

B. The rules in my relationships tend to be

____✓ **a.** nonexistent   ____✓ **b.** inconsistent

____ **c.** excessive   ____ **d.** healthy

2. Role expectations have to do with the roles that family members are expected play within the family. In the case of *poorly defined roles*, the children never receive adequate role modeling for the various activities they will need to perform as adults, and so they exist in a constant state of uncertainty about themselves. *Inflexible roles* leave individuals little choice about the roles they play. They will consistently reenact their parents' roles rather than being able to adapt to the needs of their current relationship.

If your family had *culturally inappropriate roles,* the roles might have made sense within the family but conflicted with what you saw in the outside world. Partners raised with culturally inappropriate roles do not know how to build a healthy social network, and once in a relationship, they will have trouble feeling comfortable about bringing their relationships into the mainstream of society.

A. The role expectations in my family were

____✓ **a.** poorly defined   ____ **b.** rigid

____ **c.** inappropriate   ____ **d.** healthy

B. The role expectations in my relationships tend to be

____✓ **a.** poorly defined   ____✓ **b.** rigid

____ **c.** inappropriate   ____ **d.** healthy

3. Rituals are the ways in which we celebrate those aspects of life that are important to us. Many families suffer from an *absence of rituals*. They do nothing to mark special events, occasions, or cycles within the family. They have no birthday celebrations, no birthday cakes, no recognition of Christmas or Thanksgiving. If there were no rituals in their family, partners have no way to demonstrate their love and special feelings about their partner through ritual behaviors. Other families suffer from a *disruption of rituals*. The rituals exist, but are interfered with by other problems. This is typical of families where substance abuse is present. Men and women growing up with this ritual pattern tend to have a difficult time adjusting to the rituals and observances of others. A third way rituals can be dysfunctional is if they are *rigid but empty*. In this case, rituals are perpetuated without real meaning or significance.

A. The rituals in my family were

___a. absent   _✓_b. disrupted

___c. empty   ___d. healthy

B. The rituals in my relationships tend to be

___a. absent   ___b. disrupted

___c. empty   _✓d. healthy

4. Psychological abuse, although more subtle than physical abuse, can be just as devastating. Some families hold *age-inappropriate expectations* of the children, who are expected to behave at levels of maturity beyond their capability. As adults, people subjected to inappropriate expectations will tend to expect their partner to be something he/she is not and cannot be. Other parents send *inconsistent or contradictory messages* about a child's worth. The parents communicate, "We'll decide when you're okay and when you're not and there's not much you can do about our decision." As adults, these individuals will tend to give their partner inconsistent and contradictory messages. Individuals subjected to *discounting and criticizing* in their family may be verbally abusive to their partners and constantly criticize them.

A. The form of psychological abuse I suffered in my family was

_✓a. age inappropriate

_✓b. inconsistent

_✓c. discounting and critical

___d. I did not suffer psychological abuse in my family

B. In my relationships psychological abuse is a factor because

___a. I am psychologically abusive to my partner

___b. my partner is psychologically abusive to me

_✓c. we are psychologically abusive to each other

_✓d. psychological abuse is not a factor in my relationship

5. Neglect of social training. Without social training, children never learn the skills necessary to function socially in the world. They do not know how to behave in public, how to respond to questions, or how to dress appropriately for a particular place or occasion.

A. I did not receive adequate social training in my family.
____a. true   __✗_b. false

B. My lack of social skills affects my ability to have healthy adult relationships
__✗_a. not at all   ____b. to some degree
____c. to a large degree   ____d. severely

6. Neglect of physical care. In the case of physical neglect, parents do not take proper care of the children: They do not bathe them; they do not care for their medical needs when they are hurt or sick; they do not give them adequate food; and so on. As adults, these individuals do not know how to take care of their hygiene or learn healthy eating and sleep habits.

A. As a child, my physical care was often neglected.
____a. true   ✓_b. false

B. My ability to take physical care of myself is a problem in my relationships
✓_a. not at all   ____b. to some degree
____c. to a large degree   ____d. to an extreme degree

7. Physical abuse includes *first-degree physical abuse,* such as frequent spankings that cause pain but no sustained injury. While occasional spankings may not be considered abusive, spankings become abusive when the parents use them as their primary mode of disciplining children.

Second-degree physical abuse includes spankings or other forms of corporal punishment that cause pain and create sustained injuries that do not require medical treatment, such as black eyes and bruises.

Third-degree physical abuse includes beatings and other punishment that create physical injuries requiring medical treatment.

People who were physically abused as children perpetuate the cycle of abuse in their adult relationships. It can start with verbal abuse and escalate to physical abuse. Abused children learn that there are only two possible roles in life: victim and victimizer. They typically alternate between those two roles.

A. I suffered physical abuse as a child.

    ___ a. true   ___ b. false

B. In my relationships physical abuse is a factor because

    ___ a. I am physically abusive to my partner

    ___ b. my partner is physically abusive

    ___ c. we are physically abusive to each other

    ___ d. physical abuse is not a factor in my relationship

8. Sexual abuse or incest. Sexual abuse also can be categorized in three levels.

Covert sexual abuse. The parent communicates to the child, "I am excited sexually by what I am doing with you but I deny that I am." This involves seduction and flirtation, indirect fondling, and so on.

Seductive abuse. The parent communicates, "I am excited sexually by what I do with you and because a part of you enjoys it, I'm going to blame you for it. It's your fault because you're turning me on." The parent and the child flirt and engage in low-level sexual activity.

Abusive incest. The parent's message is, "I do things to you or with you to excite myself sexually that you don't like or you find painful or offensive." This may include intercourse and oral sex.

It is important to understand that any sexual expression between a parent and a child constitutes abuse. Simply because the child may find it enjoyable does not mean that it is healthy or appropriate, or that it is not damaging. Therapists who work with sexual-abuse cases warn that the most serious damage is done by seductive sexual abuse where the child actually enjoys the sexual contact with the parent. Children are not old enough to use proper discrimination, and any sexual activity by the parent victimizes the child.

A. I was sexually abused as a child.
   ✓ **a.** true   ____**b.** false

B. Symptoms of post-traumatic stress disorder and/or other effects of sexual abuse are a factor in my relationships
   ____**a.** not at all   ✓ **b.** to some degree
   ____**c.** to a large degree   ____**d.** to an extreme degree

II. Self-assessment: The TFA (Thinking/Feeling/Acting) Triangle

1. What my parents taught me about thinking was
   ____**a.** thinking is the most important
   ____**b.** thinking is less important than acting
   ✓ **c.** thinking is less important than feeling
   ____**d.** thinking is equally as important as feeling and acting

2. What my parents taught me about feeling was
   ____**a.** feeling is the most important
   ✓ **b.** feeling is less important than acting
   ____**c.** feeling is less important than thinking
   ____**d.** feeling is equally as important as thinking and acting

3. What my parents taught me about acting was
   ✓ **a.** acting is the most important
   ____**b.** acting is less important than thinking
   ____**c.** acting is less important than feeling
   ____**c.** acting is equally as important as feeling and thinking

4. I prefer to deal with stressful situations by
   ____**a.** thinking them through
   ____**b.** trusting my feelings about them
   ✓ **c.** taking action about them

5. When my preferred style doesn't work in these situations, I usually try

    ✓ **a.** thinking them through

    ____ **b.** trusting my feelings about them

    ____ **c.** taking action about them

Chapter 3

SICK LOVE—HEALTHY LOVE

PRINCIPAL CHOICES
• To learn the essential characteristics of apathetic, compulsive, and healthy relationship styles.
• To recognize the dysfunctional habits and behaviors that may be compromising your relationships.
• To select a relationship style to achieve the consequences you want: compulsive, apathetic, balanced.

PICKING UP THE SNAKE
Once upon a time, on a very cold day, a man went walking in the woods. There before him on the road, he saw a poisonous snake that was frozen stiff as a board. The man brought the snake home with him and placed it in front of his fireplace to thaw out. He then heated some milk so the snake would have something warm to drink when it woke up. As the man placed a bowl of milk in front of the snake, it suddenly struck out and bit the man's arm, injecting a lethal dose of venom.

"How could you do this to me? How could you kill me after all I did for you?" the man asked the snake.

"Stop whining!" the snake responded harshly. "You knew I was a poisonous snake when you picked me up. What did you expect?"

Dysfunctional relationships are like poisonous snakes: manageable at first, eventually lethal. At one time or another, most of us have picked up the relationship "snake" and have been bitten. Have you ever met someone you *knew* would hurt you? One part of you said, "Stop! Don't get involved!" But you got involved anyway. You felt so attracted that you shut off your mind and let your intense emotions lead you—and you got hurt. Have you ever been in a relationship that was wrong for you? You knew you had to get out, but you just couldn't do it?

These are examples of picking up the relationship snake, which bites and injects its victims with its emotional venom. The venom works strangely, however. Before it kills you, it makes you feel wonderful, because it temporarily relieves your emotional hunger. It does this in one of two ways, depending on which of the two styles of relating you learned as a child.

In compulsive relationships, the poison ignites an intense passion and sexuality that feel so good it is difficult to believe the rational voice that warns you to avoid the relationship. Instead, the compulsion to get involved and stay involved pushes aside all rational thoughts. Almost before you know it, you are involved in a relationship that eventually hurts you, just as your rational voice told you it would.

In apathetic relationships, the venom acts in a different way: it numbs you and lulls you into a sense of well-being that you can temporarily mistake for love—until your unmet needs and isolation reawaken your emotional hunger with even greater vehemence.

If we come from a dysfunctional family, we continue to pick up the snake time after time. If we learned only destructive intimacy from our parents, we are especially vulnerable to picking up the snake, because that's all we know to do. It's as if we have no choice but to reenact the old patterns time and time again. It's all or nothing: We deal with our emotional hunger either by trying to merge ourselves with a partner or by trying to insulate ourselves from the pain of loving another person.

If both partners want the same type of relationship, whether compulsive or apathetic, the relationship may last for a long time before problems develop. But if one partner wants a compulsive relationship and the other wants an apathetic relationship, it won't be long before conflict occurs.

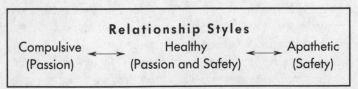

Healthy relationships form the middle ground between the compulsive and apathetic relationship styles. Healthy relationships are founded on the basis of rational choices, not a desperate attempt to relieve emotional hunger. The partners know their needs will be met and that they have the capacity to meet their partner's needs. Healthy relationships integrate passion and excitement with a sense of safety. Their love is built upon a solid foundation of shared interests and experiences, common values and life-style preferences, and mutual respect.

Before you can begin to build a healthy relationship and get love right you need to

• understand the nature of dysfunctional relationships so that you can recognize and avoid them or transform them into healthy relationships;

• understand the nature of a healthy relationship and how to build one;

• know that you have a choice, to say "no" to dysfunctional relationships and to say "yes" to healthy relationships, so you are no longer driven to pick up poisonous snakes.

By understanding the dynamic components and characteristics of both compulsive and apathetic relationships, you can learn to recognize them in your own relationships. Then you can choose what relationship style you want on the basis of the consequences you want to have.

COMPULSIVE RELATIONSHIPS: INTENSITY WITHOUT SUBSTANCE

Compulsive relationships provide intensity without substance. The unique combination of intense passion and sexuality the partners share provides an intense emotional high that blocks out or distorts other feelings. Partners in compulsive relationships feel euphoric, as if all is right with the world, and they think they must be in love. In reality, it isn't love at all. It is an intense infatuation. A good definition of infatuation is temporary insanity.

People who are infatuated wear blinders. They use emotional rather than rational reasoning. They stop thinking with their minds and think with their hormones and emotions instead. As a result, they enter relationships that eventually cause them pain.

When Daniel met Nikki, he was recovering from alcoholism and cocaine dependency. He was constantly unhappy in recovery. He felt as if there were something driving and pushing him all of the time. He called it "free-floating compulsion." Daniel believed that Nikki had the power to make that feeling go away. He confused their sexual intensity with love and made Nikki the center of his newfound recovery until his life completely revolved around her and their lovemaking.

Although both partners may share an intense infatuation with each other, they often don't have much else in common, so there isn't much of a foundation on which to build a stable, healthy relationship. In most compulsive relationships, the partners don't share a broad base of common interests, values, goals, life-style preferences, or mutual respect.

Compulsive relationships are characterized by obsession, compulsion, dependence, and loss of control. People in compulsive relationships are so obsessed with their partner and with the relationship, they often think about them when they should be thinking about other things. They also feel compelled to be with their partner, to touch them, to hold them, to talk with them or about them. This urge is sometimes so strong that they do things that are self-destructive.

"I remember feeling such a strong urge to see Nikki that I drove thirty minutes across town to have lunch with her," says Daniel. "I knew I'd be late getting back to work, but I didn't care. I ended up convincing Nikki to call in sick for the afternoon. It felt wonderful to be together, but we were both terrified that we would lose our jobs."

These obsessive thoughts and compulsive feelings lead to an irrational dependence on the relationship. For people in compulsive relationships, this dependence manifests itself as a belief that they can't live or function without the relationship. They don't *want* to be in the relationship, they *need* to be in it because they believe that if they lose the relationship, they will lose a vital part of themselves.

Daniel was terrified when Nikki threatened to leave him. "Before I met Nikki, I felt as unimportant as a pile of garbage in the corner of a large, empty warehouse. I knew that if Nikki left me, I would feel that way again. I just couldn't let her do that to me!"

Another common characteristic of compulsive relationships is loss of control. People in compulsive relationships are never sure about what they are going to do, even in specific circumstances. Sometimes they behave responsibly; other times, they are spontaneous and unpredictable.

When Daniel and Nikki were together, they could never be sure if they would do what they had planned to do, or change their minds and spend the evening making love. It was exciting for them, but created problems with their friends. Nikki said that being involved with Daniel felt like jumping out of an airplane with a parachute that might not open. It was thrilling but dangerous, because she was never sure what was going to happen next.

People enter into compulsive relationships without considering the danger that might be present in this relationship or in being with this partner. In fact, many people actually seek an element of danger in romantic relationships. The danger causes an adrenaline rush, which creates excitement.

Logically, no one wants to be involved in a relationship that poses any danger. But for people who crave compulsive relationships, this attraction to danger may have its roots in what they learned about intimacy from their parents. Both Daniel and Nikki had alcoholic fathers. As a result, they each subconsciously associated the fear and danger they felt watching their fathers drink with the emotions an intimate relationship should generate.

A sense of danger may be created in a relationship through secrecy or the unknown. A man or woman of mystery can become a blank screen upon which to project our most exciting fantasies. Compulsive relationships often begin without either partner knowing anything about the other. The sense of not knowing exactly what we are getting into can create a rush of excitement that fuels a powerful obsession to find out who our mysterious partner really is.

In some cases, real danger is present. The danger can be caused by such things as falling in love with a partner who is married to someone else, having sex in public or semipublic places, falling in love with someone who is viewed as dangerous or unacceptable by friends and family. It may be that your partner periodically threatens, scares, or abuses you.

APATHETIC RELATIONSHIPS: SAFETY WITHOUT PASSION

In many ways, apathetic relationships are the exact opposite of compulsive relationships. Apathetic relationships are characterized by minimal expectations, minimal involvement, and a strong desire to avoid conflict and pain. People in apathetic relationships do not expect very much from their partner, and they do not want their partner to expect very much from them. In apathetic relationships, the motto is, "He (or she) who does not expect cannot be disappointed."

Along with minimal expectations comes minimal involvement. People in apathetic relationships are disconnected from each other. Unlike people in compulsive relationships, those in apathetic relationships don't want to be intensely involved with each other. They both passively tend to their own needs and stay separate from each other. It's important to them not to rely on one another too much because to do so would take away their autonomy.

Apathetic relationships are "no pain" and "no conflict" relationships. People in apathetic relationships love their partner not for who they are or what they do but for what he or she will not do. They know their partner will not hurt them or openly disagree with them. They feel safe and comfortable because they don't have to deal with any intense emotions.

Their partner protects them from the demands of others. Partners in an apathetic relationship don't have to worry about meeting new people, becoming sexually active in the era of HIV infection, or moving outside their comfort zone. They have a reliable partner they can count on to pay the bills, or to clean the house, take out the garbage or handle the social obligations. Their relationship looks to all the world like a healthy, committed relationship. Only they know otherwise, because their emotional needs remain unmet.

Mary and Carl were married for sixteen years. They had two children in high school and had both settled into a comfortable rut. They had their own duties with the house and children, and routinely had sex twice a week on Friday night and Sunday morning. Each felt safe and secure with the other, but both felt an inner sense of emptiness and loneliness. They were not deeply connected. The passion they had felt in the first year of their marriage was gone. Part of each of them wanted to get the passion back, but a bigger part wanted to avoid the pain and conflict that any change would cause.

Many single people have apathetic relationships. Joanne and Paul felt extremely comfortable in their relationship because they made few demands on each other. They had an agreement that they could date other people. This meant they could sleep with those people as well, if they wanted to. But because neither of them would admit to dating or sleeping with anyone else, they were both able to pretend that theirs was an exclusive relationship and avoid the pain of feeling betrayed.

Apathetic relationships last as long as both partners want to relate in this manner, and as long as they can keep their partner inside their comfort zone: close enough to provide security and to act as a buffer against the world, but far enough away so that they won't hurt them or demand emotional honesty. These relationships typically end when one or both partners become so bored they terminate the relationship or begin to demand more from their partner.

ALTERNATING STYLES

Some people alternate between compulsive and apathetic relationships. They meet someone and fall hopelessly in love. A compulsive relationship blossoms, marked by mind-blowing highs and abject lows. When the relationship ends, they are devastated and alone. They don't have the energy for another compulsive relationship. As a matter of fact, they don't believe they will ever fall in love again, but they can't stand to be alone.

So they go to the opposite extreme. They seek out a safe and comfortable partner and start an apathetic relationship. They seek this type of relationship because apathetic relationships won't cause pain, and the relationship requires minimal commitment. The problem is, as the emotional pain from the compulsive relationship heals, they start to get bored. The new relationship is nice, comfortable, and not demanding, but it's also boring.

The need for excitement and intensity begins to build and they begin to feel cheated by the apathetic relationship. Then, one day, they meet a new one-and-only who can provide mind-blowing passion. They end the apathetic relationship and run back into a compulsive relationship, only to burn out on the intensity, and then seek another apathetic relationship in order to rest up. This cycle can continue indefinitely.

Occasionally people alternate styles within the same relationship. They have periods of intense compulsive preoccupation with their partner and then burn out on the intensity. Instead of leaving, however, they gear the relationship down by detaching from each other and taking the pressure off. Eventually, boredom brings them back into intense passionate involvement.

DYSFUNCTIONAL RELATIONSHIPS
AS ADDICTIONS

Although on the surface compulsive relationships and apathetic relationships are polar opposites, they share several qualities in common. One important similarity is that partners in compulsive or apathetic relationships use their relationships in the same way drug addicts use drugs.

People who become addicted to drugs crave one of two sensations: stimulation or calmness. Those who become addicted to uppers, such as stimulants, cocaine, or amphetamines, like them because the drugs make them feel excited by intensifying their feelings. This is what people in compulsive relationships seek. Addicts who prefer downers, such as sedatives, narcotics, or barbiturates, need the calm, safe, and secure feelings that downers create. In a similar way, people in apathetic relationships crave a sense of serenity and security, a general numbing of emotion.

Addicts become dependent upon their drug to manage their thoughts, feelings, and behavior. Relationship addicts do the same thing. They either build a romantic fantasy about their partner in order to feel good about themselves, or use their relationship to numb their emotions. In each case, the relationship works as a drug would to make them feel better by distracting them from other problems.

Both drug use and dysfunctional relationships remove the necessity of taking responsibility for ourselves and our lives. They enable us to feel better without first thinking better or acting better. They allow us to settle for short-term gratification at the expense of our long-term happiness and well-being.

WHAT IS A HEALTHY RELATIONSHIP?

Healthy relationships are very different from compulsive and apathetic relationships. In healthy relationships, partners enjoy both passion and safety. There is a shared sense of intense passion and sexuality, but they are not the key aspects of the relationship. Rather, the relationship revolves around shared values, goals, and lifestyle preferences, which create a sense of mutual respect. Healthy relationships are also based on security and trust. Each partner knows who the other really is. Their sexuality enhances this core of mutual respect and admiration.

In healthy relationships, partners balance their feelings, thoughts, and actions. They do not allow their feelings to impede clear, rational thinking, nor do they allow their feelings to be an excuse or cause for them to act irresponsibly.

Emily and Bill had a healthy relationship. They were deeply in love and had an active and satisfying sex life. Bill, however, would often overwork, pushing himself beyond the point of fatigue. When he did, he would become irritable and often overreact to Emily. He would start frequent arguments. Emily loved Bill, but she couldn't tolerate this. She explained her feelings to Bill and set definite limits. She asked Bill to change his behavior and supported his efforts to do so.

In a healthy relationship, the partners are able to think clearly about themselves, about each other, and about their relationship. As a result, they each know who they are and what they want out of life. They know who their partner is and what their partner wants. They know what their relationship is and what it is not.

In compulsive and apathetic relationships, the partners' emotional hunger prevents them from meeting their partner's needs. In compulsive relationships, the partners are so concerned with gratifying their own needs for excitement, intensity, and euphoria that they can't begin to think about their partner's needs. They don't know who he or she truly is because they project their own fantasies onto him or her in their effort to merge with another person. In apathetic relationships, partners don't want to know about their partner's needs or wants. They don't care enough to want to know who he or she is. In healthy relationships, both partners are present for the other and do their best to meet his or her needs and wants.

Partners in healthy relationships are satisfied with themselves as people and satisfied with their partners. As a result they are pleased by the relationship they have built together. They have realistic expectations about what their relationship can and cannot do for them. And, most important, these realistic expectations allow them to be happy and satisfied with what they have. This is not magical happiness, it's realistic. They are not expecting the relationship to change them or fix their lives.

This doesn't mean that they have a perfect or problem-free relationship. Even the healthiest relationships have problems. We get love right by learning how to recognize and solve common relationship problems.

RELATIONSHIP CHARACTERISTICS

Although there are extreme compulsive or apathetic behaviors present in many relationships, most people find that their relationships have a combination of characteristics that falls somewhere in the middle, varying between compulsive and apathetic tendencies. The relationship may be compulsive in some ways and apathetic in others. One partner may switch back and forth between compulsive and apathetic behaviors, while the other compensates by behaving in the opposite manner, thus maintaining the precarious balance that allows them to believe theirs is a stable, meaningful relationship.

There are eight specific areas that differ among compulsive, apathetic, and healthy relationships. By assessing your relationship style you can identify areas that are problematic for you or your partner.

In examining your own relationships, past and present, the goal is not to classify them rigidly as either compulsive or apathetic but to ask such questions as: "Do my relationships tend to have compulsive or apathetic characteristics that are causing problems?" Once these characteristics are identified, you can choose to adopt alternative behaviors to change and improve your current relationship (if you are presently involved) or your future relationships.

The eight common problem areas that affect relationships are:

1. Expectations—what we expect our partner to do or be; what our partner expects us to do or be; what we expect the relationship to do or be.

2. Gratification—the type of pleasure or reinforcement we seek from the relationship.

3. Communication—our ability to be open with our partner; what we can and cannot talk about in the relationship.

4. Influence—issues of leadership, power, and control in the relationship and the ways we go about getting our needs met within the relationship.

5. Trust—our belief in our partner's honesty, reliability, and integrity.

6. Boundaries—the knowledge of where we stop and our partner starts, what thoughts and feelings belong to us and what thoughts and feelings belong to our partner.

7. Sociability—the way we build our social life and friendships within and around the relationship.

8. Consequences—the result of the ways in which we interact with our partner.

Expectations

We all have expectations about ourselves, other people, and the way things work. In our relationships we also have certain expectations: I expect my partner to do or be certain things; I expect the relationship to work in certain ways. My partner also has expectations.

Problems arise in a relationship when our expectations are not or cannot be met. This can happen for a number of reasons.

> **Expectation Questions**
> What do I expect from my partner? What does my partner expect from me? What roles are we expected to fulfill? What kinds of things are we required to do or not to do in order to make the relationship work?

One reason is that many people, particularly those from dysfunctional families, are unaware of their needs. Their emotional hunger has left them with a general feeling of want, need, or deprivation. They feel motivated to do something to make these feelings go away, but because they don't know what their needs are, they can't develop a rational plan to do so. Because they don't know what they are feeling or thinking, they can't express their needs to their partner.

> **Expectations**
> Compulsive = Magical
> Balanced   = Rational
> Apathetic = Minimal

Another reason people's expectations may not be met is that these expectations are unrealistic. In compulsive relationships the expectations are too high—they are magical and exaggerated. Partners in a compulsive relationship expect the relationship to act as a magical cure-all. No matter what we need or expect, the right lover or the right relationship will meet the need. We expect our partner to fulfill an ideal image or to be something that he or she is not as a condition of loving us.

Sometimes this involves asking our partner to act in ways he or she doesn't normally act and which may even be contrary to their basic nature.

My friend Brian bought a cat. The next time I saw him, I asked him how they were getting along.

"Terribly," he said. "I'm so angry at this cat, I'm ready to give up."

"Why?" I asked.

"That animal walks all over everything! It climbs on bookshelves and the drapes. It walks on the table. I've been beating that lousy cat to keep him off the furniture and keep him off the drapes but it doesn't do any good. Nothing I do will get that cat to stay off my furniture."

"Why are you trying to do that?" I asked.

"I had a dog that never did that."

Brian expected the cat to violate its basic nature because he wanted it to. No matter how much he wanted that, he couldn't actually change the cat's fundamental nature. People have fundamental natures, too. You cannot get somebody to change their fundamental nature, just because you want him or her to. If somebody's nature doesn't fit yours, you're not going to change it.

If Brian had taken the time to figure out what he wanted in a pet he would have been better off. He might have said, "I want a small, affectionate, furry animal that stays off my furniture." In that case, he wouldn't have bought a cat; he would have bought another dog, and both he and his pet would have been happier for it.

Just because someone loves you doesn't mean that they will magically change their basic nature. Before we commit to a relationship, we need to know what our general expectations are, and then find a partner capable of meeting them.

Carol was deeply in love with Chris, a successful accountant with a bright career ahead of him. He was a compulsive worker who routinely worked twelve-hour days. Carol was a homebody who enjoyed quiet evenings in front of the television or fireplace. She expected Chris to change because he loved her. When he didn't, she was hurt and outraged. "How could he prefer his spreadsheets to me?" she asked her counselor. "Doesn't he know that love means wanting to spend time together? What's wrong with him? When I complain, he gets mad! I never thought he'd be this way."

Carol hadn't fallen in love with Chris. She fell in love with a fantasy of what she wanted Chris to be and then expected him to make her dream come true. When we don't take the time to get to know our partner before we commit to the relationship, we often expect him or her to do or be things he/she can't.

In an apathetic relationship, the expectations are minimal. People in apathetic relationships don't expect much from their partners, and don't want their partners to expect much from them. They remain separate from each other and, as a result, they are emotional strangers.

Ellen and Ray were both busy with their careers. They wanted the benefits of a steady relationship, a social life, and a sex life, but they didn't want any of those to interfere with their work. Because they were compatible in their relationship goals, they became involved with each other, lived together, and eventually got married. The unspoken arrangement was, "We'll love each other as long as the relationship doesn't interfere with our careers." When Ellen received a promotion and was transferred by her company to their headquarters in Singapore, she told her friend, "I can't expect Ray to give up his job, especially just now. We'll just have to make the best of it and see what happens." Over the next eight months, Ellen and Ray gradually became more and more out of touch with one another, until eventually the relationship died.

In a healthy relationship, the expectations are realistic. Each partner has taken the time to assess his or her relationship expectations, needs, and wants and waited until he or she found a partner who seemed likely to be capable of fulfilling them. They then spent time together building the relationship and getting to know one another in a variety of situations. They know what their partner is likely to do or not do, so they do not expect him or her to act out of character in the relationship.

Roberta fell in love with and married Matt, a race-car mechanic who loved machinery and felt alive only when he had grease on his hands. During the week, he worked as a mechanic for a car dealer, and on weekends he worked on race cars. Roberta knew how important cars were to Matt. She shared his interest in racing and enjoyed spending time at the track. When they decided to have children, the family organized its life around events involving three-wheel motorcycles and took vacations touring the national race circuit.

Roberta wasn't jealous or resentful of Matt's love for cars and racing. She loved him for it. "I get so excited by his enthusiasm. When he gets a car working just right he's ecstatic!" There were times when Roberta had to set limits. "If it were up to him, he'd get lost in an engine and never come out!" said Roberta. "But I'd never expect him to change. I love him and want him to be happy, and that means he has to love what he's doing."

Roberta's expectations were realistic. She married a mechanic who loved cars, and she expected him to spend a lot of his time and energy on cars. Since she enjoyed the lifestyle her husband loved, she accepted the problems that came along with it.

When our expectations are realistic, they are more likely to be met. When we expect something of our partners that they are unwilling or unable to give, we become frustrated and angry. When we expect little or nothing, we become bored and alienated.

Gratification

> ### Gratification Questions
> What type of gratification do I want from my partner? Physical? Emotional? What does my partner want from me? How often do we expect to receive gratification? How much gratification do we want in our relationship?

Most people want their partners to give them pleasure by satisfying their needs, wants, and desires. If people want the type of pleasure that their partner is willing and able to give, this area of their relationship works well. Problems develop when people desire a type or level of gratification that their partner is unwilling or unable to give.

In most relationships, partners share two types of pleasure—physical and emotional. Physical pleasure occurs when our needs for physical safety, comfort, affection, sensuality, and sexuality are met. Emotional pleasure occurs when our needs for loving, caring, warmth, and affirmation are met. In a healthy relationship both partners are willing and able to met each other's physical and emotional needs. Some people, however, channel their need for gratification into either physical or emotional expression at the expense of the other.

Louise wanted to be loved and cared about for who she was. She wanted affirmation and respect and expected Ed to think about her. She was uncomfortable with physical affection and had difficulty being sexually responsive. She wanted emotional gratification and was out of touch with her need for physical pleasure.

Ed was the opposite. He wanted physical and sexual pleasure from Louise, but didn't think it was important to gratify her emotional needs. He was sexually aggressive and demanding and wanted physical affection, back rubs, shared baths, and lots of sex. He didn't feel a strong need to be emotionally gratified, so he couldn't understand what Louise was asking for. Because of their different needs for gratification, Ed felt unloved and neglected, while Louise felt used and abused.

Gratification

Compulsive = Instant/Constant
Balanced   = Long-term
Apathetic = No Pain

In compulsive relationships, both partners expect instant, even constant, gratification. They expect their partners to change their mood on demand, to fix them, and to make them feel whole and complete. They want their partner to make them feel powerful and to transform them into what they want to be, instantly, no questions asked. There is a general attitude of "I want what I want when I want it." If their partner can't do it, then there's something wrong with their partner, with themselves, or with the relationship. Unless the relationship is providing constant and intense gratification, it's not okay.

When a relationship is centered around the need for instant gratification, both partners believe it is their job to make each other feel good on demand. As long as they can do it, they're viewed as a good partner. When they can't, they're seen as a bad partner because they are not loved for themselves but for how they make their partner feel.

The problem with this situation is that your partner isn't responsible for your feelings. You are. Only you can control your feelings. When you expect your partner to manage your feelings, you avoid taking responsibility for yourself and blame your problems on your partner.

Pat and Jack had a compulsive relationship that centered around hot sex and frequent romantic escapes. They expected intense sexual passion during each encounter. They both wanted the same thing and were able to deliver until Jack was in a motorcycle accident and had his leg in a cast for six weeks.

"During those six weeks I saw Jack in a new way," said Pat. "Since we had difficulty making love with his cast on, we spent time doing other things. I found out things about him I had never known before." Unfortunately, Pat had mixed feelings about some of the things she learned. As the passion fell into the background of their relationship, she got to know Jack as a person. She was surprised to discover she was more in love with the intense sexuality than she was with Jack.

In an apathetic relationship, the partners really don't expect intense gratification of any kind. Their sense of gratification comes from feeling safe and comfortable with their partner. If their partner doesn't threaten or hurt them, they're satisfied.

Ethel and Jake married soon after graduating from high school. Jake got a good job at the quarry and they were careful with their money. Soon they bought their first house and started a family. Year after year, their lives continued in much the same pattern. Every night when Jake would come home, Ethel would have dinner ready. After dinner they would sit together and watch television. They were content to snack and nibble their way into obesity. Nice, safe. No intense pleasure. No real pain. They lived this way for forty-four years. When her daughter asked Ethel if they had had a happy marriage, Ethel replied, "Oh yes. Jake is so reliable. Always had a steady job. Never beat me or embarrassed me. He is a good man, your father."

In healthy love relationships, people expect their partners to meet their needs for gratification, but not necessarily the instant they want it. When one partner does something to make the other angry or sad, he or she does not stop loving his/her partner. Healthy people love their partners even when they don't make them feel good. Healthy love transcends the momentary here and now. Each loves his/her partner and wants what is best for him/her, regardless of how they feel at the moment.

Instead of instant gratification, partners in a healthy relationship expect long-term gratification. They realize that relationships have ups and downs, good days and bad days. They realize there are moments of intense love and passion, and there are quiet, gentle times. They learn what their partner enjoys and regularly include that in their plans. They don't need to have what they want immediately. Healthy partners can wait until the appropriate time, because they know that eventually they will get what they want.

Communication

Communication Questions
How open and honest are my partner and I with each other? What is okay to talk about openly? What kinds of things do we need to hold back and hide? How honest can we be with our thoughts and feelings? How much do we have to hold back or lie about?

Honest communication is the foundation of true intimacy. Communication in a relationship involves sharing ideas, thoughts, emotions, and opinions with your partner.

Many people want to be honest with their partners but are afraid of hurting and getting hurt. "Honesty is a good thing," Jerry told me in counseling. "But it can be dangerous. If I tell Ann what I am really thinking and feeling, she may not like what I say. I could hurt her and she might even leave me!"

This is a conflict for many people. "Do I let my partner know who I really am and how I really feel, or do I hold back because I fear the consequences?" By choosing honesty, we assume the risk of finding out if our partner loves us for who we really are. By choosing to keep our thoughts and feelings secret, we condemn ourselves to live in a constant state of fear and doubt. "Am I loved for who I am?" If I were honest, would my partner still love me?" These questions are constantly in the back of our minds.

Many people confuse the desire for honesty with the desire to be told what they want to hear. One day Arnold was quiet and withdrawn. "What's the matter?" asked Ruth. "I know you're upset and I want to know why." Arnold was reluctant to be honest because he didn't want to hurt Ruth's feelings.

After Ruth assured him that she could handle anything that he said, Arnold told her that he was upset by how dependent she was upon him. He was feeling drained and taken advantage of, and would like her to become more independent. Ruth was hurt and outraged. She accused Arnold of blaming her for his problems. Ruth really didn't want to know what Arnold was thinking and feeling. She wanted Arnold to tell her only those things that wouldn't upset her.

In compulsive relationships, communication is dishonest. Both partners lie about or hide aspects of themselves that they believe would diminish the intensity of their relationship.

Communication

Compulsive = Deceptive
Balanced = Honest
Apathetic = Withheld

The unspoken policy in a compulsive relationship is "I'm not going to tell you the truth. I'm going to tell you what you need to hear in order for you either not to abandon me or to do what I want you to do." They edit what they tell their partners to make themselves look better. Both partners tend to focus on minor issues and blow them out of proportion, while minimizing or ignoring other, often major, problems.

Most people view themselves as honest about "important" things. They rationalize that they only hold back or lie about little things that don't make any difference. Unfortunately, most relationships are not destroyed by one major lie; they die slowly as the results of hundreds of little lies about unimportant things.

Valerie was in the process of a vicious divorce. She was dating a man named Ted and told him in detail all of the awful things that her ex-husband was doing to her. She magnified every detail of her husband's abusive behavior. She neglected, however, to tell Ted about her temper tantrums, the angry phone calls she made to her ex at two in the morning, or her instructions to her attorney to "take the jerk for every penny that he's got!"

Partners in compulsive relationships often want instant intimacy. Their motto is "the faster, the better; the more intense, the better." In order to get that intensity they are willing to take the risk of opening themselves up to people they don't know.

Premature self-disclosure is one way of creating that intensity. It involves telling another person all our strengths and weaknesses. Negative self-disclosure means telling others about our problems or character defects. It is important for us to be honest about ourselves, but timing is critical.

The process of communication in an apathetic relationship is also dishonest. Here the unspoken policy is "I'm not going to lie. I'm not going to con. I'm not going to hustle. I'm just not going to tell you very much. The less you know about me the less able you are to hurt me. So you're not going to know anything about me that I value highly enough to be hurt by as a consequence."

So apathetic partners withhold information and carefully select what they let their partner know. It's not what they tell their partner that's important, it's what they don't tell. They are dishonest by omission.

Bruce worked in the vice president's office in his accounting firm, but he wasn't the vice president. Whenever Carla called him at work, his secretary answered the phone saying, "Office of the vice president," then connected her to Bruce. "I've never told her I'm not the vice president," says Bruce, "but she thinks I am. I'm not going to tell her otherwise unless she asks. It isn't my fault she made the mistake."

In a healthy relationship, the communication is honest. Both partners know that intimacy is founded on honest communication shared in a context of trust and safety. They realize that it is important to choose the appropriate time to share information about themselves. They know that the premature sharing of personal secrets is not necessarily a sign of intimacy and can be dangerous with an unsafe or unknown partner.

Before healthy people make a commitment to a relationship, they want to now who their partner really is. They honestly want to know their partner's strengths and weaknesses. They do this because they know that love is a decision, based on rational choices about getting involved and staying involved.

Partners in a healthy relationship know that learning about each other is a process that takes time. It doesn't all happen on the first date. They also know that as they learn new things about their partner, they can decide to renegotiate the relationship, either by moving closer and increasing their commitment or by backing off and decreasing the level of commitment.

Influence

Influence deals with leadership, power, and control. The issue of leadership is present in all relationships. The basic questions are, who's in charge and what do they do to stay in charge.

Influence Questions

Am I comfortable sharing leadership? Do I always need to be in charge? Am I a perpetual follower or always the loyal servant? Do I need to force my partner to conform to what I want him or her to be? Does my partner force me to conform to what he or she wants me to be?

It is rare to find two people who agree about everything or act in perfect accord. When disagreements occur, a power struggle can ensue with both partners attempting to dominate. Who makes the decisions for the couple? Who decides how time should be spent, how joint resources should be used, or when to get together with friends and family? Issues can range from where to go to dinner to whether or not to start a family or terminate the relationship.

There are three distinct styles of resolving these power struggles—overt control, abandonment and passive compliance, and negotiation based upon shared power.

Influence

Compulsive = Control
Balanced = Shared Power
Apathetic = Abandonment

In compulsive relationships, one or both partners feel the need to overtly control the other by manipulating the way their partner thinks, feels, and acts. The controlling partner believes that the only way to be safe in the relationship is to have absolute control over it. They say to themselves: "If I can make my partner think what I want him/her to think, feel what I want him/her to feel, do what I want him/her to do, then and only then will our relationship work."

Jennifer was an executive secretary who ran her home, like her office, on a precise and rigid schedule. If anyone in the family was late or disorganized, she took it as a personal insult. Her husband, Ralph, liked her being in charge. He was more than willing to follow Jennifer's rules because she made things work so well. The rules of their relationship in terms of influence were rigidly set—Jennifer led and Ralph followed.

Jennifer needed to dictate her family's activities so that the household and relationship were under her firm control. Ralph abdicated his responsibility for his own decision making to follow Jennifer's lead. Consequently, when Jennifer left him, Ralph was at a loss to provide these functions for himself.

In apathetic relationships, control is exercised by abandonment and passive control. One partner makes the other guess at what he or she wants, instead of taking responsibility for communicating in a straightforward manner.

When Agnes told Jim she wanted more closeness and intimacy, Jim listened in silence, got a sad look on his face, and withdrew deeper into his shell. Agnes instantly knew that she had done something wrong. "I shouldn't have asked Jim directly," she said to herself. "I just should have hinted at it instead of coming right out and saying it." Jim's silence and unwillingness to communicate were his major means of conveying disapproval and controlling Agnes.

Partners in an apathetic relationship are unwilling to put themselves on the line. They don't tell their partner what they are really feeling. They control their partner and the relationship by *not* talking about their hurts, disappointments, angers, fears, and needs. They don't let their partner see how they are experiencing them or the relationship. Apathetic relationships commonly fall into a repeating cycle of alienation:

Step 1: I want to avoid pain, so I close off and find an apathetic relationship.

Step 2: I make you guess about my perceptions in the relationship.

Step 3: You guess wrong.

Step 4: That proves to me that you are dangerous and don't really understand me. I have to close off even more.

In a healthy relationship, there is no need for one partner to force the other to do what he or she doesn't want to do. When conflict arises, healthy partners know how to work together to resolve the conflict, how to compromise and still get what they need. It is a matter of voluntary shared power. Power struggles don't exist for long because both partners participate in making decisions. Neither partner is trying to prove that he or she is better than, or smarter than, or stronger than the other. They don't need to do that because they respect each other's skills, fears, and vulnerabilities. They support each other's strengths. They are able to give up their need to control because they trust their partner. They know that when a conflict occurs, it will be resolved according to the needs and wishes of both partners. They feel safe in the knowledge that their partner would never do anything to deliberately and intentionally hurt them.

Myra had been working long, hard hours for a month for the

year-end review at the office. Although she and her boyfriend, William, had not planned a vacation, Myra decided she really needed to take a few days off. She brought up the subject over dinner.

"What do you think?" she asked after she had explained her feelings and her ideas about the vacation.

"I don't know," William replied doubtfully. "I don't feel comfortable taking time off work right now."

"What if I rent a motel room in the mountains for a week, and you come up on the weekend?"

"That sounds good. I could take one day off, I guess, and make it a three-day weekend."

Both Myra and William were able to state their needs clearly and work toward a common solution that met both requirements. Myra was clear about what she needed for herself but understood that William had his own commitments and priorities at work. He was willing to understand her need to get away and thought of a plan to spend time with her and still put in the necessary time at work.

Trust

Trust Questions
Are you honest with your partner? Is your partner honest with you? Do you honor your commitments? Does your partner honor his/her commitments? Do you present yourself honestly to your partner, or do you try to appear to be something you're not? Does your partner honestly present him/herself? Does your partner's personality change under pressure?

Trust is a feeling of confidence and safety regarding the honesty, character, ability, and strength of another person. There are two types of trust—rational and irrational. Rational trust is based upon evidence that the other person is trustworthy, which in turn is based on sufficient knowledge of who that person is and what he or she is doing. Irrational trust is based upon ignorance or denial. When trust is based upon ignorance, we trust someone that we don't know. When our trust is based upon denial, we decide to ignore or rationalize evidence that that person is not trustworthy.

Trust is a matter of choice. In a relationship, we choose whether or not to trust our partner. If I choose to distrust you in spite of evidence that you are trustworthy, or if I trust you in spite of evidence that you are untrustworthy, then my trust is irrational.

The former wife of a Mafia boss was being interviewed on a national talk show. She said she had been married to her husband for twenty years. When her husband was arrested for murder and extortion, she instantly divorced him. The interviewer asked her why suddenly, after twenty years of marriage, she had chosen to divorce her husband.

"I didn't know what he did for a living," she said. "I was shocked. If I had known that I was with someone like that, I never would have stayed married to him."

How do you stay married to a murderer for twenty years and not know it? The only way to do that is to become a master of denial, trapped by irrational trust. She chose to trust her husband although he was not trustworthy.

Rational trust is not something you can create by yourself. Trust in a relationship emerges over time as a consequence of the interaction between partners. One partner must behave in a trustworthy manner, and the other partner must perceive the behavior as trustworthy. Both must honestly participate in the process or rational trust cannot develop.

Even though somethe is not trustworthy you act as though mignn)

Trust

Compulsive = Irrational
Balanced = Rational
Apathetic = Not Needed

In a compulsive relationship, trust is irrational: "As long as I feel good around my partner, I trust him or her regardless of the evidence," they seem to say. "As soon as the good feelings begin to fade, my suspicions run rampant and I stop trusting." As a result, many people in compulsive relationships vacillate between feelings of intense, unshakable trust, and feelings of paranoid suspicion, doubt, and jealousy.

Sandra was going through her husband's suits to take them to the cleaners. Mack traveled a good deal on business, which Sandra often resented. As she piled up the suits, a business card dropped out of one coat pocket and she saw "Laura 555-8372" handwritten in a scrawl on the back. Sandra felt as if she had been struck. "How could he do that to me?" she thought. "He's obviously having an affair!" She thought of all the things she would tell him when she confronted him with the evidence that evening.

An apathetic relationship, by definition, is based on profound distrust. Neither partner trusts the other to meet his or her needs and neither trusts the other not to hurt him/her. Each partner is so well defended that there is no need to develop trust.

Julianne wrote in her journal regularly and kept it in the large drawer in the dining room. She never told Tim not to read her journal and never asked if he did. She was careful, however, to write nothing in her journal that she would not want Tim to read.

Julianne didn't need to rely on Tim's honesty because she didn't trust him in the first place. This is typical of apathetic relationships in which people prefer to coexist in safety rather than risk intimacy with their partner.

Healthy partners want to develop rational trust, so they communicate about who they are, what is important to them, and what they can be relied upon to do. They take responsibility for their actions and for the consequences of their actions. As the relationship deepens and their knowledge of one another increases, trust develops also.

Jonathan offered to pick Joan up from work and take her to the airport for her early-evening flight. He assured her that he would get her to the airport in plenty of time for her overseas check-in. Joan knew from their numerous dates that Jonathan was a punctual and conscientious person. He seldom disappointed her and the one time he had, there were extenuating circumstances that Joan understood. Joan felt she could trust Jonathan to get her to her flight on time.

As fallible human beings, we are all untrustworthy from time to time. Healthy relationships can survive a violation of trust because the partners know that even though there will be times when they will fail those whom they love, it will be the exception, not the rule.

How we deal with the accidental violations of trust in our relationship is an essential test of a healthy relationship. The key issue is to know that your partner did not intentionally mean to hurt you. Perhaps he or she was out of control, or made a mistake in judgment, or did not anticipate the consequences. When you know that it was not done with an intent to hurt you, it becomes possible to survive it and move ahead. Violations of trust that are repetitive, conscious, and intentional, however, should not be overlooked. They indicate that the partner is not trustworthy and the relationship should be reexamined in this light.

Boundaries

> **Boundary Questions**
> Are we able to be our own person in the relationship? Are we able to surrender within the context of the relationship without losing our sense of self, or without expecting our partner to give up their sense of self?

A boundary is a barrier that establishes where one person ends and another person begins. Boundaries are essential to a healthy relationship. Without them, you cannot distinguish between the three necessary entities of a healthy relationship: *me*, the individual self, who I am as a person; *you*, the partner, who he or she is as a person; and *us*, the couple, who we are together.

Dysfunctional families frequently have difficulty teaching children about healthy boundaries. As a result, people growing up in dysfunctional families bring these difficulties into their adult relationships. Healthy people have boundaries. They have developed an identity that is separate and distinct from other people.

In compulsive relationships personal boundaries are poorly defined. The partners' emotional hunger drives them to try to merge with another human being in an attempt to overcome the emptiness they feel in being themselves. Both partners either seek to lose themselves in their partner or expect their partner to become lost in them.

Wayne felt that he was better than Marla. He was better educated, had more widely varied experiences in life, and was a good organizer. He wanted her to merge with him and become a part of who he was, to do things the way he did them, and to enjoy what he enjoyed. He needed an extension of himself to make him feel more important. "I can help her be a better person if I tell her what to do and how to do it," Wayne thought.

Marla tended to feel insecure. When she met Wayne she was impressed by his strength and intelligence and felt inferior. "I have to do what he expects," Marla thought. "He's so much smarter than I am, I'd just look dumb if I challenged him!" Marla tried to become an extension of Wayne. She wanted to merge with him and lose herself in him. "At times I felt that if I could just get close enough, I could forget about who I was and the problems that I was having."

A lack of boundaries frequently means that one partner takes on the emotional state of the other. If Wayne feels sad, Marla should, too. If Wayne doesn't feel like going out with friends, Marla shouldn't want to either. The identity of the partners as individuals is lost. There is no *you* and *I*, there's only *us*. Two thirds of the relationship is missing.

In an apathetic relationship, there is no *us* as a separate entity. Each partner is a self-contained unit superficially interacting with the other. Each has fixed boundaries. The partners stay in the relationship but set up firm rules to keep from getting too close to each other. It's as if they are walking down a railroad track on separate rails. They are traveling in the same direction but they're not really together. Neither wants to reach out too far to the other person because they will fall off their own rail.

In a healthy relationship, all three entities—*me, you,* and *us*—are fully developed and strengthened. Together the couple can be stronger than either individual is alone. The partners share their personal power with each other, and when personal power is shared, it is magnified, amplified, and intensified. Instead of draining them, the relationship energizes them.

In healthy relationships, boundaries are flexible. The partners can walk hand in hand; they can walk separately or close together. There's a lot of freedom in healthy relationships. Both partners have choices. In being together they don't lose their individual identity. When one partner is angry or hurt, the other doesn't need to mirror that emotion. They may be sympathetic to their partner's anger or pain, but they don't need to take it on as their own.

People in healthy relationships are comfortable changing boundaries. They can lower their boundaries and become very close and intimate with their partners. They can also establish emotional distance, putting up a barrier to keep their partner away if they want or need to. This ability to have flexible boundaries allows for both intimacy and safety. People with healthy boundaries are capable of detaching from others and protecting themselves from abusive behavior. They can be intimate when appropriate or back away when they need to feel safe.

When Peter lost his temper, Abby refused to talk with him. "I am not going to talk with you while you are so upset. I will not be insulted by you or put up with your accusations. When you are ready to talk in a reasonable manner, let me know. Until then, I am unavailable." When Peter regained control, he and Abby discussed the problem.

Sociability

> ### Sociability Questions
> How do I integrate my friendships with my relationship? Am I allowed to have friendships that are mine, independent of the relationship? Does my partner have his or her own friends? Do we share friends as a couple? Does either my partner or I feel bad when the other spends time alone with his or her friends?

Sociability is the way we build friendships around our relationship. The way we include our friends and acquaintances in our lives reflects our relationship style. Just as there are me, you, and us in a healthy relationship, there are me and my friends, you and your friends, and us and our friends.

In compulsive relationships, the couple is isolated. It's "you and me against the world." Since the compulsive couple believes that nobody understands them, they refuse to share what they have together with others. They aren't interested in developing a network of mutual friends; they are content and complete within themselves. "I become lost in you, you become lost in me, we become obsessed with each other—no one else matters."

I had a friend named Dean. When he wasn't in a romantic relationship, we'd spend a lot of time together. Periodically, he'd disappear for weeks at a time. No calls. No communication. He just wasn't around. Where was he? He was in love again! When the relationship ended, generally in four to ten weeks, he was back on my doorstep expecting our friendship to continue as though it had never missed a beat.

This is a common experience for women. Many have told me of making plans to spend an evening with a girlfriend and getting a last-minute telephone call canceling out. Why? You guessed it. She met Mr. Right. Her priorities shifted, and a near stranger became more important than a close friend. That's the power of a compulsive relationship. That's how these relationships create conflict and isolation from friends.

When a couple isolates themselves in a relationship, there are often very good reasons for this isolation. Have you ever introduced your partner to your friends, and nobody liked him or her? They came to you privately and asked, "Why are you involved with someone like that? Don't you know that he (or she) is not right for you?"

At this point, people in compulsive relationships have two choices: to listen to their friends and end the relationship, or ignore their friends and keep the relationship. People who tend to get involved in compulsive relationships usually keep the relationship and create distance between themselves and their friends. They think that their friends and family don't understand.

Partners in an apathetic relationship are socially separated. If they live together, they may share the functional day-to-day chores of living together but they don't have many mutual friends. If they live apart, they lead separate lives and have separate friends. Their shared social life is minimal.

Marshall and Rachel met and married in their mid-thirties. Their social activities were already well established. Rachel would stay in the city once or twice a week to have dinner with her friends from work. Marshall would work out at the gym two to three nights a week. On weekends, Marshall played softball and soccer. Rachel was free to indulge in her mystery reading and gardening.

Healthy relationships are socially integrated. They parallel our relationship boundaries. There are your friends, my friends, and our friends. Each partner has his or her separate friends, and together they have friends as a couple. This creates a healthy, balanced, stable social network.

Consequences of Relationship Styles

> **Consequences Questions**
> Does the relationship cause you progressively
> more pain? Does it cause you to feel progressively
> more alienated, isolated, and alone? Or does the
> relationship cause you to feel progressive levels of
> connectiveness, meaning, and fulfillment?

In each relationship style, there is a cycle of repetitive steps that produces predictable consequences or outcomes.

In compulsive relationships, there is a repeating cycle of pain. As the relationship develops, it goes through a series of phases. First, there is a period of intense pleasure, followed by pain and problems. The magical expectations are shattered and one or both partners feels intense pain. This leads to disillusionment.

When pain or disillusionment hits, some people get out of the relationship and look for someone else. Others try desperately to re-create the intense pleasure of the early days of their relationship and fix the relationship. These efforts may result in another period of intense pleasure before the cycle begins again.

> **Consequences**
> Compulsive = Pain
> Balanced   = Contentment
> Apathetic = Isolation

In apathetic relationships, there is a cycle of alienation or isolation. Initially, both partners are comfortable. Their relationship is moving along in a pain-free style. Then a problem occurs. They may, in part, want to try to work it out but don't think it's worth the effort. So they don't try. Or they may try to work it out, only to be disappointed if their partner is unwilling. So they lower their expectations even further and, as a result, they get even less from the relationship until, finally, they are just going through the motions.

In a healthy relationship, the cycle is one of contentment. There is an ebb and flow. In this cycle, when one or both partners encounter a problem, they don't immediately experience fear that it will cause the relationship to end. They trust that they will be able to work it through. Even though they may not know the answers, they don't give up. They keep talking. Why? Because they know that by talking, they are going to discover some answers.

Every time they encounter a problem and solve it, their trust deepens. Each partner's self-respect and respect for their partner grow because they are able to be true to themselves and to their values. As a result, there is a deepening cycle of contentment, respect, admiration, love, and caring. As a result, the relationship grows more special, and the bond that they share with their partner is strengthened.

Relationship Scorecard			
	COMPULSIVE	HEALTHY	APATHETIC
EXPECTATIONS	Magical	Realistic	Minimal
GRATIFICATION	Instant/Constant	Enduring Satisfaction	No Pain
COMMUNICATION	Deceptive	Honest	Withheld
INFLUENCE	Control	Shared Power	Abandonment
TRUST	Irrational	Rational	Not Needed
BOUNDARIES	Merged	Flexible	Rigid and Distant
SOCIABILITY	Isolated	Integrated	Separate
CONSEQUENCES	Pain	Contentment	Alienation

USING RELATIONSHIP STYLES FOR CHANGE

The goal of examining your current relationship style is to help you identify problems and to set goals for change. It is important to remember that there is no such thing as a perfect relationship. All relationships have problems and rough edges. The goal is not to develop a perfect relationship but to work toward positive change.

There are no clear-cut dividing lines between compulsive, healthy, and apathetic relationship traits. These traits operate on a continuum and most relationships involve a mixture of compulsive, balanced, and apathetic characteristics. In the chart below, each common characteristic is followed by a scale which ranges from very compulsive ($+10$) to very apathetic (-10). This scale allows you to construct a profile of your relationship to identify the areas that need work.

Brent and Judy, for example, decided that they scored a plus ten in terms of expectations because neither could possibly live up to the highly romanticized ideal they had set for each other. In terms of gratification, they rated themselves as a plus five because both of them expected the relationship to feel good but realized there would be problems and bad days.

They rated each other a minus five on communication. They both felt that they kept too many secrets and tended to avoid talking about sensitive issues that might cause a disagreement.

Relationship Characteristics

	COMPULSIVE	HEALTHY	APATHETIC
1. EXPECTATIONS	Unrealistic x5	Realistic	Minimal
	$+10$ ←――――――――― 0 ―――――→ -10		
2. GRATIFICATION	Instant	x5 Long-term	No Pain
	$+10$ ←――XXXXX 0 ―――――→ -10		
3. COMMUNICATION	Dishonest	Honest	Withheld
	$+10$ ←――――――― 0 ―――――→ -10		
4. INFLUENCE	Control	Shared Power	Abandonment
	$+10$ ←――――XXX 0 ―――――→ -10		
5. TRUST	Irrational +9	Rational	Not Needed
	$+10$ ←――――――― 0 ―――――→ -10		
6. BOUNDARIES	Merged	Flexible	Rigid
	$+10$ ←――――XXXXX 0 ―――――→ -10		
7. SOCIABILITY	Isolated	Integrated	Separated
	$+10$ ←――――――― 0 XXXXXXXX―→ -10		
8. CONSEQUENCES	Pain	Contentment	Alienation
	$+10$ ←――――XXXX 0 ―――――→ -10		

In terms of influence, they rated themselves as a plus three because Brent tended to be the recognized leader of the relationship, but they also shared most of the problem solving. In terms of trust, they rated themselves as very balanced (a zero) because they felt they knew each other well and could rely completely upon each other.

In terms of boundaries, they rated themselves as a plus five because Brent tended to expect Judy to merge with him, and Judy had a tendency to want to lose herself in Brent. In terms of sociability they rated themselves as a minus eight. They both had a lot of friends as individuals, but they never built a shared social network. Brent had his friends and Judy had her friends. When they spent time together they were generally alone. In the area of consequences, they rated their relationship at a plus three because they tended to feel frustrated and hurt when they couldn't resolve problems and felt that the relationship was accumulating pain and frustration as it went along because they weren't good at problem solving.

They constructed the following profile of their relationship.

Relationship Characteristics

	COMPULSIVE	HEALTHY	APATHETIC
1. EXPECTATIONS	Unrealistic	Realistic	Minimal
	+10 ←——XXXXXXXXXX 0————→ -10		
2. GRATIFICATION	Instant	Long-term	No Pain
	+10 ←———XXXXX 0————→ -10		
3. COMMUNICATION	Dishonest	Honest	Withheld
	+10 ←——————— 0 XXXXX————→ -10		
4. INFLUENCE	Control	Shared Power	Abandonment
	+10 ←——————— 0————→ -10		
5. TRUST	Irrational	Rational	Not Needed
	+10 ←——————— 0————→ -10		
6. BOUNDARIES	Merged	Flexible	Rigid
	+10 ←———XXXXX 0————→ -10		
7. SOCIABILITY	Isolated	Integrated	Separated
	+10 ←——————— 0 XXXXXXXX——→ -10		
8. CONSEQUENCES	Pain	Contentment	Alienation
	+10 ←——————— 0————→ -10		

Notice that instead of trying to label their relationship as compulsive, balanced, or apathetic, they were able to do an inventory of their relationship. They evaluated their relationship in each of the eight characteristics, discussed their personal evaluations, and came to an agreement about which areas of the relationship needed work.

It is easy to exist in an unhealthy relationship for years. Sometimes we may not even recognize the relationship as unhealthy or realize how hurtful it is. Other times we do, but may not know what to do about it. Unfortunately, in unhealthy relationships our needs don't get met. We're not honest with ourselves and we can't feel good about who we are. We can't feel good about who our partner is. We stop learning and growing as people. We may have glimpses of happiness, but they are the exception. In the end, we pay a high price for dysfunctional relationships, and each of us deserves much more than that in life.

Healthy relationships are not an unattainable ideal. It is possible to have a rewarding and fulfilling relationship. It is possible to have rational expectations of our partners; to have a relationship based upon rigorously honest communication and shared power and influence without either controlling or abandoning our partners. It is possible rationally to trust our partner to be who and what he/she is, to have flexible boundaries so that we can relate to our partner without losing ourselves or seeking to change who our partner is. We can develop a balanced and integrated social life. And we can create a growing cycle of contentment and satisfaction.

Chapter 4

GETTING TO KNOW YOURSELF: REVIEWING THE PAST

PRINCIPAL CHOICES
• To become conscious of your past influences and how they affect your ability to get love right.
• To examine past relationship patterns and learn from them.
• Whether to live out the patterns you've established or to break free of them.

Many people think that getting love right begins in the wonderful moment you find Mr. or Ms. Right and the relationship proceeds to magically unfold. In reality, a healthy relationship begins long before that moment. It begins with you and the type of person you are, the life experiences you've had, and the relationship decisions you make based on your needs and wants. If you don't know who you are or what options are available to you, you won't have the information you need to get love right. When you know who you are and what you want, you can use that information to make healthy choices that will give you the relationship you want.

Kerrie met Ryan at her sister's Christmas party. Ryan seemed as interested in her as she was in him and they spent the evening talking together. They began seeing one another. On their third date, Ryan said, "Kerrie, I'm really enjoying being with you. I like you a lot. I think you should know, therefore, that I'm only teaching here at the university for one semester. It's true that they might offer me a permanent position, but I'm not going to accept it if they do. I'm committed to my work in Florida, and I plan to return when my work here is done. I'm telling you this to let you know that I'm not interested in a long-term relationship. I like you and I would like to date you while I'm here, but I have to be honest with you."

Kerrie heard what Ryan said, but she didn't believe him. She knew they were a good match and hoped that their relationship would develop into a long-term commitment, perhaps marriage. Surely if he was in love with her, Ryan would change his mind and accept the university position.

Three months later, Ryan began to tell her about his plans to move and talked about ending their relationship. Kerrie couldn't believe her ears. What did she do wrong? Why did Ryan betray her that way? Over the next weeks and months, Kerrie tried to figure out what she had or hadn't done that led to the failure of their relationship. It had seemed so good. What had caused him to act that way?

Kerrie didn't realize that there was only one problem in her relationship with Ryan, but it was a fatal problem: She was looking for a long-term, committed relationship and Ryan was looking for a short-term relationship. As much as he liked Kerrie, Ryan was not interested in becoming involved with her in a long-term, committed way.

Often people's inability to find satisfaction in their relationships is due to the fact that they don't know what they want or what their partner wants. When Ryan told Kerrie what his expectations were, Kerrie had three options. She could have said, "Ryan, I really like you and I would really like to be involved with you, but I'm looking for a long-term relationship, perhaps marriage and a family. I'm afraid this won't work between us."

Or she might have accepted Ryan's offer of a short-term, high-quality relationship according to the terms he set. Instead, Kerrie chose the third option, which was to ignore the information Ryan had given her about himself and his expectations for the relationship and to hold on to her magical thinking that he would change his mind. The result was she got hurt.

All relationships are not the same. To get love right, we need to be aware that there are several types of relationships that can serve different purposes in our lives. There are both long-term and short-term relationships; some require high levels of commitment and others do not. We have the choice to select the type of relationship that will meet our current needs. For most people, the relationship they want at age twenty will be different from what they want at forty. We also need to consider who we are and what we want to do in our lives and select the type of relationship that fits our personality. What it means for a person who is career oriented to get love right may be very different from someone who is family oriented, whose most important goal is to raise and nurture children. Ryan put his career as a research scientist first and his relationship with Kerrie second. He wanted a relationship that would meet his needs for intimacy but also allow him the flexibility to pursue his research. Kerrie's priority was to find a partner for a long-term, committed relationship that would eventually lead to marriage and a family.

Even before you meet a potential partner, you need to know the type of relationship you want. If you don't, you won't be able to tell if a particular person has the potential to meet your relationship goals. Knowing the type of relationship you want requires you to know yourself—who you are and what past experiences you have had that may affect your needs and relationship choices.

Sometimes we fail to make the best decisions about our intimate relationships in spite of our best efforts to do so. One reason may be out of self-ignorance. We may not have considered how our relationships fit into the larger context of our life, the goals and values we hold, and what we want to do in life. We may also make poor decisions because we are unconsciously re-creating patterns established by earlier experiences, particularly in our family of origin. We may not even be aware of the influence these earlier experiences have on our ability to make healthy relationship choices. The Personal History assessment in this chapter will assist you in examining your past experiences and uncovering some attitudes and beliefs that may be operating in your life without your conscious knowledge.

Another important area of personal exploration includes past relationships. What types of relationships have you had? Did they tend to be long-term or short-term? How do you feel about them? What did you gain from them? What would you like to do differently?

Had Kerrie known that there are different types of relationships, she would have realized that she and Ryan had fundamentally different relationship goals. She would have spared herself a great deal of heartbreak and self-blame. If she had completed her own Personal History, Kerrie may have been able to understand the origins of her lifelong desire for stability and long-term commitment. Her Relationship History could have shown her how her relationship problems stemmed from her repeated attempts to find this stability with partners like Ryan who could not provide it. Aware of these patterns in her life, Kerrie could have chosen to change the way she went about building relationships. As it was, she didn't know what had gone wrong, so she couldn't understand how to keep from repeating the same error in the future.

RELATIONSHIP CHOICES

When we think of adult relationships, we, like Kerrie, may think primarily in terms of committed relationships, perhaps marriage and family. We might say: "I am (or am not) ready to settle down"; "I am (or am not) looking for a potential marriage partner." We overlook the fact that there are types of relationships other than the traditional long-term, "til-death-do-us-part" arrangement. Love relationships can be divided into four broad types: experimental dating, transitional and committed relationships, and intimate encounters.

Experimental dating, transitional relationships, and intimate encounters are all short-term relationships that last from several days to several months and are generally not expected to grow into long-term committed relationships. These short-term involvements each meet particular relationship needs. Experimental dating relationships give us new experiences that allow us to gain the knowledge we need to make sound relationship choices in the future. Transitional relationships provide valuable support during the difficult period after the end of a long-term committed relationship. Intimate encounters are unique relationships outside the normal context of our lives that meet our here-and-now needs for intimacy.

Two essential factors in all healthy relationships are awareness of your own and your partner's expectations and your honesty of motive. You must first be aware of the type of relationship you are or are not looking for and then be willing to discuss your expectations with your partner in the early stages of the relationship. If you are unsure of exactly what type of relationship you want, you can communicate that, too. Your partner also must talk about his or her expectations. This will give both of you an opportunity to decide if involvement, under those terms, will meet your relationship needs. This is especially important in transitional relationships and intimate encounters, when a misunderstanding of expectations and motive can be emotionally devastating.

Although you think you know what type of relationship you are ready for, your relationship goals may change when you become involved with a particular person and your feelings toward him or her evolve. You can never be certain at the outset how a relationship will turn out. Don't be afraid to change your expectations as your feelings change, but realize that if they do, you need to let your partner know and renegotiate the terms of the relationship. Remember, just because you change your expectations doesn't mean your partner will change his or hers.

These relationship categories are not absolute. They are important primarily to help you clarify the essential nature of the short-term relationships so that you can have a way of determining what you are seeking in a particular relationship and talk about it with your partner. There are times these categories will overlap, and you may find they are less definite in practice than in theory.

Experimental Dating Relationships

The most common form of experimental relationships is dating. We become involved in this type of relationship to learn something new or to have a certain experience we have not had before. It gives us an opportunity to get to know different types of people and how to handle the intense feelings love relationships involve. Experimental dating prepares us to make sound decisions about the type of partner and relationship that can best meet our needs.

Although there are many reasons for experimental dating, people are most likely to enter into this type of relationship as young adults, when they are first learning about love relationships and partners.

Tom began dating when he was eighteen years old. His first girlfriend, Norma, was serious and conservative. Tom liked her but quickly grew bored and felt pressured by her serious nature.

He then met Elaine, an exciting free spirit who wanted fun and adventure. They dated for three months and Tom fell madly in love. When he told Elaine about his feelings, she ended the relationship. "I'm not ready to get tied down," she told him. "I just want to enjoy myself and have a good time." Tom was crushed. It was his first heartbreak. He thought he'd never get over it, but he did.

Over the next four years, Tom had three other serious relationships with three very different women. Each time he was drawn into the relationship by a sense of curiosity about this person and what it would be like to be with her. These experiences helped Tom learn about women and relationships so that he developed realistic expectations about love. As a result, when Tom was ready for a committed relationship, he had the information and skills he needed to make a healthy choice.

Many people bypass the experimental relationships of adolescence. They fall in love and marry their first partner and never have any other romantic relationships. In later years, these individuals may be curious about what other romantic relationships would be like. They may even feel they have missed some important life experiences.

Gwen married Stan, her high school sweetheart. She never dated anyone else. They had three children and built a happy life together. "Even though I'm happy," she confided to a friend, "I still feel like there's something missing. I love Stan and he's a great husband and provider, but a part of me wonders what other men are like!"

Many people who marry their first lover come to believe that somewhere in the world there is a mystical, ideal partner with whom life would be magically and blissfully better—the "grass is greener" syndrome. Because they never went through the process of dating different types of partners, these individuals were unable to learn for themselves that all relationships are a trade-off and that no partner is perfect or without faults. Consequently, they may have a desire to experiment with other partners later in life, either in the form of extramarital affairs or by ending the relationship in search of a better one.

Experimental dating is not only for adolescents and young adults, however. It is valuable for anyone who wishes to experience new relationships. This includes individuals who are interested in changing their relationship patterns and learning new ways to experience love and intimacy. Many people who have had trouble with relationships in the past undertake a program of personal growth and change and enter into a period of experimental dating to gain new relationship skills. If you are not in a committed relationship and choose to follow through the relationship-building process in this book, you will probably find it valuable to engage in experimental relationships for a period of time.

Transitional Relationships

After ending a long-term committed relationship, it is common for people to go through a period of emotional instability and unwillingness to commit. During these periods, people often look for short-term, supportive relationships that will help them deal with the aftermath of the previous relationship and help prepare them emotionally for their next relationship. Although some transitional relationships grow into permanent, committed relationships, most do not, and partners should never expect that they will.

Transitional relationships differ from experimental dating relationships because partners are not looking for new experiences but for a safe environment in which to heal from past hurts. People looking for transitional relationships therefore are drawn to the types of partner they already know and with whom they can feel secure.

People who don't know about transitional relationships, or who believe that these relationships are wrong, feel they need to make them more than they really are. This type of unhealthy transitional relationship can be called a rebound relationship. People in a rebound relationship cannot accept it for what it really is—a relationship where healing and preparation for a future relationship can take place. Instead, one or both partners feel the need to force the relationship to be something that it really isn't and cannot be.

In a healthy transitional relationship, both partners know they have limited expectations for the relationship and openly communicate their needs and wants from the start. If one person wants a transitional relationship and the other wants a permanent committed relationship, conflict will ensue. If, however, the couple discuss their needs and wants, the relationship can be terminated before serious damage is done. If one or both partners is dishonest, he/she can mislead the other and create serious emotional problems.

Margaret was recently divorced from her husband of fifteen years. She did not want a divorce, but her husband felt stifled and decided to end the marriage. Margaret was devastated and went through a period of depression and severe emotional pain. Four months after her divorce, she decided to date again but felt she could not trust men. Psychologically, Margaret was not prepared to make another commitment. She needed time to heal and to readjust to her new position in life. She needed a supportive, loving male companion who could help her through the transition. She was looking for a relationship experience that would allow her to reenter the dating world and reestablish her self-concept as a woman so she could become comfortable interacting with men.

One of Margaret's biggest fears was of being dishonest and hurting the men she was dating. She was afraid, however, to express her desire for a short-term, transitional relationship. When her desire for honesty overcame her fear of rejection, she began communicating openly and honestly with her partners about her needs and the limitations she saw in the relationship. She became better able to select appropriate partners who would not hurt her or be hurt by her as the relationship developed, ran its course, and ended. This combination of self-awareness, honesty and communication made it possible for Margaret to date a series of men, heal the damage from her broken marriage, and prepare herself to once again take the risk of making a commitment in a relationship.

Intimate Encounters

Intimate encounters are short-term relationships which occur within a special or unusual context outside the normal flow of our lives. Traditionally referred to as affairs, they frequently involve intensity and excitement. Two people meet on a singles' cruise to Europe and have an intense romantic relationship for two weeks. When the cruise is over, they return to their normal lives and the relationship ends. Intimate encounters also can occur when one or both partners are involved in another relationship.

People who choose to have an intimate encounter do so to meet their needs for here-and-now intimacy. This type of relationship is not incompatible with other relationships: for example, an intimate encounter may or may not also be an experimental relationship, providing partners with new experiences; or it may serve as a transition between committed relationships. What distinguishes an intimate encounter is its focus on immediacy and the special nature of the context in which it occurs.

Although many people may disapprove of them, intimate encounters in the form of extramarital or extrarelationship affairs are fairly common. It is important to understand what these relationships are and the options people have in coping with them. We will return to this subject in chapter 8, "Sexuality in Relationships."

Committed Relationships

People seeking a long-term relationship begin with the expectation that the relationship will "go somewhere" if all goes well. As the partners interact and spend time together, they learn more and more about each other. They evaluate their partner as to his or her suitability for a long-term commitment and, if they are compatible, usually proceed to make personal, financial, and legal commitments to one another. The most commonly recognized committed relationship in the United States today is marriage.

Yet "long-term" is not necessarily forever, even in the case of marriage. The majority of committed relationships today last somewhere between seven and eleven years. Approximately one third of all people maintain committed relationships for the rest of their lives.

We have a tendency in this society to think that long-term committed relationships are the only truly meaningful relationships to have. This is not true. You don't have to be in a lifelong one-and-only committed relationship to get love right. Many times people have their relationship needs met by serial monogamy: they are in meaningful relationships that span anywhere from several years to a decade but then decide to uncouple because, for one reason or another, they are no longer meeting each other's needs in a new stage of life.

When a relationship ends, it need not be seen as a tragedy or failure. Often, it is an indication of the individual growth of each partner. It is very important, however, that partners end their relationship responsibly, as we will discuss further in chapter 11, "Relationship Transformation: Evaluation, Renegotiation, and Termination."

PERSONAL HISTORY

Making healthy relationship decisions requires having as much information as possible. This means knowing who you are and how your past experiences may be affecting your ability to make healthy choices. As we have seen, our family of origin can cause us to unconsciously follow certain behavioral patterns, which, if destructive or dysfunctional, can trap us in dysfunctional relationships time after time.

In fact, the influence of our past experience may be so strong that many of the problems we experience in our adult relationships have less to do with the current situation than with unresolved issues from the past. Constructing a Personal History can help you identify significant and potentially problematic issues that may be keeping you from developing healthy relationships.

Your Personal History helps you analyze the sequence of key events in your life and the ways in which those events have affected your relationships. When you answer the questions pertaining to the following significant periods in your life, you will be able to understand what it is about you that has led you to adopt certain relationship styles and behaviors in the past and what you can do differently in the future. There are seven areas to examine:

Early Childhood

Questions about Childhood

1. Describe your childhood: Was it happy, sad, troubled?
2. What kind of person was your mother? Describe your relationship with her.
3. What kind of person was your father? Describe your relationship with him.
4. How do you remember your brothers and sisters? How did you fit in with them?
5. Describe the friends you had.
6. What kind of person were you at this age? What did you believe the world was like?
7. How did you feel about people of the opposite sex? About people of the same sex? How did you feel about members of your peer group?
8. How did your early childhood experiences affect your image of yourself as a boy/girl?
9. How do you think your childhood experiences affected your ability to have close, intimate relationships later in life?

On the basis of what we see and learn in our family of origin, we develop deeply entrenched beliefs about ourselves, other people, and the world in general. However painful or dysfunctional these earliest experiences may have been, they become the norm against which we judge everything else. In the context of our family of origin, we learn to believe that we are or are not worthwhile human beings worthy of being loved and that we are or are not able to cope with the world successfully. We also develop definite impressions about other people and about the type of men and women to whom we are attracted. We develop an intuitive sense of whether the world is a friendly or hostile place. We come to believe that life will be either satisfying or painful.

Grammar School

Questions about Grammar School

1. How do you remember grammar school?
2. What kind of person were you in grammar school?
3. How did you view people of the opposite sex in grammar school? How did you view people of the same sex? How did you view members of your peer group?
4. How did you get along with your teachers and other people in authority?
5. How did you do academically? What were your favorite subjects? What were your least favorite subjects?
6. How did your grammar school experiences affect your image of yourself as a boy/girl?
7. What experiences did you have in grammar school that reinforced the basic beliefs that you learned in your family?
8. What experiences did you have in grammar school that conflicted with or challenged what you learned in your family?
9. How did your grammar school experiences enhance your ability to have successful, intimate love relationships?
10. How did your grammar school experiences hinder your ability to have successful, intimate love relationships?

When we begin grammar school, our world expands to include new experiences. Some of these experiences reinforce our early childhood beliefs by confirming what our family taught us. These reinforcing experiences also tend to support our automatic behaviors—ways of thinking, feeling, and acting we learned from our family that have become so ingrained in us, we are often unaware of them.

Other experiences, however, challenge our childhood beliefs. We are exposed to new ideas and ways of thinking that may show us flaws in what we learned from our families. These new and challenging experiences may conflict with our automatic behaviors. When we act in ways we learned in our families, we may come into conflict with other people who criticize our behaviors. When this happens, we are confused because the truth, as we know it, is that our behavior is appropriate and our family is right, but our experiences tell us otherwise. This establishes an inner conflict that will continue throughout adolescence. When what we learn about the world seems to contradict what we were taught in our families, it forces us to choose whether we are going to reconcile this conflict by aligning with our parents against the world or with the world against our parents.

High School

Questions about High School
1. How do you remember high school?
2. What kind of person were you in high school?
3. How did you view people of the opposite sex? People of the same sex? Your peer group?
4. How did you get along with your teachers and other people in authority?
5. How did you do academically? What were your favorite and least favorite subjects?
6. How did your high school experiences affect your image of yourself as a teenager?
7. What experiences did you have in high school that reinforced the basic beliefs you learned in your family?
8. What experiences did you have in high school that conflicted with what you learned in your family?

> **9.** How did your high school experiences enhance your ability to have successful, intimate love relationships?
> **10.** How did your high school experiences hinder your ability to have successful, intimate love relationships?

The ongoing task of adolescence is to become our own person. High school brings teenagers an even broader range of new experiences which aid the process of developing independence. Adolescents enjoy more freedom and begin to associate with a more influential peer group.

High school experiences tend to further reinforce or challenge childhood beliefs. Teenagers may have experiences that give them a view of life totally different from what they experienced within their families. When the contrast is extreme, teenagers have a choice. They can decide their families' beliefs are true and align themselves with their families against the world, isolating themselves from others. Or they can separate themselves psychologically from their families and begin to identify with a new belief system that allows them to affiliate with their friends. When this happens, they begin to develop identities that are separate from that of the family system.

College

> **Questions about College**
> **1.** What was college like for you?
> **2.** What kind of person were you in college?
> **3.** How did you view people of the opposite sex during college? The same sex? Members of your peer group?
> **4.** How did you get along with your instructors, professors, and other people in authority?

5. How did you do academically? What were your favorite/least favorite subjects?
6. How did your college experiences affect your image of yourself as a man/woman?
7. What experiences did you have in college that reinforced the basic beliefs you learned in your family?
8. What experiences did you have in college that conflicted with what you learned in your family?
9. How did your college experiences enhance your ability to have successful, intimate love relationships?
10. How did your college experiences hinder your ability to have successful, intimate love relationships?

In college students begin to learn about different life philosophies and the rules of logic. They also are exposed to new values and cultural norms. The college atmosphere often involves teenagers in a subculture of higher education that supports experimentation with new behaviors and different life-styles. Some of these behaviors are healthy and productive; others, such as alcohol and drug use, are potentially dangerous.

Some of an individual's college experiences will support what he or she learned as a child, while others will tend to conflict with those early lessons.

Military

Questions about the Military
1. What were your military experiences?
2. What kind of person were you in the military?
3. How did you view members of the opposite sex? Members of the same sex? Members of your peer group?

4. How did you get along with your commanding officer and others in authority?

5. Were you in combat? If you were, did you suffer any negative aftereffects from your combat experiences?

6. How did your military experiences affect your image of yourself as a man/woman?

7. What experiences did you have in the military that reinforced the basic beliefs you learned in your family?

8. What experiences did you have in the military that conflicted with what you learned in your family?

9. How did your military experiences enhance your ability to have successful, intimate love relationships?

10. How did your military experiences hinder your ability to have successful, intimate love relationships?

Service in the military can produce a fundamental change in a person's identity and world view. This is especially true when the person is involved in combat or combat-related activities, such as being a medic or working in a field hospital.

It is important to recognize the significance of your military experiences. Boot camp is designed to produce personality changes by altering values and instilling a radically new way of viewing the world. Combat experiences may be shocking and dramatic, often creating serious aftereffects, such as post-traumatic stress disorder, which can cause recurrent nightmares, feelings of being dissociated from yourself, and feelings of shame and guilt.

It is important to reconstruct your military history thoroughly, especially if you were in combat situations. Many people find that their military experience has the potential to seriously affect their ability to love and be loved. Unresolved post-traumatic stress disorder especially can be a serious obstacle to getting love right.

Adult Work History

Questions about Your Work Life

1. Describe your adult work experiences.

2. Describe the kind of person you were when you began your first adult job and the person you are today.

3. How do you view members of the opposite sex in the context of your current career? How do you view members of the same sex? How do you view members of your peer group at work?

4. How do you get along with your boss and others in authority?

5. How have your work experiences affected your image of yourself as a man/woman? How do they affect your image of yourself today?

6. What experiences have you had at work that have reinforced the basic beliefs you learned in your family?

7. What experiences have you had at work that have conflicted with what you learned in your family?

8. How have your past adult work experiences enhanced your ability to have successful, intimate love relationships? How do your current work experiences do this for you?

9. How have your past adult work experiences hindered your ability to have successful, intimate love relationships?

10. How do your current work experiences do this for you?

Work is the primary social outlet of most adults in the United States. We tend to build our identities around our career and our work. Our career selection is often based upon our personality preferences, our capabilities, and the opportunities available to us.

Our social life and our later relationships often revolve around our career.

Adult Friendship History

Questions about Adult Friendships

1. How many close, personal friends have you had from childhood to the present? List them by name and briefly describe each relationship.

2. What kind of friend have you been in the past? What kind of friend are you today?

3. How many of your close, personal friends were men? How many were women?

4. How do you feel about your male friends? How do you feel about your female friends?

5. If you have not ever had a close, personal friend of the opposite sex, do you think it is possible for you to have one? Why or why not?

6. How do you get along with your male friends? How do you get along with your female friends?

7. How have your friendships affected your image of yourself as a man/woman? How do they affect your image of yourself today?

8. How have your friendships reinforced the basic beliefs you learned in your family?

9. How have your friendships conflicted with what you learned in your family?

10. How has your social life helped your ability to develop successful, intimate love relationships?

11. How has your social life hindered your ability to develop successful, intimate love relationships?

Friendships and social activities are the least reinforced social outlets for most adults in the United States. These are often alcohol and drug centered as a result of cultural role modeling. Many people in the United States develop no close, lasting, personal friendships. Others have a limited number of friends and no active social networks. Without social skills, we become desperate for attention and vulnerable to falling in love with anyone who will spend time with us and accept us. As a result, we are vulnerable to having relationships with people who are not really high-quality partners. We get what we settle for.

Another important truth is that if you are unable to build a healthy friendship, you cannot build a healthy relationship. If you don't have a healthy social network, you're going to go places where other people who don't know how to have relationships and friendships go to look for partners—namely, bars, singles clubs, or cruising the supermarkets. You are not going to have a social network with which to come in contact with potential partners.

When you have written down your answers to the questions in each of these seven areas, look them over and see what significant patterns or themes you can detect in your descriptions of the events and people in your life. Do you see something you hadn't realized before? Take a moment to write down your observations, especially as they pertain to the goal of becoming a healthy choice maker. Keep your Personal History at hand to refer to from time to time as you read through later chapters in this book.

RELATIONSHIP HISTORY

Your Personal History gives you information about who you are and where you've been in your life in general terms. Completing your Relationship History gives you more specific information about your past relationships. Combining the information of both assessments will let you see the ways in which the general issues in your life may be affecting your ability to get love right. This information can prove valuable in changing the way you go about building relationships.

When Rose came into counseling, she wanted to understand why she had such terrible luck in getting love right. She believed that her past relationships had failed due to a series of random problems, one after another. After she completed her Relationship History, she recognized that her relationships, while involving different partners, shared several common patterns.

Relationship problems hurt. Yet frequently the pain is only partially related to the current problem—it is often connected with unfinished business from previous relationships as well. In compiling your Relationship History, you will consciously examine each romantic relationship you have had. As you do this, you will begin to see the ways in which each relationship was both similar to and different from other relationships, and thereby discover your own relationship patterns.

Your Relationship History will also help you plan for change. It will help you identify past strengths and problems in your relationships so that you can set appropriate personal and relationship goals. It can help you make changes in how you think and feel about yourself, your partner, and your relationships, so then you can make changes in the way you act on the basis of those thoughts and feelings.

Your Relationship Calendar

Before going into detail, it is useful to construct a brief overview of the types of relationships you have had in the past. Have you tended to have intimate encounters, or committed, transitional, or experimental relationships?

The Relationship Calendar is a one-page visual display of all of your relationships. Your adult relationships are divided into solo periods, experimental relationship periods, transitional relationship periods, intimate encounter periods, and committed relationship periods.

Make a copy of the blank Relationship Calendar grid. In the first column fill in the years you have been involved in adult relationships. Record your age in the second column. Then, using Steve's Relationship History as an example, fill in the following:

* Began dating

− Experimental dating (short-term relationships that give us new experiences and skills)

X Committed relationships (long-term relationships)

0 Solo periods (periods when we were alone and did not date)

+ Transitional relationships (short-term relationships that provide valuable support during the difficult period after the end of a long-term committed relationship)

RELATIONSHIP CALENDAR

Year	Age	Jan.	Feb.	Mar.	April	May	June	July	Aug.	Sep.	Oct.	Nov.	Dec.

STEVE'S RELATIONSHIP CALENDAR

Year	Age	Jan.	Feb.	Mar.	April	May	June	July	Aug.	Sep.	Oct.	Nov.	Dec.
1968	18									*	−	−	X
1969	19	X	X	X	X	X	X	X	X	X	X	X	X
1970	20	X	X	X	X	X	X	X	X	X	X	X−	−
1971	21	−	−	−+	+	+	+	+	+	+	+	X	X
1972	22	X	X	X	X	X	X	X	X	X	X	X	X
1973	23	X	X	X	X	X	X	X	X	X	X	X0	0
1974	24	0	0	0	−	−	−	−	−	−	−	−	−
1975	25	−	−	−	−	−	−	−	−	−	−	X	X
1976	26	X	X	X	X	X	X	X	X	X	X	X	X
1977	27	0	0	0	0−	−	−	−+	+	+	+	+	+
1978	28	X	X	X	X	X	X	X	X	X	X	X	X
1979	29	X	X	X	X	X	X	X	X	X	X	X	X
1980	30	X	X	X	X	X	X	X	X	X	X	X	X
1981	31	X	X	X	X	X	X	X	X	X	X	X	X
1982	32	X	X	X	X	X	X	X	X	X	X	X	X
1983	33	X	X	X	X	X	X	X	X	X	X	X	X
1984	34	X	X	X	X	X	X	X	X	X	X	X	X
1985	35	X	X	X	X	X	X	X	X	X	X	X	X
1986	36	X	X	X	X	X	X	X	X	X	X	X	X
1987	37	X	X	X	X	X	X	X	X	X	X	X	X

= Intimate encounters (short-term unique relationships outside the normal context of our lives that meet our here-and-now needs for intimacy)

When you have completed your Relationship Calendar, note the different relationships you have had. Then ask yourself if they were what you needed at the time, or if you chose partners or types of relationships that did not meet your needs.

Your Relationship History

Your Relationship History is a more detailed description of your past relationships. In addition to identifying the type of relationship, you will give each period a descriptive title and then further describe it in several short phrases, as in the example of Steve's Relationship History on page 111.

After reading the example, take a sheet of paper for each relationship and use the following format for your own history.

Your Relationship History

Title: _____

Your age at time of relationship: _____

Type of relationship: _____

Partner's name: _____

Partner's age: _____

Duration: _____

Dates: From _____ To _____

Short description (including how you met, compulsive-apathetic characteristics, reason for ending):

—

—

—

—

—

—

—

—

—

—

Steve's Relationship History

Steve called his first solo period "Afraid to Love." This lasted from the time he was born until he was eighteen years old. During this time, he felt lonely, angry, and scared. He wondered if he would ever fall in love, but he didn't want to get trapped, like his parents, in a destructive relationship. Steve had few friends and poor social skills. He believed he would be alone forever, and, in a way, he was grateful because he believed that then he could avoid the pain of a conflictual relationship. In another way, he was sad and defeated because he really wanted to love and be loved.

Steve summarized his first alone period as follows:

Steve's Relationship History

Title: _____ *Afraid to Love* _____

Your age at time of relationship: _____ *Before age 18* _____

Type of relationship: _____ *Solo period* _____

Duration: _____ *Before age 18* _____

Dates: From _____ *1950* _____ To _____ *9/68* _____

Short description:

_ I was lonely, angry, and scared.

_ I wondered if I'd ever fall in love.

_ I was afraid of getting trapped like my parents.

_ I was alone, without any friends, and thought I would be alone forever.

_ I was isolated and had poor social skills.

_ A part of me was glad to avoid the pain of having a relationship.

_ Another part felt sad and defeated; I wanted to love and be loved.

When Steve was eighteen, he began to date. He called this period of his life "Giving It a Try." During this two-month period, Steve was afraid that no one would like him. He felt lonely, isolated, and unattractive, but tried hard to be liked. He acted more confident than he really was. When he dated, he went through the motions but didn't reveal much about himself. He dated women he wasn't attracted to because he believed that attractive women would reject him.

Steve summarized this period as follows:

Steve's Relationship History

Title: _____ *Giving It a Try* _____

Your age at time of relationship: _____ 18 _____

Type of relationship: _____ *Experimental dating period* _____

Partner's name: _____ *(various)* _____

Partner's age: _____ *(various)* _____

Duration: _____ *3 months* _____

Dates: From _____ *9/68* _____ To _____ *11/68* _____

Short description:

    — I was scared and afraid no one would like me.

    — I was lonely, isolated, and felt unattractive.

    — I tried hard to be liked.

    — I acted more confident than I felt.

    — I dated women I didn't like.

    — I was afraid of being rejected by women I liked.

Steve was still eighteen when he fell in love with Suzy. Their relationship lasted two years. This was the first time Steve felt he was in love. He was surprised that Suzy loved him, too. He was infatuated and felt as if he was living a fantasy come true. He and

Suzy were emotionally close and affectionate. They were both immature and had no previous sexual experience. They engaged in petting but didn't have intercourse.

As their relationship unfolded, Steve shifted between feeling intense infatuation and euphoria and feeling trapped. Suzy refused to practice birth control for moral reasons. She was also reluctant to have sex. She believed petting was as far as she could go without committing a mortal sin.

Steve began to feel increasingly trapped. Suzy had many traits that reminded him of his mother. He began to have fears of becoming dominated and tied down by unwanted children as his father was, so Steve decided to end the relationship. It was a difficult thing to do, and he was upset, but he was also excited about dating other women. This led him into another dating period.

Steve summarized his relationship with Suzy as follows:

Steve's Relationship History

Title: _First Love_

Your age at time of relationship: _18_

Type of relationship: _Committed_

Partner's name: _Suzy_

Partner's age: _18_

Duration: _2 years_

Dates: From _12/68_   To _11/70_

Short description:

_ This was the first time I felt I was in love.

_ I was surprised that Suzy liked me. It felt like a fantasy come true.

_ We were emotionally close and affectionate.

_ We only petted and didn't have intercourse.

_ I began to feel trapped; Suzy reminded me of my mother in some ways.

_ It was hard but I ended the relationship rather than be trapped in a destructive relationship.

Steve called his second dating period "I Want It All." He wanted freedom, sex, and excitement. He wanted to live life in the fast lane. This period lasted for five months.

Steve described this period as "mad-dog dating." He engaged in many short-term, intense relationships. He drank heavily and smoked marijuana. He experienced soaring highs and crashing lows. He was very excited but also devastatingly lonely.

At times, he felt guilty because he treated women like sexual objects and used them. At other times, his feelings were hurt when he dated a woman who used him. He enjoyed dating but began to tire of the intense highs and crashing lows. He began to want more than he was experiencing.

Steve summarized this period as follows:

Steve's Relationship History

Title: _____ *I Want It All* _____

Your age at time of relationship: _____ 20 _____

Type of relationship: _____ *Experimental Dating* _____

Duration: _____ *5 months* _____

Dates: From _____ *11/70* _____ *To* _____ *3/71* _____

Short description:

    _ I called it heavy "mad-dog dating."

    _ I had short-term, intense relationships.

    _ I drank heavily and smoked marijuana.

    _ I had soaring highs and crashing lows.

    _ I was excited but lonely.

Steve met Angie through mutual friends at one of the many college parties he attended at this time. He and Angie were immediately attracted to each other. Since they both enjoyed parties and nights on the town, their dates were fun and exciting. They were very compatible sexually and sex was a major part of the relationship. They both recognized this as a transitional period in their lives and enjoyed it for what it was. Steve liked having a steady relationship without the fear of entrapment. When Steve landed a job in the city, he moved and the relationship ended. Steve summarized this period as follows:

Steve's Relationship History

Title: _____ *Getting Ready* _____

Your age at time of relationship: _____ 21 _____

Type of relationship: _____ *Transitional* _____

Partner's name: _____ *Angie* _____

Partner's age: _____ 21 _____

Duration: _____ *8 months* _____

Dates: From _____ *3/71* _____ To _____ *10/71* _____

Short description:

— I met Angie at a party with friends from college.

— We had lots of fun together going to parties and bars.

— Sex was exciting and a major part of the relationship.

— We both knew the relationship wouldn't go anywhere and I liked that.

— We broke up when I moved to take a job in the city.

Soon after moving, Steve fell in love with Julie, who was twenty-six. Their relationship lasted approximately two years. Steve described this as his first mature, sexual relationship. Julie was a wonderful lover, far more sexually experienced than Steve, and their sex life was, in Steve's opinion, great. In addition, Steve felt a deep love for Julie and enjoyed her companionship. He believed that Julie loved him for who he really was and he felt he could be himself when he was with her.

In spite of his feeling of safety, Steve once again began to feel trapped as the relationship progressed. Julie wanted a family and children, and this terrified Steve, who was career oriented and wanted to be successful in his field. He was going to school nearly full time and working full time as well. He didn't have time for a family. Besides, he knew what having kids could do to a couple because his parents had told him, in no uncertain terms, that they would have been happy if they hadn't had children.

Finally, Julie ended their relationship because she wanted to have a family and realized that Steve didn't.

Steve summarized this relationship as follows:

Steve's Relationship History

Title: _____ *Real Love* _____

Your age at time of relationship: _____ 21 _____

Type of relationship: _____ *Committed period* _____

Partner's name: _____ *Julie* _____

Partner's age: _____ 26 _____

Duration: _____ *2 years* _____

Dates: From _____ *11/71* _____ To _____ *11/73* _____

Short description:

 _ This was my first mature, sexual relationship.

 _ We had great sex, love, and companionship.

 _ We had a life-style conflict. I wanted a career and she wanted a family.

 _ I feared being trapped.

 _ She left to find a family man.

When Julie left, Steve felt devastated and stopped dating for a period of four months. He was seriously depressed and could hardly work. He isolated himself from his friends and spent a lot of time alone. He believed he would never find another woman who would love him. He vacillated between feeling deeply hurt, guilty, and ashamed. He knew that he had somehow failed. He believed that if he hadn't been so afraid of intimacy their relationship wouldn't have ended. There were also times when Steve felt anger and rage toward Julie. He reasoned that if she really loved him she wouldn't have left. He would also rage at all women. "Women are no good, why bother to try?" When his depression began to lift, he began to date again.

Steve summarized this as follows:

Steve's Relationship History

Title: _____ Crushed _____

Your age at time of relationship: _____ 23 _____

Type of relationship: _____ Solo period _____

Duration: _____ 4 months _____

Dates: From _____ 11/73 _____ To _____ 3/74 _____

Short description:

    _ I felt emotionally crushed.

    _ I was depressed.

    _ I could hardly work.

    _ I isolated myself from my friends.

    _ I was too hurt and angry with women, in general, to date, so I didn't.

Steve began dating again in April 1974 when he was twenty-four. He continued to date heavily through October 1975 (approximately 1½ years).

During this period, Steve was out for good times. He sought short-term fun relationships. He didn't want any commitments. He never got too close and quickly ended a relationship if the woman started to get too close to him. He dated so many women during this period that he can't remember how many there were. On the surface, he was having a good time but underneath he was angry, bitter, and lonely.

Steve summarized this period as follows:

Steve's Relationship History

Title: _____ *Confirmed Bachelor* _____

Your age at time of relationship: _____ 24 _____

Type of relationship: _____ *Experimental* _____

Partner's name: _____ *(various)* _____

Partner's age: _____ *(various)* _____

Duration: _____ *1 year, 7 months* _____

Dates: From _____ *4/74* _____ To _____ *10/75* _____

Short description:

— I was out for a good time.

— I had short-term, fun relationships.

— I didn't want a commitment.

— I used women.

— I never got close to any of them.

— Everyone thought I was having fun, but I was angry, bitter, and lonely.

During this period, Steve met Ann, a ballet and jazz dancer who liked to live close to the edge. She was an experienced lover. In Steve's words, she was "hot."

Steve experienced intense sexual highs with Ann, more intense than he'd ever known was possible. He was totally committed to their relationship but scared by the possibility that Ann could hurt him emotionally.

As his infatuation began to wear off, he realized that he and Ann had little in common. She liked dance, ballet, opera, and rock and roll. He didn't enjoy any of those things.

He was career motivated. She wasn't. Her only desire was to earn enough money to maintain her social and recreational lifestyle.

Steve and Ann had put each other on pedestals. Ann saw Steve as a powerful, rugged, he-man. She cast him as a hero who would sweep her off her feet and make all of her problems disappear. Steve cast Ann as a sex goddess. He believed she was the embodiment of sexuality, love, and passion. He believed that he could lose himself in her and that she would make his problems disappear and enhance his success.

As their relationship continued, Ann began to realize that Steve was a fallible human being. Every time Steve expressed vulnerability, Ann became angry and outraged. She felt let down. "You're supposed to be strong," she would yell at him. "If you're not strong, how will you take care of me?"

Finally, their relationship ended when Ann broke up with him and told him that she had lost all respect for him. Steve entered his third solo period after Ann left him.

Steve summarized this relationship as follows:

Steve's Relationship History

Title: _____ *Addicted to Love* _____

Your age at time of relationship: _____ 25 _____

Type of relationship: _____ *Committed* _____

Partner's name: _____ *Ann* _____

Partner's age: _____ 27 _____

Duration: _____ *1 year, 1 month* _____

Dates: From _____ *11/75* _____ To _____ *11/76* _____

Short description:

_ We had great sex and were intensely passionate.

_ I was totally committed but scared.

_ We had nothing in common.

_ We put each other on pedestals.

_ She wanted a superman.

_ She couldn't handle my fallibility.

_ She left to find a "strong" man.

When Ann left, Steve was devastated again. He didn't date for nearly four months.

Steve described himself as emotionally crushed and depressed. He felt no good. He didn't trust women and he knew that love would never work out right for him. He vacillated between intense anger and depression. He didn't want to have a relationship and often would jokingly say that he was going to join a monastery.

Steve summarized this period as follows:

Steve's Relationship History

Title: _____ *Crushed Again* _____

Your age at time of relationship: _____ 27 _____

Type of Relationship _____ *Solo period* _____

Duration: _____ *4 months* _____

Dates: From _____ *1/77* _____ *To* _____ *4/77* _____

Short description:

   _ I felt emotionally crushed.

   _ I was depressed.

   _ I felt no good.

   _ I was angry and depressed.

   _ I didn't want a relationship.

As time wore on, the intense pain and anguish Steve was feeling dissipated and he became ready to date.

Steve began dating again in April 1977 and continued to date approximately four months. He was twenty-seven years old and desperately wanted to have a relationship. He was tired of being alone. His anger had dissipated. He entered therapy and learned how to change his relationship style. In the past, he had always focused on finding an intense, sexual partner. He now selected his partners carefully and avoided women with emotional problems or intense, destructive life-styles. He summarized this dating period:

Steve's Relationship History

Title: _Another Approach_

Your age at time of relationship: _27_

Type of relationship: _Experimental_

Partner's name: _(various)_

Partner's age: _(various)_

Duration: _4 months_

Dates: From _4/77_ To _7/77_

Short Description:

— I started personal therapy to deal with the issues.

— I was tired of the high excitement and bad ends.

— I was tired of being alone.

— I was no longer angry.

— I started experimenting with different types of partner.

— I selected my partners carefully and avoided women with emotional problems of intense, destructive life-styles.

Steve decided to change his style and focus more on his partner than on the sexual experience. Then he met Jeri at work. He tried to build this relationship slowly. He was reluctant to get involved with a woman who inflamed him to intense passion. For Jeri he felt a quiet, gentle feeling of caring. He realized that although his relationship with Jeri was less intense, it was safer and healthier. For the first time in his life, he felt he could be involved in a relationship without getting torn apart.

Steve summarized this as follows:

Steve's Relationship History

Title: _____ *Willing to Try Again* _____

Your age at time of relationship: _____ 27 _____

Type of relationship: _____ *Transitional* _____

Partner's name: _____ *Jeri* _____

Partner's age: _____ 24 _____

Duration: _____ *5 months* _____

Dates: From _____ *7/77* _____   To _____ *12/77* _____

_ I wanted to have a successful relationship.

_ I selected my partner carefully.

_ I met Jeri through work.

_ I focused on the person, not the sexual side of the relationship.

_ We had a lot of things in common and spent a lot of casual time together.

_ I built the relationship slowly.

_ Our relationship was less intense but safer and healthier than previous relationships.

_ We broke off the relationship when we both wanted to pursue new relationships.

Steve met Marge when he was twenty-eight. She was a 32-year-old nurse who worked at a local hospital. She was going to school part time to earn a master's degree in psychology. She had been divorced for two years, had gone through therapy after her divorce, and had a stable life-style.

Their relationship begin slowly and pleasantly. They met through mutual friends, spent time together, and shared social activities. At first, Steve felt their relationship was comfortable but not exciting. He enjoyed Marge's company but didn't feel sexually attracted to her. Over time, as they grew closer emotionally, Steve began to feel drawn to Marge sexually. They became sexy friends and lovers. There were no firecrackers and no intense highs, but there were also no crashing, heartbreaking lows. Steve described their relationship as a low-intensity roller-coaster ride —feeling good and then feeling empty. He felt their relationship was fulfilling, but he wasn't getting emotionally torn apart. He had what he believed to be a functional relationship, but he felt disillusioned. He felt he was trapped, doomed forever to have either high-intensity relationships that would cause him pain, or comfortable, safe relationships that lacked the intensity he desired. Eventually, Steve sought therapy to find out what he could do to bring more satisfaction into his life and his relationship. He felt that he wanted to work to make his relationship better or end it.

Steve described this relationship as follows:

Steve's Relationship History

Title: _____ *Love and Marriage* _____

Your age at time of relationship: _____ 28 _____

Type of relationship: _____ *Committed* _____

Partner's name: _____ *Marge* _____

Partner's age: _____ 32 _____

Duration: _____ *Ongoing* _____

Dates: From _____ 1/78 _____ *To* _____ *present* _____

Short description:

    — We have a functional relationship.

    — It is safe but not exciting.

    — We are good friends.

    — There are no firecrackers.

    — It's not fulfilling.

    — I feel it's important at this stage either to work to make it better or end it.

Steve's Evaluation of His Relationship History

Looking through his Relationship History gave Steve some important information about his previous and current relationships. It let him see first of all that they were not random. Each of the relationships fulfilled a definite purpose at a particular stage in his life. He could also see that in several significant ways he had not taken full, conscious responsibility for what he was doing in his relationships. When a relationship ended he would blame his partner rather than taking time to see his own contribution to the situation. Steve learned that he needed to take more responsibility for deciding what he wanted in his life instead of just meeting someone and saying, "We'll see what happens."

Steve noticed that in most cases, his partners left him, rather than the other way around. He now asked the question, "Why did they leave?" This led him to another question, "What am I doing to invite them to leave?" Steve was beginning to understand the role that he played in what his partners did. Although he blamed them at the time, he saw that he did in fact participate in their decisions to leave. He came to see that if he had chosen his partners more carefully, his relationships would have been more successful.

Another observation Steve made was that his solo periods were launched because of his fear of relationships. He decided to be alone because he was afraid of getting involved and didn't know what to do. He noted this as an area for improvement.

Steve also learned that he didn't deal with rejection very well. When a relationship ended, he would go into a period of blame and depression. In essence, Steve realized, he somehow felt he had to punish himself for failing before he could go on. Here was another area Steve needed to work on: his ability to deal with the pain and the grief of an ended relationship. This pattern contributed to his fear of becoming involved in new relationships and kept him from taking healthy risks. As a result, he would take no risk at all or take too many irrational risks, only to retreat into lengthy solo periods. In this way, Steve was caught in a cycle many people experience. First, in self-protection, he would isolate himself until his deep hunger for affirmation and physical intimacy grew unbearable. Then, when he met a likely partner, he would overreact, let down all of his barriers, and throw himself head over heels into an unsafe relationship.

From an objective evaluation of his Relationship History, Steve saw this pattern for the first time. He realized that each time a relationship ended he had foolishly hoped that a long period of abstinence would prepare him for the next relationship, which, he hoped, would somehow work out right. Unfortunately, his abstinence had the opposite effect. He was like a tennis player who didn't know why, after not playing tennis for three months, he wasn't any better at the game then he was when he stopped playing.

In looking over the various types of relationships he had had, Steve saw that none of his relationships could be described as an intimate encounter. All his relationships fell into the categories of experimental dating, transitional, or long-term committed relationships. Steve had not consciously decided against having an affair, and thought he would not have minded having an intimate encounter during times when he was uncommitted. He knew, however, that he would feel uncomfortable about becoming involved with another woman while he was committed to someone else.

His Relationship History also gave Steve the impetus he needed to seek therapy for his current relationship problems in his marriage. He decided first to go into personal therapy to solve some of his own problems before he asked his wife to work with him to address their relationship problems as a couple.

HOW TO EVALUATE YOUR OWN RELATIONSHIP HISTORY

Once you complete your Relationship History and have spent some time in considering what lessons it contains, be sure to talk about it with someone, such as your therapist or sponsor, a support group, or a trusted friend. As you tell someone about your experiences and your feelings both then and now, more memories, more feelings, and thus more insight will inevitably surface.

As you work with your Relationship History, you will experience many emotions, both positive and negative. These may include nostalgia for the past or for a time of life that is over. You may feel regret or anger. The memories of past relationships can be very painful. This is normal and can even be helpful. An important reason to construct your Relationship History is to look back on past relationships in the spirit of reconciliation. Be ready to forgive yourself for the past and accept past relationships, not as failures but as meaningful, positive parts of your life.

If you are like many people who believe that lifelong commitment is the ultimate goal in a relationship, you may be especially vulnerable to self-blame and regret over relationships that fell short of this goal. Yet the value and quality of a relationship cannot be determined solely by how long it lasts. Some of the highest-quality relationships last only a few months or years. On the other hand, some unhealthy relationships last a lifetime.

Chuck and Tara were in a committed relationship they both thought would be forever, but it ended after only ten years. For eight of those ten years, they were both very happy. They built a fulfilling life together that met their mutual needs for challenge and personal development. As they pursued their chosen careers, they found that they themselves changed, too. Finally, they had changed to such an extent that their relationship needs changed also and they parted as friends. Some of their family and friends expressed great sorrow over their divorce. Yet instead of viewing those ten years as a "waste," Chuck and Tara chose instead to see their relationship as a valuable, important period of their lives, a time when they learned and grew as individuals and as a couple. Because of their relationship, they were very different from when they first met. Both had had many positive experiences that, in the long run, significantly and permanently enhanced their lives.

The best way to reach your relationship goals is to become a healthy choice maker and take responsibility for the choices you make. As you look over the relationships you've had, consider the benefits each relationship brought with it. How did you grow? What did you learn about yourself, your partner, about people in general, and about getting love right? What choices do you want to make in the future?

Now that you have a sense of where you have been and the

types of relationships you have had in the past, take a moment to ask yourself about your current relationship goals. The following self-assessment should help you in this.

Self-Assessment: Relationship Types and Needs Questionnaire

What type of relationship do you want at this point in your life? Once you know the answer to this question, you will be able to communicate that clearly to your partner and find out the kind of relationship your partner wants. This can save both of you later heartbreak and disappointment.

1. What type of relationship do you want to have?

___✗ **a.** experimental dating

_____ **b.** committed

___✗ **c.** transitional

_____ **d.** intimate encounter

2. Why do you want this type of relationship?

_____ **a.** I am not ready to be in a committed relationship.

_____ **b.** I have been in experimental or transitional relationships and am now ready for a committed relationship.

___✗ **c.** I was in a relationship that ended recently and am not ready for anything more serious than a transitional relationship that I can use to heal the pain and prepare myself for a committed relationship.

_____ **d.** I do not want commitment of any kind and so an intimate encounter is enough for me.

_____ **e.** other

3. If you are currently in a relationship, how would you describe that relationship?

If you are single, how would you describe the last relationship you had?

My current relationship is/My last relationship was

_____ **a.** experimental

_____ **b.** committed

_____ **c.** transitional

___✗ **d.** an intimate encounter

___ e. other

Why did you answer as you did?

although I felt it was a genuinely committed relationship, it was not

4. **I believe my partner would say/would have said our current relationship is/was**

___ a. experimental

___ b. committed

_✓_ c. transitional

_✓_ d. an intimate encounter

___ e. other

Why did you answer as you did?

_____

_____

_____

II

BUILDING

A HEALTHY

RELATIONSHIP

Chapter 5

BUILDING THE
RELATIONSHIP: *ME*

PRINCIPAL CHOICES
Whether or not to assume responsibility for:
- who you are
- what you do
- the consequences of what you do

Some years ago, I decided I was ready for a high-quality relationship with a high-quality partner. When it didn't materialize, I went into therapy to find out why.

I weighed 245 pounds. I was working eighty hours a week. I was obsessed with my work; I could not communicate because I would monopolize conversations talking about it. I had underlying anger and hostility.

I told the therapist a bit about my life and that I was ready to find a high-quality partner to begin a relationship. The therapist asked, "What kind of partner are you looking for?"

I said, "I want a young, attractive woman, nice personality, athletic, she has to be athletic. She has to have a lot of interests, a lot of friends, good social activities, and be sports minded."

He listened to me and nodded. When I was through, he looked at me and said, "Terry, I'm going to ask you a question."

I said, "Yes?"

He hesitated a moment and said, "You may not like it."

I said, "Well, okay, go ahead."

"Are you sure you can handle it?"

I said, "Yeah, I'm sure."

"Terry, what would a woman like that want with somebody like you?"

I fired that therapist on the spot. There are plenty of therapists in this world. I didn't need that kind of screwy thinking messing up my life.

Of course, years later, I discovered he was right. He was telling me a fundamental truth about getting love right. You can't attract a high-quality partner if you yourself are not a high-quality person. You cannot have a high-quality relationship, if you and your partner are not high-quality people, capable of meeting one another's needs.

RELATIONSHIP AS A TRIANGLE: *ME, YOU,* AND *US*

All relationships are triangles consisting of three separate entities: me, you, and us. There is *me:* who I am as a person. There is my partner, *you:* who you are as a person. Then, as we begin to relate to one another, a third entity is created, *us:* who we are as a couple. All three components of this equation are important and each is distinct from the other two. I am responsible for who I am. You are responsible for who you are. Together we are responsible for what the relationship is.

Problems in relationships also fall into three distinct categories: my problems, your problems, and our problems. You can't fix my problems, only I can. I can't fix your problems, only you can. You or I alone can't fix our problems; only we together can fix them. For a relationship to succeed, therefore, I must be functional, you must be functional, and we must relate to each other in a functional way.

In building a relationship, many people focus only on the *you* of the equation. Just as I did years ago, they think a good relationship depends on the quality of their partner. So they have a list of the qualities they want their partner to have and they focus on finding Mr. or Ms. Right, who will embody all of them.

Paula's dream was to find Mr. Right. Paula lived with her mother because she couldn't find any good reason not to. Paula had no friends, no social life at all. She hated her job, but she knew that jobs were hard to come by, so she stayed on with the company year after year. Paula's happiest moments were spent dreaming about meeting the man who would free her from all of her troubles. She never bothered to develop hobbies or attend social organizations where she might meet Mr. Right. She never lifted a finger to change the negative things that made her life intolerable. Instead, she invested all her energy into imagining the wonderful things she and her partner would do together in the future once she met the perfect *you*.

Paula wanted Mr. Right to fix her problems, and yet no one but Paula could do that. Even if Mr. Right were to enter her life, Paula's ongoing problems would probably make it impossible for her to build a healthy relationship with him.

Other people focus on *us*. They think all they need in their life is a good intimate relationship and everything else will fall into place. Time after time, people hope that the *us*, this wonderful entity created by our relationship, will fix them and the way they live their lives. Unfortunately, this, too, is an idle fantasy.

Brad was a young man who was unemployable because he was irresponsible. He fell in love with a high-quality woman and had a satisfying intimate relationship with her. Brad was still unemployable, however, because he didn't take his work seriously. He refused to learn job skills. He got into arguments with his boss. His relationship did nothing to change any of that. Nothing else about Brad changed, except that he was in a relationship.

People who focus on *you* or *us* are overlooking the essential first step in relationship building, the first part of the equation, *me*. If I am not a healthy person, I will not be able to attract a healthy partner or build a healthy relationship.

If you have consistently had problems in relationships, you need to take a closer look at what it is about you that causes this. While you were constructing your Relationship History in the last chapter, if you saw that you have consistently chosen partners who did not and could not meet your needs, you should ask yourself why this happens time after time. What is it about you that keeps you trapped in dysfunctional relationships, even though you know you need to get out?

A woman named Anne came into counseling with me. She said, "I don't understand it. Every time I meet a guy, within six weeks he slaps me around. I don't know what's going on."

I said, "Well, where do you meet these guys?"

She said, "Bars."

I said, "Bars?"

"Well, yeah, you know, leather bars."

"Leather bars?"

"Yeah, you know the kind where bikers go."

I said, "Well, why do you go to these types of places to meet men? Don't you think you're at pretty high risk for picking a man in there who's physically abusive?"

She said, "Well, to be quite honest, other men bore me."

Anne's relationship problems stemmed from her unwillingness to reexamine the type of relationship choices she continued to make, even though she had been hurt by them time after time. She refused to change the way she sought partners or to deal with her attraction to dangerous men. She wanted the danger and the attraction without the consequences. Each time she met a man at one of these bars, she wanted him to turn out to be someone other than what he was or could be expected to be. Because Anne refused to give up her magical expectations, she was caught up in one dysfunctional relationship after another.

PREPARING FOR A RELATIONSHIP: *ME*

Many people are so anxious to be in a relationship, they can't think of anything else. All their time and effort go into thinking about Mr. or Ms. Right.

When healthy people are single, they are not obsessed with finding a partner. They concern themselves with becoming a person who is worthy of healthy love. They don't believe they have to compulsively hunt out somebody to love them, because they know that if they put the same energy into developing themselves into a high-quality person somebody will find them.

To become a person worthy of being in a relationship means that you are not afraid to take a look at what is wrong with your relationships or afraid to work to change them. No one has trouble-free relationships and no one is so perfect that he/she cannot improve. The difference between people from healthy families and those from dysfunctional families is that healthy people know how to think clearly, logically, and rationally about their problems and work productively to resolve them.

Healthy people know that caring begins with *me,* the self: first the self, then the possibility of intimacy with another person. For people from dysfunctional families, this may be a very hard lesson to learn because they may have been taught that they are not valuable or worthy of care and respect. Yet what kind of friend can you be if you are not first a friend to yourself? What kind of a lover, if you don't love yourself enough to act in your own best interest?

The way you care about yourself will be the way you care about others. If you care about yourself in a way that destroys you, the love you give to others will inadvertently destroy them.

Julia came in to see me. She was married to an actively drinking alcoholic who had been physically abusing her for years and physically abusing their children as well.

She told me, "I loved him so much I couldn't leave." Then she couldn't understand why three of her five children were alcoholics and the two nonalcoholics were in a penitentiary. In therapy she began to see that she had loved her husband and her children the way she loved herself.

"Maybe," she said sadly, "if I had loved differently, the outcomes would have been different."

I told her that was a real possibility. If you love yourself in a way that produces constant pain and dysfunction, you will bring that pain and dysfunction into your relationship when you try to love another person. Entering into a program of personal recovery, making a commitment to personal growth and change, may be the most important step you can take toward a healthy relationship because it is an investment in yourself and what you will ultimately bring to your relationships.

Personal-development programs take many forms because people have very different needs. Some people can work on personal change independently because they are entirely self-motivated. Their problems are relatively minor and they come from fairly functional families. They are self-disciplined and possess skill in introspection and self-change.

Most people, however, require a structured program of growth and change that can provide them with motivation, support, and accountability. Motivation is important because it is hard to keep working through painful relationship issues and most people need someone outside themselves to keep them at it. As the pain begins to surface, people need someone to lend emotional support in a difficult time. People also need someone to hold them accountable, to keep them moving ahead, to make sure they follow through on what they commit to and know they need to do.

Personal therapy, group therapy, and support groups, such as various twelve-step programs and other similar groups, can provide the needed motivation, support, and accountability. It may be that you will find a combination of these helpful in giving you what you need to bring about your own personal growth and change. Because support and therapy groups are organized to address a wide diversity of issues and problems, from incest and sex addictions to eating disorders and substance abuse, you can locate a group to meet your needs in any particular area.

BREAKING THE CYCLE

When you begin to care for yourself in a healthy way, you can believe enough in yourself to say "no" to the dysfunctional partners, relationships, and behaviors that are creating problems in your life. When you believe in yourself, you can learn to say "no" to short-term relationships that will not give you what you want, because you are getting yourself ready for something better.

If you are serious about building healthy relationships, you need to abstain from becoming involved with partners who do not share your relationship goals and who cannot give you the type of relationship you want. This is especially true if you want to find a high-quality partner to share a serious, committed relationship.

Joel, in his twenties, could not make his relationships work, so he decided to talk with a therapist.

The therapist asked, "How many people are you dating?"

Joel thought about it and said, "Oh, about five."

The therapist asked, "Do you think any of these current relationships has the potential to become a really intense relationship for you?"

Joel says, "I doubt it."

"Why?"

"Well, none of these women are really into committed relationships. They're fun people to be with, but they're not really the kind of person I'd like to settle down with."

The therapist then asked, "If you don't think any of these women can give you what you want, why are you wasting your time with them?"

Joel had no answer for this; the question had never occurred to him.

If you are currently involved in a relationship, this is a question you need to ask yourself. Are the people you are presently involved with capable of giving you what you want in a relationship? Do you share similar expectations for the relationship? There are other important questions to ask: Are you currently involved with someone who has the potential to be a healthy partner? Is he/she willing to work on building a healthy relationship? Does he/she want a close relationship with you? Does he/she have personal problems that would prevent him/her from making the commitment? Do you love him/her? Does he/she love you? Do you respect and love him/her or do you feel a need to change, fix, and make him or her a different person as a condition of the relationship?

In his eagerness to be in a relationship, any relationship, Joel never considered any of these questions. He practiced what I call "mad-dog dating." He was dating several women, none of whom he cared much about. None of these partners had the capacity to help Joel to grow, to deal with himself in any new way, or to develop his intimacy skills. None of them was a high-quality partner for Joel. They met his needs for companionship and sex, but that was all. Joel didn't expect any of the relationships to go anywhere because he chose partners he didn't value enough to want to share a quality relationship with.

Unlike dead-end relationships, quality relationships give us a chance to discover more about ourselves, our partners, and about intimacy itself. This is the essential difference between mad-dog dating and healthy, experimental dating. To get love right, you need to stop wasting your time on relationships and partners who are unable or unwilling to build a quality relationship.

Joel's next step was to look for a potential partner who shared his relationship values and goals. Rather than rushing to become involved again as soon as possible, he needed to proceed slowly so that he could make healthy choices about his next relationship.

There is an important difference between abstaining from dysfunctional or dead-end relationships and abstaining from all relationships. We may be tempted to abstain from all relationships out of fear that we can't make them work. We don't want to be in another bad relationship, but we don't know how to build a good one. So we decide we won't get involved at all. This is often a poor choice for two reasons: First, the goal of abstaining from dysfunctional relationships is to become ready for a quality relationship by working on the issues that have kept you from healthy relationships in the past. For that you need skills, and you can't develop relationship skills by refusing to be in a relationship. Second, when we abstain from all relationships, we make ourselves more vulnerable to repeating dysfunctional habits.

Maryann realized that she was picking losers as partners. She decided to abstain from dysfunctional relationships, but she went too far. Instead of abstaining from destructive relationships with partners that obviously couldn't meet her needs, she decided to abstain from all relationships.

"This is it," she said after a fight with her boyfriend, "never again. As a matter of fact, I've had it with relationships in general. I'm not going to go out with anybody ever again."

The first month was fine, but then she started getting lonely. The second month, she started getting horny. The third month she began to get desperate. Finally, she was so lonely, so horny, and so desperate that she couldn't stand it. She started thinking irrational thoughts such as, "I can't stand living all alone. I can't stand not getting affection. I can't stand not having sex. I can't stand this; this is terrible. This is recovery?"

Maryann was so miserable, she thought, "Gee, maybe I'll try a relationship just one more time." But now she was desperate, and desperate people do desperate things. She began looking for a partner. She felt she needed to find somebody, anybody, to make her loneliness go away and to make her feel whole and complete.

One night Maryann was at a party. All kinds of people were there, but there *he* was, Mr. Right, the type of person she was always attracted to, the type of person she always had a dysfunctional relationship with. All of a sudden—bong! The bell went off and she was drawn to him. The old feelings suddenly overwhelmed her and she went on automatic pilot. It was as if she were hypnotized or drawn by a magnet. Then the next thing Maryann knew, she was standing right in front of him.

A part of her knew something was wrong. "Don't do this!" it said. "Leave! Run! Go the other way. This is going to blow up in your face. He is just like every other person that's always done this to you. Don't do this!" But then there was another part of Maryann that said, "What the heck. I'm lonely. I haven't had sex in three and a half months now. I deserve better than this. And besides, this time I'm going to control it. I'm desperate, I'm deprived, but I can handle it. I'll get in and I'll get out before I can get hurt." And there she was again, beginning a relationship with someone she didn't know and who probably would end up hurting her just like all the others before him.

This is what I call the Big Bang Theory of finding a relationship. It's a three-step process:

Step 1. You meet Mr. or Ms. Perfect.

Step 2. Your emotions go bang! Your brain shuts off.

Step 3. You fall in love and make a commitment to a relationship that probably won't work.

The longer you are not in a relationship, the more intimacy deprived you become. The more intimacy deprived you become, the more vulnerable you are to the type of person that can set you off. Like Maryann, you increase your vulnerability to dysfunctional relationships.

Deciding to abstain from dysfunctional relationships does not mean learning how to be comfortably alone for the rest of your life. The goal is to learn how to build a healthy, productive relationship with a partner who can meet your needs. If you do abstain from relationships, it is vitally important that you use the time to work on making yourself into someone who truly believes that he or she is worthy of being loved by another high-quality person.

If you are already in a committed relationship, beginning a program of personal change and development means abstaining from dysfunctional behaviors. The first dysfunctional behavior you need to give up is placing unrealistic expectations on your partner. That is, expecting your partner to fix you. Ask yourself, "What do I expect my relationship to do for me?" Then ask, "Is it realistic?"

Debra weighed 150 pounds, but her ideal weight was 124. Debra was in a good relationship, but her good relationship didn't make her lose weight. To her dismay, it was just as hard to take off the excess weight now that she had a good relationship as it had been when she didn't. Her partner did not rescue Debra from the consequences of her actions. Only Debra could make the commitment to lose weight.

The second dysfunctional behavior to abstain from is the spontaneous expression of anger. You have to stop surprising your partner with anger and criticism. This is known as "dropping bombs." Healthy partners do not explode suddenly and vent their anger on their partner, nor tolerate their partner's sudden anger and criticism.

Healthy partners know that criticism and anger need to be discussed openly and honestly, but in a caring and rational way. This is best done by appointment. When healthy partners feel anger, they examine their thoughts, feelings, and urges so they can determine their source and figure out what they need to resolve.

Of course, nobody is totally rational all the time, nor is it highly desirable to be. It is important, however, to practice techniques and ways of dealing with emotionality that contain and channel it so that it doesn't become destructive. I encourage couples to use a six-part communication process, a Couple's Dialogue, as outlined in chapter 10.

These techniques require practice. Abstaining from dysfunctional behaviors requires becoming skilled in managing feelings and emotions so we can stop dropping bombs or reacting to the bombs our partner drops on us. It means learning to think clearly about ourselves and our partner, doing away with unrealistic demands and irrational beliefs about what we should think, feel, or be, and what our partner should think, feel, or be.

To improve your existing relationship or the quality of future relationships, you need to learn how to think better and act better before you can feel better. These are basic skills necessary for healthy relationships.

THINKING AND RELATIONSHIPS: MANDATES AND INJUNCTIONS

Without the ability to think clearly and reason on the basis of logical criteria, dysfunctional families teach children to think in terms of mandates and injunctions. Mandates are irrational beliefs that we "must," "should," or "have to" think, feel, or do something a certain way. Injunctions are irrational beliefs that we "cannot," "should not," or "must not" think, feel, or do something a certain way.

Mandates and injunctions are irrational because they operate outside the natural law of consequence. Whether something is good or bad is determined by the consequences it produces. If an action usually causes a negative consequence, we can generalize to say, "It is bad to do this." If the consequence *always* happens, a mandate or injunction is valid: "You must never drop an electric radio into the bath water while you are bathing, or you will be electrocuted."

Most mandates and injunctions, however, are true only some of the time. "Never give your address to a stranger," Trudi's mother told her when she moved into her first apartment. How can Trudi take a cab? Fill out a job application? There are appropriate situations in which she can and will choose to give her address to a stranger if she is to function in the real world. In each situation, she will have to decide if it is prudent to give out her address or if she should refuse. People *can* do things, but certain behaviors and actions may cause adverse consequences.

Sometimes these mandates and injunctions are generalized statements such as "Men mustn't cry," or "Women should not be strong." They may take the form of personalized statements about ourselves such as "I must do everything myself because I am the only person who can do it right." Or "I can't let anyone see me cry because they will think I'm weak."

When we learn them from our parents, mandates and injunctions tend to be so strong they defy all reason and logic.

There was a man who believed he was dead because his parents taught him he must be dead or he is worthless. Like any of us trained in irrational mandates, he went through life believing he was dead.

At the age of forty, he came to the attention of a famous behavioral psychologist. This psychologist decided that he was going to cure the man of the belief that he was dead. He had the man write on a blackboard hundreds of times, "Dead men don't bleed." At the end of each day, the doctor hooked the man up to a lie detector and asked him to repeat the phrase "Dead men don't bleed" to see how strongly he believed it. They did this every day for ninety days. By the end of this time, the man had the most intense belief you could ever have that dead men don't bleed. At that moment, the psychologist grabbed the man's hand, took a pin, pricked the man's finger, squeezed out a huge drop of blood, and held it out before him.

The psychologist asked, "Now what do you think of that?"

The man who believed that he was dead began to shake and tremble; he turned white as a ghost. He stared at the blood coming out of his own finger and said, "My gosh! Dead men *do* bleed!"

This is how strongly mandates and injunctions affect us. We will adjust our perception of reality to accommodate the mandate or the injunction rather than the other way around. Instead of believing ourselves dead, we may think in terms of certain attributes "real men" and "real women" must have or certain things they must do: "real men do this" and "real women do this."

Frequently, people who are taught to believe mandates and injunctions are so accustomed to following them they simply don't see how irrational they really are. How many times did your parents tell you to eat everything on your plate, even when you were no longer hungry? Do you remember the "reason" they gave you? "Eat everything on your plate. There are children starving in China." Where is the logic in that?

Others may know that the mandates and injunctions they believe are irrational, but they have a deep-seated feeling that something awful will happen if they don't follow them. In some cases, they know that their lives could be improved if they lived differently, but they can't. It would be wrong. They have been taught that they must do certain things, and that they can't do others, even though they could improve their lives and the lives of those they love by deviating from that teaching.

Betty was raised by a father who needed to act strong and could never show weakness. Her mother, a very competent woman, deferred constantly to her husband's wishes. When Betty would ask her mother why she let Dad treat her that way, her mother would say, "He treats me that way because he loves me." She would then explain that in order to keep a good man like her father, a woman needed to make him feel important by doing what he wanted and not challenging him.

Betty learned to accept male aggression as an expression of love. She also learned that a woman's place in life is to defer to a man. These mistaken beliefs had serious consequences for Betty in her adult relationships.

"I don't know why," Betty told her therapist, "but I'm attracted to strong, insensitive men who try to control me!" Betty didn't feel attracted to sensitive or caring men. She somehow felt they didn't love her because they didn't seek to dominate her or control her.

Betty was blindly following the mandates and injunctions her mother transmitted to her: "To be loved, you must allow your partner to control you!" "You must do everything he asks and constantly defer to him." "You must make your partner feel important!" "You must not challenge your partner." "Real men must be strong and insensitive." "A man must try to control you or else he doesn't love you."

People continue to comply with mandates and injunctions because they believe that a variety of awful consequences may or will occur if they don't. Some mandates and injunctions have relatively mild consequences. The person believes that by violating the mandate or injunction he or she is no good and feels ashamed and guilty. Betty believes that she must follow the injunctions and mandates of her mother in order to be in a relationship with "a good man." In the most severe cases, the person believes the consequence of violating the mandate or injunction will be annihilation. When he or she tries to do things differently, he/she experiences fear and anxiety that borders on panic.

CHALLENGING OUR MANDATES AND INJUNCTIONS

Functional families teach children how to make healthy decisions on the basis of a realistic appraisal of the likely consequences. As adults they are free to make their own choices rather than blindly follow the will of others. They think for themselves, and they operate in the real world, aware of the law of consequence. Children from functional families are choice makers. They are also risk takers, willing to challenge irrational mandates and injunctions in order to attain better results.

Mandates and injunctions inhibit a person's ability to choose a rational course of action. Some people have such deeply entrenched mandates and injunctions they are not even aware that choices are available to them. To become a choice maker, you must train yourself to identify mandates and injunctions and convert them into choice statements.

Suppose you say to yourself, "I must never let anyone know when I'm sad." This is a mandate; it is not true. To begin to convert this to a choice statement, you can find its opposite. "I must always tell everyone immediately when I am sad." These are the two extremes: never and always. Between them lie many choices from which to choose, among them: "I can let my friends know when I'm sad." "I can let my family know when I'm sad." "I can let my partner know when I'm sad."

Suppose you believe "I can't tell my partner what I am really feeling!" To convert this into a choice statement, you can find its opposite, "I can always tell my partner what I am really feeling." From experience, you have probably learned that there are times when your partner may be tired or preoccupied and that these times are inappropriate for the disclosure of your feelings. Having considered the two extremes, you can simply affirm to yourself, "I can choose when it is safe to tell my partner what I am feeling, and when it is safer to keep my feelings private!"

Another way choice makers challenge mandates and injunctions is to subject irrational demands to rational evaluation. They use four questions to examine their mandates and injunctions so that they can choose whether or not to act upon them.

1. *Who taught me that I must, should, or have to do this? Who told me that I can't, shouldn't, or mustn't be a certain way?* By establishing the source of authority, it is often possible to determine whether a mandate or injunction is rational or irrational.

2. *Is it possible that I was taught incorrectly?* Most of us learned these mandates and injunctions from our parents, fallible human beings who can make mistakes. Perhaps they were wrong when they taught us this.

3. *What will happen if I continue to act out this mandate or injunction?* We are often afraid to challenge our mandates and injunctions because of our fear that something terrible will happen. But we often ignore the terrible things that occur when we continue to act on irrational mandates that make our lives miserable. We need to consider all options and choose the best.

4. *If I challenge this mandate or injunction and act differently, what will most likely happen?* You might find it helpful to ask this question in three ways: *If I challenge this mandate or injunction, what is the best thing that could happen? What is the worst thing that could possibly happen? What will most probably happen?*

MANAGING FEELINGS

In many ways, the art of relationship building is the art of emotional expression. To get love right, we must be able to communicate our most intimate, loving, and caring feelings in our love relationships. We also need to be free to express our negative and painful feelings. In healthy love, partners share their emotions, both pleasant and unpleasant. They celebrate together and they mourn together. At times, they feel joyful, caring, or fulfilled, and at other times they feel sorrowful, angry, or frustrated. When you know how to get love right, you can talk about your feelings and emotions with your lover. You also know how to hear, understand, and affirm your partner's feelings and emotions. This allows both of you to express all of your emotions without shame, guilt, or fear of rejection.

When we mismanage our primary feelings, it affects our relationships. Most people, from time to time, mismanage their feelings. This is normal and human. Yet when emotional mismanagement becomes the norm in a relationship, healthy intimacy becomes impossible. People from dysfunctional families who have never learned the basic principles of emotional management control their feelings so poorly that they jeopardize their ability to achieve healthy intimacy. Often they exist in a constant state of low-grade emotional crisis. They experience painful feelings almost all of the time.

BASIC PRINCIPLES OF EMOTIONAL MANAGEMENT

Healthy emotional management is based on four basic principles.

1. It is normal and natural to have feelings. Human beings are feeling oriented. We are born with the capacity to experience physical sensations and emotions. We are also rational beings who can reason and remember. Healthy people use both their capacity to feel and their capacity to think when determining whether to act on their feelings.

2. Feelings have a purpose. Feelings are emotional signals that give us information. Just as physical pain is a sensation that tells us there is something wrong with our bodies, painful emotions are signals that tell us that something is wrong in our lives and causing us pain. We need to discover and understand the cause. If your pain is due to the fact that your partner is abusive and leaves you feeling bad about yourself, you need to recognize this. When you do, you can take action either to set limits on his or her behavior or to end the relationship. When you put an end to the abuse, you can begin to feel better.

Sometimes, however, we experience deep, painful emotions that are normal and healthy, such as grief at the loss of a loved one. If we understand the source of the pain, we can decide how to cope with this feeling, knowing that the intense grief will pass in time. Painful feelings are a fact of life, but they should be the exception in our lives, not the rule.

Even in the presence of strong emotions, healthy people use intellect to deal with them effectively. They use communication skills that allow them to communicate responsibly and not abusively.

In the case of an abusive relationship, we must use our rational mind to recognize that we will continue to feel bad as long as the abuse continues. Then we can take action to end the abuse. In the case of grief, we use our rational mind to know that it will pass and that we can help ourselves by affirming our feelings, not by becoming lost in them.

Unfortunately, in an effort to cope and feel good, many children from dysfunctional families have not learned that thinking and acting better are the primary ways to effect healthy changes to make them feel better. Instead, they have learned to try to feel better by turning off or ignoring their painful feelings. Others learned to exaggerate or artificially create pleasurable feelings, or to make desired feelings more intense. They have perfected these skills as adults to the extent that they no longer can understand the messages their feelings need to convey.

3. Feelings alone can be deceptive. It is natural to want to feel only pleasant feelings and never experience pain or discomfort. When we allow ourselves only to feel good, we not only shut out valuable information we need to conduct our lives in a healthy way but we may be choosing to feel good now at the expense of our later good. Many things that are harmful can initially feel good but cause pain later. This pattern makes it difficult to identify the source of our pain. We associate the activity with the initial pleasure, not with the resulting pain. As a result, we have a hard time believing that something that makes us feel so good in the beginning can actually be the cause of our pain later on.

This tendency to indulge in pleasurable activities and avoid pain goes hand in hand with a need for instant gratification. We want to take something, or do something, or love someone who will instantly remove our pain and create pleasure for us, without our taking the responsibility for thinking better or acting better. We want our pain to go away without having to do anything about the thoughts, behaviors, and situations causing it.

Many relationships produce short-term pleasure only to cause long-term pain and dysfunction. As a result, we can't rely upon our feelings as the only tool for deciding if a relationship is good for us. We must also use our rational mind to think about it. In order to protect ourselves, we sometimes have to abstain from dysfunctional relationships that have the power to make us feel good now but will hurt us later. Or we must accept the pain of ending a relationship that ultimately cannot meet our needs in order to find a partner who will meet our needs.

4. Feelings are neither "good" nor "bad." There is no such thing as a "bad" feeling. At worst, there are unpleasant or painful feelings that give us important information about ourselves and what is happening around us. Since both pleasant and unpleasant feelings have a definite purpose, it is dangerous to ignore or repress them.

This is most true in dysfunctional families, which teach children to deal with their emotions through mandates and injunctions. These families teach children to turn off their feelings in one of three ways. In some dysfunctional families, children are taught not to feel anything: "Good children don't get excited or upset!" As a result, the children learn never to express strong feelings. When they do feel a strong emotion, they are overcome by shame and guilt and try to hide it.

Other dysfunctional families teach their children that only pleasant feelings are acceptable. In essence, they say, "Tell me how wonderful you feel, but keep any bad or unpleasant feelings to yourself!" In such families, children learn to act happy and calm and to mask the unresolved anger and pain that stays beneath the surface.

In still other dysfunctional families, children learn that unpleasant feelings are acceptable, while pleasant or happy feelings are forbidden. The underlying belief is: "Life is unfair and made for suffering. You can't be happy and that is just the way things are!" As a result, the children learn to make themselves feel miserable. They learn that pain and suffering are virtues and that constant anger is justified because the world is unfair.

EFFECTIVE EMOTIONAL MANAGEMENT

You can learn to deal effectively with your feelings by following a four-step process: (1) recognize your feelings, (2) accurately label your feelings, (3) affirm your feelings, and (4) communicate your feelings to others when it is safe to do so.

1. Recognize your feelings. We recognize our feelings by taking a deep breath and noticing the sensations that are going on within our bodies. It is useful to get started by noticing the feelings that begin in the pit of your stomach and move on up through your esophagus into your throat. Once you connect with your sensations, you can identify related emotions by mentally imagining that sensation and then noticing any memories or fantasies that are connected with it.

2. Label your feelings. To do this, you need an emotional vocabulary. People from healthy, functional families learn to use a rich emotional vocabulary. They learn words with which to describe their feelings and how to link these words to their emotions and tell others about what they are feeling.

Three-year-old Rusty showed his mother the house he had built with blocks. "That's a very good house, Rusty. You must feel proud." Rusty learned to associate the feeling of pride with the word *proud*. When Rusty felt that way again, he knew the word to describe it.

Most people from dysfunctional families have learned to distort feelings and never have the words necessary to express their feelings to others.

3. Affirm your feelings. If, for example, you know you are unhappy, say to yourself, "I feel unhappy and it is all right to have this feeling." This is a simple step that is crucially important to people raised in dysfunctional families, who may have learned that it is not all right to feel certain feelings.

"I hate you, you're mean!" Rachel screamed at her mother when she would not let her watch more television. Her mother became furious and slapped her. "How dare you get angry at me? I want you to apologize at once or no more television for a week!"

"I'm sorry," said Rachel, although she did not feel sorry but was in fact very angry at her mother. Rachel learned that however angry she felt, she must not let her mother and others see the anger that seethed inside her.

A very different lesson would have been taught if her mother had said, "I know you are angry now. You would like to watch the next program, too, but two hours is the limit that we agreed on." In this case, her mother affirmed her anger, even while remaining firm about the limit. As she matures, Rachel will be able to recognize and affirm her immediate anger and frustration at not getting what she wants, and how to accept limits without acting out her anger and frustration.

When people are taught that certain emotions are not acceptable, they feel guilty, ashamed, or anxious when they begin to experience those emotions. By practicing an affirmation that says it is all right to experience this feeling, you validate your emotional life.

4. Communicate your feelings. You need to tell somebody else what you feel, the thoughts related to that feeling, and the urges to act created by that feeling. When we have the vocabulary to do this, and learn that we are allowed to experience our feelings, we can communicate our feelings and open the way for healthy intimacy.

EMOTIONAL MISMANAGEMENT

As a result of their early training, many people start with strong, healthy primary feelings and then distort them. Distorted feelings are more difficult to deal with because they are extremes of healthy feelings. These distorted feelings result from the way the individual mismanages the expression of the primary feelings. There are five typical ways that couples mismanage their emotions in their relationships. These are:

1. Blocking feelings. Many people refuse to experience certain feelings in their relationships. When these forbidden feelings begin to rise, they try to push them down. As the unwanted feeling begins to emerge, they mask the feeling with muscle tension. They hold their breath, tense their muscles, and attempt to stifle the feeling physically.

The next step in blocking is cognitive distraction. To avoid dealing with the feeling, they think about something else. When all else fails, they use behavioral distraction. They do something else to take their minds off the unwanted feeling. The goal is to forget about the feeling and pretend it does not exist.

The problem with blocking feelings is that they always come back. Remember, when we experience an emotion it is a signal that tells us how we are managing our emotions. If we ignore these signals, the next time we feel that way, it will return with more intensity and force. If we try to push it down when it comes back, we will temporarily feel better, only to have the emotion emerge again at a later time with even more intensity. This can become a vicious cycle that results in intense, unmanageable emotions.

2. Judging the feelings. The second way to mismanage emotions is to judge the feeling. When we become aware that we are feeling something, we may say to ourselves, "This feeling is bad, it is morally wrong, it is awful and terrible to feel this way. This feeling is unbearable and I can't stand it." By judging the feeling negatively, we tend to intensify what we are experiencing and add feelings of shame and guilt.

Many people attempt to block the feeling, and when it emerges they judge it as bad or negative, mix it with shame and guilt, and then attempt once again to block it. The result is that the feeling keeps returning in a more intense and distorted form.

3. Judging the self. Such judgments basically go: "Since this is a terrible feeling and I am having it, I must be a terrible person." "Since this is a bad feeling that I am having, I must have done something wrong to deserve it." "I lack courage and strength. If I were a stronger person, I wouldn't feel this way." "I must be crazy for having this feeling. Only people with emotional problems would feel the way that I feel." "I must be inferior for feeling this way. The fact that I am having these feelings proves that I am inferior to others."

4. Mandating the emotion. We begin to believe that we must feel a certain way all the time or else something awful will happen. As a result, we attempt to force ourselves into specific emotional states, whether we feel that way or not. Many people turn to the discipline of a positive mental attitude. They use such affirmations as: "I am feeling joyful. I am feeling alive and well. I am feeling better each day." Although these affirmations can have very powerful short-term effects, they can also be used as tools of repression. If we are feeling sad, scared, or angry about some real issues going on in our lives and we use positive affirmations to turn those feelings off, we do not help ourselves. We simply block the genuine emotion, ignore the life situations that are causing it, and program ourselves with an artificial feeling that will be temporary. In the long run, the negative feeling, aggravated by our behavior, will return.

5. Forbidding the emotion. We begin to believe, "I must not feel this way or else I will be no good or something awful will happen and I will die." This forbidding of certain feelings results in further attempts to block the emotion, and the cycle of mismanagement occurs all over again.

THE CONSEQUENCES OF EMOTIONAL MISMANAGEMENT

There are three logical consequences of emotional mismanagement: repression, exaggeration, and distortion.

We experience *repression* when our feelings are blocked from our awareness; we are not aware of what we are feeling. We may feel only positive feelings and repress or block out the negative. Or we feel only negative feelings and repress or block out the positive. At still other times, we become emotionally numb and feel nothing at all.

Exaggeration is the result of magnifying, amplifying, and intensifying feelings and emotional experiences. As a result, we emotionally overreact. We experience a problem that warrants mild anger and we feel extreme anger. We experience a situation that would normally elicit moderate sadness and we become suicidally depressed. It feels as if any emotion we experience is ten times more intense than it should be.

Emotional mismanagement also results in the *distortion* of feelings. Instead of having clear, solid, healthy feelings, we distort them.

To stop mismanaging our emotions, we need to understand our emotional habits and patterns. We can begin by becoming familiar with the primary feelings and how they relate to other feelings, both healthy and distorted. When we can recognize an emotion, understand it and what it is telling us to do, we can act on it for our own good. We can affirm the emotion and communicate it.

THE PRIMARY FEELINGS AND THEIR DISTORTIONS

Distorted Feeling		Primary Feeling		Distorted Feeling
Grandiosity	←	Strength	←→ Weakness	→ Helplessness
Obligation	←	Caring	←→ Anger	→ Resentment
Mania	←	Joy	←→ Sorrow	→ Depression
Complacency	←	Security	←→ Fear	→ Panic
Self-indulgence	←	Fulfillment	←→ Frustration	→ Hopelessness

As you can see from the above chart, the primary feelings each have a counterbalancing or opposing feeling. When we fully experience and express an intense feeling, it eventually dissolves or gives way to its opposite. Each primary feeling also has a distorted form. The goal is to recognize and acknowledge the healthy primary feelings and to manage these feelings so that distortions do not occur.

Strength and Weakness

Strength is the feeling of high energy, power, and potency. It is normal and natural to feel strong sometimes and to act upon it, and then to swing in the opposite direction and feel weak. Both are healthy, natural feelings that reflect basic needs.

Grandiosity ← Strength ←→ Weakness → Helplessness

When strength is distorted and exaggerated, it transforms into grandiosity, an experience of extreme strength and power brought on by the conviction that it is impossible for anyone or anything to hurt or defeat us. It can create the perception of "I am always right, and you are always wrong." When a partner starts to feel grandiose, he or she begins to act in a one-sided fashion and tends to put his or her partner down.

Weakness is distorted into helplessness. When we feel helpless, we experience an extreme sense of weakness caused by the conviction that we are so powerless that we are unable to defend or take care of ourselves. This helplessness is usually an exaggeration or distortion of a healthy feeling of weakness.

When two grandiose people attempt a relationship, a power struggle generally ensues. The relationship is often intense, but it is also usually conflictual and marked by powerful arguments. When two helpless partners come together, they cling to each other and expect to be protected and taken care of. When their partner doesn't do for them what they want, they feel disillusioned and leave to find someone stronger.

When a grandiose person gets into a relationship with a helpless person, there is often a powerful attraction. The grandiose person wants a partner who will affirm how wonderful he or she is and who will acquiesce to his/her desires and demands. The helpless person wants to be taken care of by a powerful caregiver. This match often temporarily meets both partners' needs. The partners enter into an unconscious arrangement. The weak partner allows the other to be grandiose as long as he or she doesn't challenge his/her helplessness. The grandiose partner allows the other to be weak as long as he or she doesn't challenge his/her grandiosity.

Caring and Anger

When we feel caring toward someone, we want to look after him or her. When he or she rejects or refuses to accept our caring, we may get angry. We are willing to let ourselves get close to him/her and to lower our defenses. This is why the people we care the most about have the greatest potential to hurt us, and when they hurt us, our typical reaction is anger.

As a result, it is essential that any couple interested in developing a healthy relationship learn how to recognize and communicate both caring and anger. Couples who are accustomed to communicate only caring tend to ignore, or repress, feelings of anger when they arise. Anger becomes a forbidden feeling. Although they still feel it, the partners don't allow themselves to talk about or share their anger. As a result, both partners feel an undercurrent of anger that can begin to reach explosive levels.

Some relationships are just the opposite. Anger is allowed, but the expression of caring is prohibited. When both partners are only free to express anger, the caring goes unspoken and there is no affirmation of the foundation of love that exists between them.

Obligation ←—— Caring ←——→ Anger ——→ Resentment

Anger can be distorted into resentment, a sense of intense anger or hostility that will not go away or diminish. We get angry and we stay angry even though we may know that it is unjustified. In short, we carry a grudge. We don't finish or resolve the anger; we keep recycling it over and over again.

Resentful partners tend to be victimizers. They take out their anger on others who often don't deserve it. It is difficult to deal with resentful partners because they are always angry, and their anger generally has little to do with the immediate situation.

Feelings of caring can be distorted into an unhealthy sense of obligation. When we feel obligated, we feel such a strong sense of caring that we believe we must neglect or sacrifice ourselves in order to demonstrate our caring to others. We tend to make excessive commitments. We feel like a martyr. We believe we are obligated to sacrifice ourselves for the well-being of somebody else.

It is difficult to deal with a partner who feels obligated. He or she attempts to please but not out of a desire to do so. The obligated partner attempts to please out of a sense of duty.

Chronically resentful people tend to be attracted to martyrs. Martyrs feel obligated to tolerate their partner's irrational resentment. Conversely, the resentful person feels their anger is justified because the obligated person acts like a subservient victim.

Joy and Sorrow

The biblical saying "The Lord giveth, and the Lord taketh away" reflects the nature of joy and sorrow. When we receive something of value, we experience joy. When we lose it, we experience sorrow. Because we are mortal human beings, all things in our earthly existence are temporary. No matter what we have or value, we will ultimately lose it. This is most true of those we love. The ultimate confrontation with this reality was summarized by Ernest Hemingway when he said, "All true stories end in death."

It is this fear of losing the people or things that they value most that often causes people to repress their feelings of joy. They think, "If I don't value it too much, it won't hurt too much when I lose it." The fear of loss can prevent us from appreciating the most valuable people and things in our lives and from attaining our most heartfelt goals.

Mania ◄— Joy ◄—► Sorrow —► Depression

Joy is often exaggerated and distorted into mania. When we feel manic, we are so overjoyed that we experience a sense of intoxication and agitated delight. We experience an extreme mood sweep that is out of context with what we are actually feeling. Manic partners are difficult to deal with because their expressions of joy are inappropriate. They also use their manic mood to intrude upon others.

Sorrow is often distorted into depression. When we are depressed, we feel so sorrowful, anguished, and grief-stricken that we have difficulty functioning normally. Our energy levels are so low we find it difficult to get out of bed.

Depressed people are difficult to relate to because they are a constant drain. Their low energy and negative mood become grating. Their inability to feel joyful, happy, or content can easily affect the mood of their partner.

Security and Fear

Security is one of the basic human needs, and we all strive for it. Fear is an inner experience of agitation caused by the anticipation of danger. The ultimate fear, often called the existential fear, is the fear of our own mortality, the fear that we are going to die.

Since we must meet the conditions necessary for happiness and survival on a day-to-day, hour-to-hour, and at times minute-to-minute basis, it is inevitable that we will lapse into periods of fear and insecurity. This fear is a signal that we need to do what is necessary to secure our life and our well-being.

Complacency ◄─── Security ◄──► Fear ──► Panic

Security is often distorted into complacency. When we feel complacent, we feel so secure and satisfied that we lose our sense of motivation. We feel there is no challenge or excitement left in life. We feel as if there is nothing we can do to get our edge or excitement back.

Complacent partners are stuck in a rut. They tend to want to stay the way they are. They resist change and refuse to recognize or deal with problems.

Fear is often distorted into panic. When we experience panic, we are so afraid that something terrible or awful will happen that we have difficulty functioning well. This panic may result from an identifiable threat, or it may result from a generalized feeling that something awful is about to happen. In essence, this panic is based upon the belief that we will not be able to manage what happens to us.

Panicky partners are scared or apprehensive about everything. They don't want to take risks because they expect the worst. They easily overreact or are frightened by any change in the relationship.

Fulfillment and Frustration

Fulfillment and frustration operate on a continuum. When we desire something that we cannot get, we feel frustrated. The frustration motivates us to find solutions to overcome the obstacle. When we figure out how to get what we want, our frustration is replaced by a feeling of fulfillment. If we are unable to get what we want, the frustration can become so intense that it motivates us to give up. In giving up, we stop wanting the object and accept that we cannot have it.

Self-indulgence ◄——— Fulfillment ◄———► Frustration ———► Hopelessness

Healthy frustration is often distorted into hopelessness. When we feel hopeless, we experience severe frustration caused by the conviction that we will never be able to get what we want or need. We feel as if insurmountable obstacles face us and no matter how hard we try, nothing will ever work.

A healthy feeling of fulfillment is often distorted into a feeling of self-indulgence. We feel self-indulgent if we continue to seek pleasure and pleasurable experiences when we need to do other things to maintain our health and well-being.

Shame and Guilt

When we distort primary feelings, we may also feel shame or guilt. People who come from dysfunctional families are more prone to experience shame and guilt than others. These emotions can result from the distortion of any other feeling or emotion. Guilt is based upon the deep-seated belief that we have done something wrong. While it can be a healthy response to violating a personal value, it may be inappropriate when it stems from an irrational conviction that we have done something wrong when we haven't.

Shame results from the conviction that we are defective as a person. It is not that we have *done* something wrong; we *believe* we are wrong.

PHYSICAL FACTORS THAT AFFECT FEELINGS

How we feel and how we express our feelings affect our relationships. When we feel well, we are more able to respond appropriately to our feelings and thoughts. If we feel terrible, it is easier to lash out at the world and people around us. If we want to have a healthy relationship based on an honest exchange of feelings, we need to first take care of ourselves.

The five major physical factors that affect our emotional state are poor diet, fatigue, high stress, lack of exercise, and illness.

Poor diet. A poor diet, one that includes too much sugar, too many stimulants such as caffeine and nicotine, can create the tendency to overreact to little things. These overreactions can create serious relationship problems.

Fatigue. A constant state of fatigue can set the stage for emotional overreaction or emotional numbness. When we numb our feelings in an effort to ignore the fatigue, we also turn off our other feelings and we may appear distant and remote to our partners.

High stress. High stress distorts feelings, especially for people who live a chronic high-stress life-style that puts them under constant pressure. Other people are stressed by the boredom of being underchallenged and understimulated by their life-style. People under high stress often live on an emotional roller coaster marked by euphoric highs and crashing, tension-filled lows. These changes in mood, prompted by the inability to cope with the chronic high stress, can devastate relationships.

Lack of exercise. Lack of exercise affects our mood, our thinking, and can eventually lead to physical problems. By contrast, aerobic exercise is the best stress manager you can invest in. Walking, running, jogging, swimming, and aerobic classes can all help you get rid of stress. Sharing these exercise activities with your partner can strengthen your relationship.

Illness. High stress can also lead to chronic illnesses such as colds, the flu, and general low energy. Although healthy couples are able to nurture and support each other through periods of illness, chronic illness caused by a lack of self-care can be frustrating to a partner.

Sam would work himself into the ground. He'd never rest, and when he would take a vacation he'd get sick. He'd be so sick, he and his wife couldn't enjoy themselves. Sam said it wasn't his fault, but his wife, Shirley, wasn't impressed. "Anyone could see that Sam would get sick because he beat himself into the ground," said Shirley. "After a while I got tired of it. Who wants to live with someone who always gets too sick to enjoy the benefits of his work?" Living in chronic high stress strains the immune system and sets us up to get sick. When we are physically ill, we are emotionally on edge.

MANAGING EMOTIONS IN A RELATIONSHIP

Healthy intimacy requires a feeling of safety. I must feel that it is safe to tell my partner what I feel, and my partner must feel safe telling me about his/her feelings. To be able to listen to, understand, and affirm our partner's feelings and emotions, we must know what we ourselves are feeling. This means we must learn to identify, appropriately label, and communicate our own feelings to our partner. We must also make a commitment to listen to the feelings that our partner is attempting to share with us.

We may judge our partners harshly for having certain feelings. Since we can't understand why our partners feel this way, we may even begin to think they must be crazy for feeling as they do. As a result, we encourage them to judge themselves and put themselves down for feeling certain ways. We can also mandate what our partners feel in certain ways. We expect them to be happy when we're happy and sad when we're sad. We tell them, in essence, that it is their job to put themselves into the mood that we want them to be in. We go one step further by forbidding them to feel certain ways. There are certain forbidden feelings and we communicate this verbally and nonverbally. "You don't have a right to get mad at me!" At other times we will communicate, "Don't be hurt by what I did, I didn't mean it!" Again, we fail to honor and affirm our partners in their feelings and emotions, and we project onto them the same emotional mismanagement strategies that we use.

Other people feel so overwhelmed or threatened by their partners' emotions that they criticize and judge them out of a need to bring these overwhelming emotions under their control.

It is easy to tell our partners to suppress their feelings; we often do it automatically. "You shouldn't feel that way, Abe," said Sally. "I didn't mean to hurt your feelings and I think it's very immature of you to take it that way." Sally dismissed Abe's feelings and told him to repress or deny them. In essence, she told Abe that his feelings don't count.

"You shouldn't feel lonely," Andy told Sarah. "You knew I had to work late tonight, so there's no reason for you to feel alone. What are you, crazy?" Andy is judging Sarah's feelings. He is telling her that what she is feeling is wrong.

"You have no right to be afraid of me," Tom yelled at Ellen. "I've never hit you and I won't have you feeling that way about me!" Tom is forbidding Ellen to have her feelings. She'll still feel them, however, she just won't tell Tom about them. They will grow further apart because Ellen can't share certain aspects of her emotional life with Tom.

To succeed in our relationships, we must learn to manage our own feelings effectively and to encourage and support our partners in the healthy and effective management of their emotions.

Self-assessment I: Identifying Your Mandates and Injunctions

Mandates and injunctions are destructive when they intrude on our lives and prevent us from choosing the best options available. Nowhere are they more destructive than in relationships, and yet this is the area in which many people rely most frequently on the mandates and injunctions they learned as children.

The following questionnaire will help you identify the mandates and injunctions that may be interfering with your ability to get love right. There are no right or wrong responses. Complete each sentence as quickly as you can with as many answers as you can that come to mind.

For example, the first sentence stem is: "Men must . . ." One man completed it this way: "Men must: be strong, take care of women, not show their feelings, be good providers, be warm and sensitive, be able to take care of themselves, be rugged, be willing to take chances, know how to win, and be willing to work for what they get."

If you have a friend who is willing to help you, you can complete the sentences out loud and ask your friend to write them down.

As you complete the sentences, strong feelings or past memories may pop into your head. Write these memories and feelings down and talk about them with a friend or counselor. Most mandates and injunctions are driven by unfinished emotions and painful past memories. To free yourself from them, you need to think and talk about them.

Mandates and Injunctions about Men
1. Men must, should, or have to be . . . (Give 10 answers)
2. Men can't, shouldn't, or must not be . . . (Give 10 answers)
3. Men would be better off if they would . . . (Give 10 answers)
4. Men will probably never change because . . . (Give 10 answers)
5. The three most important male mandates are:
6. The three most important male injunctions are:
7. The three most important things that I expect men to change are:
8. The three most important reasons why men probably won't make the changes I want are:

Mandates and Injunctions about Women
1. Women must be . . . (Give 10 answers)
2. Women can't be . . . (Give 10 answers)
3. Women would be better off if they would . . . (Give 10 answers)
4. Women will probably never change because . . . (Give 10 answers)
5. The three most important female mandates are:
6. The three most important female injunctions are:
7. The three most important things that I expect women to change are:
8. The three most important reasons why women probably won't make the changes I want are:

Mandates and Injunctions about Myself
1. I must be . . . (Give 10 answers)
2. I can't be . . . (Give 10 answers)
3. I would be better off if I would . . . (Give 10 answers)
4. I will probably never change because . . . (Give 10 answers)
5. The three most important mandates about myself are:
6. The three most important injunctions about myself are:

7. The three most important things that I expect myself to change are:

8. The three most important reasons why I probably won't make the changes I want are:

Mandates and Injunctions about My Partner

1. My partner must be . . . (Give 10 answers)

2. My partner can't be . . . (Give 10 answers)

3. My partner would be better off if he or she would . . . (Give 10 answers)

4. My partner will probably never change because . . . (Give 10 answers)

5. The three most important mandates about my partner are:

6. The three most important injunctions about my partner are:

7. The three most important things that I expect my partner to change are:

8. The three most important reasons why my partner probably won't make the changes I want are:

Mandates and Injunctions about My Relationships

1. My relationship must be . . . (Give 10 answers)

2. My relationship can't be . . . (Give 10 answers)

3. My relationship would be better off if my partner would . . . (Give 10 answers)

4. My relationship will probably never change because . . . (Give 10 answers)

5. My three most important relationship mandates are:

6. My three most important relationship injunctions are:

7. The three most important relationship changes that I want to make are:

8. The three most important reasons why my relationship probably won't change in the ways I want are:

When you have completed the questionnaire, here are two additional exercises to help you to evaluate your mandates and injunctions.

Exercise 1: Go back over your answers and ask yourself the following four questions:

1. *Who taught me that I must, should, or have to do this? Who told me that I can't, shouldn't, or mustn't be a certain way?*

2. *Is it possible that I was taught incorrectly?*

3. *What will happen if I continue to act out this mandate or injunction?*

4. *If I challenge this mandate or injunction and act differently, what will most likely happen?*

Viewed from this perspective, your mandates and injunctions may appear quite different, and you will be in a position to evaluate whether the consequences of adhering to this mandate or injunction are more beneficial than the potential consequences of violating it.

Exercise 2: Take the most significant mandates and injunctions and convert them into choice statements by creating three to five options you can substitute for this mandate or injunction. Then subject each mandate and injunction to the three-step decision-making process demonstrated on page 147.

These two exercises will allow you to stop blindly responding to preprogrammed, irrational mandates and injunctions and begin to make the responsible, mature, and healthy choices that functional families teach their children to make.

Self-Assessment II: Emotional Management Questionnaire

Instructions. The following questionnaire is designed to help you evaluate how well you manage your feelings in your current relationship. If you are not presently in a relationship, complete the answers on the basis of past relationships. If you have a partner, set up a meeting and compare your answers with your partner's. Whether you complete this exercise alone or with a partner, it can show you those emotions you feel you are able to communicate effectively and those emotions that create communication problems for you.

Completing the questionnaire should enable you to become more aware of your feelings and what you choose to do about them on a daily basis. Observe your partner's emotional communications.

Watch for patterns and habits that may signal emotional mismanagement and think of alternative reactions and responses to these
situations. As you become more aware of what you feel and what
these feelings make you want to do, you can practice effective
emotional management.

Rate each question with a number from 1 to 5 (1 = very; 5 = not
at all).

1. Strength

____ a. How comfortable do you feel expressing feelings of strength
to your partner?

____ b. How skillful is your partner at affirming you when you are
feeling strong?

____ c. How comfortable is your partner in expressing feelings of
strength to you?

____ d. How skillful are you at affirming your partner when he or she
is feeling strong?

2. Weakness

____ a. How comfortable do you feel expressing feelings of weakness
to your partner?

____ b. How skillful is your partner at affirming you when you are
feeling weak?

____ c. How comfortable is your partner in expressing feelings of
weakness to you?

____ d. How skillful are you at affirming your partner when he or she
is feeling weak?

3. Anger

____ a. How comfortable do you feel expressing feelings of anger to
your partner?

____ b. How skillful is your partner at affirming you when you are
feeling angry?

____ c. How comfortable is your partner in expressing feelings of
anger to you?

____ d. How skillful are you at affirming your partner when he or she
is feeling angry?

4. Caring

____ **a.** How comfortable do you feel expressing feelings of caring to your partner?

____ **b.** How skillful is your partner at affirming you when you are feeling caring?

____ **c.** How comfortable is your partner in expressing feelings of caring to you?

____ **d.** How skillful are you at affirming your partner when he or she is feeling caring?

5. Joy

____ **a.** How comfortable do you feel expressing feelings of joy to your partner?

____ **b.** How skillful is your partner at affirming you when you are feeling joyful?

____ **c.** How comfortable is your partner in expressing feelings of joy to you?

____ **d.** How skillful are you at affirming your partner when he or she is feeling joyful?

6. Sorrow

____ **a.** How comfortable do you feel expressing feelings of sadness or sorrow to your partner?

____ **b.** How skillful is your partner at affirming you when you are feeling sad or sorrowful?

____ **c.** How comfortable is your partner in expressing feelings of sadness or sorrow to you?

____ **d.** How skillful are you at affirming your partner when he or she is feeling sad or sorrowful?

7. Security

____ **a.** How comfortable do you feel expressing feelings of security to your partner?

____ **b.** How skillful is your partner at affirming you when you are feeling secure?

____ **c.** How comfortable is your partner in expressing feelings of security to you?

_____ **d.** How skillful are you at affirming your partner when he or she is feeling secure?

8. Fear
_____ **a.** How comfortable do you feel expressing feelings of fear to your partner?
_____ **b.** How skillful is your partner at affirming you when you are feeling fearful?
_____ **c.** How comfortable is your partner in expressing feelings of fear to you?
_____ **d.** How skillful are you at affirming your partner when he or she is feeling fearful?

9. Frustration
_____ **a.** How comfortable do you feel expressing feelings of frustration to your partner?
_____ **b.** How skillful is your partner at affirming you when you are feeling frustrated?
_____ **c.** How comfortable is your partner in expressing feelings of frustration to you?
_____ **d.** How skillful are you at affirming your partner when he or she is feeling frustrated?

10. Fulfillment
_____ **a.** How comfortable do you feel expressing feelings of fulfillment to your partner?
_____ **b.** How skillful is your partner at affirming you when you are feeling fulfilled?
_____ **c.** How comfortable is your partner in expressing feelings of fulfillment to you?
_____ **d.** How skillful are you at affirming your partner when he or she is feeling fulfilled?

11. What primary feeling are you most comfortable expressing?
_____ 1. strength   _____ 2. weakness
_____ 3. anger   _____ 4. caring
_____ 5. joy   _____ 6. sorrow

_____ 7. security   _____ 8. fear
_____ 9. frustration   _____ 10. fulfillment

12. What primary feeling is your partner best at affirming when you express it?

_____ 1. strength   _____ 2. weakness
_____ 3. anger   _____ 4. caring
_____ 5. joy   _____ 6. sorrow
_____ 7. security   _____ 8. fear
_____ 9. frustration   _____ 10. fulfillment

13. What primary feeling does your partner have the most difficulty affirming when you express it?

_____ 1. strength   _____ 2. weakness
_____ 3. anger   _____ 4. caring
_____ 5. joy   _____ 6. sorrow
_____ 7. security   _____ 8. fear
_____ 9. frustration   _____ 10. fulfillment

14. What primary feeling do you believe your partner is most comfortable expressing?

_____ 1. strength   _____ 2. weakness
_____ 3. anger   _____ 4. caring
_____ 5. joy   _____ 6. sorrow
_____ 7. security   _____ 8. fear
_____ 9. frustration   _____ 10. fulfillment

15. What primary feeling are you best at affirming when your partner expresses it?

_____ 1. strength   _____ 2. weakness
_____ 3. anger   _____ 4. caring
_____ 5. joy   _____ 6. sorrow
_____ 7. security   _____ 8. fear
_____ 9. frustration   _____ 10. fulfillment

16. What primary feeling do you have the most difficulty affirming when your partner expresses it?

_____ 1. strength   _____ 2. weakness
_____ 3. anger   _____ 4. caring

____ 5. joy   ____ 6. sorrow

____ 7. security   ____ 8. fear

____ 9. frustration   ____ 10. fulfillment

17. What primary feeling do you want to become better at expressing to your partner?

____ 1. strength   ____ 2. weakness

____ 3. anger   ____ 4. caring

____ 5. joy   ____ 6. sorrow

____ 7. security   ____ 8. fear

____ 9. frustration   ____ 10. fulfillment

18. What primary feeling do you want to become better at affirming when your partner expresses it?

____ 1. strength   ____ 2. weakness

____ 3. anger   ____ 4. caring

____ 5. joy   ____ 6. sorrow

____ 7. security   ____ 8. fear

____ 9. frustration   ____ 10. fulfillment

19. What primary feeling do you want your partner to become better at expressing?

____ 1. strength   ____ 2. weakness

____ 3. anger   ____ 4. caring

____ 5. joy   ____ 6. sorrow

____ 7. security   ____ 8. fear

____ 9. frustration   ____ 10. fulfillment

20. What primary feeling do you want your partner to become better at affirming?

____ 1. strength   ____ 2. weakness

____ 3. anger   ____ 4. caring

____ 5. joy   ____ 6. sorrow

____ 7. security   ____ 8. fear

____ 9. frustration   ____ 10. fulfillment

21. What are the two major distorted emotions that you tend to experience?

____ 1. grandiosity   ____ 2. helplessness

____ 3. obligation   ____ 4. resentment

____ 5. mania   ____ 6. depression

____ 7. complacency   ____ 8. panic

____ 9. hopelessness   ____ 10. boredom

____ 11. shame   ____ 12. guilt

22. What are the two major distorted emotions that you believe your partner tends to experience?

____ 1. grandiosity   ____ 2. helplessness

____ 3. obligation   ____ 4. resentment

____ 5. mania   ____ 6. depression

____ 7. complacency   ____ 8. panic

____ 9. hopelessness   ____ 10. boredom

____ 11. shame   ____ 12. guilt

23. What are the three feelings (either primary or distorted) that you and your partner communicate about most easily?

a. _____   b. _____   c. _____

24. What three feelings (either primary or distorted) cause the most communication problems?

a. _____   b. _____   c. _____

Chapter 6

BUILDING THE
RELATIONSHIP: *YOU*

P R I N C I P A L C H O I C E S
• To become consciously aware of the types of partners you are attracted to; the basis of that attraction; what this type of partner can and cannot give you.
• To build a social network.
• To determine your relationship needs.

"**I** really don't understand it," said Catherine. "I met this guy Peter. We started a relationship and he walked out on me after six months."

I said, "Tell me about the relationship."

"Well, Peter's kind of an insecure guy. He was physically battered as a child by his mother. He doesn't trust women. I remember the first time we sat down to have coffee, he told me, 'You don't want to get involved with me. I'm a runner. If we get sexually involved, we'll be together for a while. I'm going to use you and then I'm going to dump you. You don't want to be involved.' "

"What happened?" I asked.

"I got involved and he dumped me."

I said, "I'm confused. He told you this on the first date. He told you, 'This is my agenda. This is what I'm going to do to you. I've done it to all other women. I'm going to do it to you. Don't expect me to be any other way.' Why did you continue the relationship?"

"I thought it would be different this time. I thought if he really loved me he would change."

In his film *Chalk Talk,* Father Joseph Martin gave an excellent definition of addictive insanity. He said somebody is addictively insane if he or she expects different consequences from the same behaviors. By this definition, when we make the same relationship choices again and again, only to have the relationship end in dismal failure each and every time, we're crazy. We are locked into a cycle of repetitive self-destructive behavior. If you have consistently used the same behavior and gotten the same disastrous result, it's time to try something new.

Partner selection is a primary reason for relationship failure. Like Catherine, if you continue to select partners on the basis of irrational fantasies about changing their fundamental natures, you are going to be hurt, just as she was. Instead of repeating old patterns, however, you can learn how to build a relationship slowly and systematically with a partner who has the capacity to meet your needs in a safe and responsible fashion.

Relationships are not simple. They are driven by very powerful, primitive urges that follow an unconscious, emotional logic. This is why we find ourselves, against our better judgment, attracted to partners who hurt us or cannot give us what we need. This is the reason we need to develop sound relationship skills. It pays to go slowly, to think clearly about what we are doing in our relationships, what we want, and who our partner is.

All relationships are risky. Healthy people are able to accept the risks involved in developing love relationships because they have a variety of ways to protect themselves. There is always risk, but, when we get love right, there is also safety.

DETERMINING YOUR NEEDS

Building safety into a relationship begins before we ever meet our partner. We do this by knowing in advance what type of relationship we want and need: a long-term committed relationship, experimental dating relationships, transitional relationship, or an intimate encounter.

BUILDING A SOCIAL NETWORK

Single people often ask me, "Where can I go to meet partners?" The answer is, you don't "go" anywhere. You invest time and energy in building a healthy social network that will bring you into contact with many potential partners who share common friends and interests.

People obsessed with finding a partner frequently have the mistaken belief that they have to go somewhere special to meet one, usually to bars. In reality, bars are an especially poor place to meet people. Most bars are frequented by three types of people: alcoholics, socially isolated people, and healthy, functional people.

Alcoholics or problem drinkers go to bars to drink and get high. Even if they are interested in forming a relationship, their drinking problem gets in the way.

Socially isolated people don't know where else to go to meet people. They typically come from dysfunctional families and have never learned how to build a social network. They build superficial associations with other people, but they have difficulty developing long-term, lasting friendships or intimate relationships. As a result, they are not healthy potential partners.

Healthy, functional people go to bars with a group of friends to enjoy the music, dance, or socialize. They arrive as a group and they leave as a group. They are not usually open to inviting strangers to join their social network.

John came into therapy because he couldn't find a partner for a love relationship. He was socially isolated and had few friends. He had tried a dating service for a while, but even though there were plenty of women, none of them was suitable for the type of relationship John wanted to develop. He met the few friends he had at bars. Although John had never developed a meaningful relationship with anyone he'd met at a bar, he kept returning, looking for Ms. Right.

I asked John to reinvest his time and energy in building a social network based on activities that interested him. This presented a problem for John, who was a workaholic and tended to build his life around his job. He had never taken the time to figure out what he enjoyed doing outside work.

To help John identify activities that interested him, I asked what he would do on his ideal day off, what types of activities he would enjoy doing if he were to retire, and what his idea of an ideal vacation was. John said that he thought he would enjoy outdoor activities, such as fishing, hiking, and camping.

Once John targeted his interests, the next step was to find people who also enjoyed these activities. John did this by using the telephone yellow pages and looking up clubs, associations, and organizations that focused on these outdoor recreations.

John decided to call the Sierra Club. He attended a Sierra Club meeting, but came to his next therapy session disappointed. "There were hardly any woman at that meeting," John told me. "What's the point of going if there are no eligible women?"

"You're missing the point," I told him. "The goal is not to go somewhere to meet eligible partners. The goal is to join a club so you can build a social network."

Building a social network is a long-term goal. It involves more than meeting a partner because it involves creating the kind of life-style that can build and support many relationships with many different people, including friends and acquaintances, as well as lovers.

Once John understood this concept, he made a commitment to attend several Sierra Club meetings and to become an active member. At the meetings, he got to know several men. Sometimes he went out for coffee with them afterward. As they spent more time together, John realized they shared other interests, such as the same tastes in music and movies. Over a period of months, he cultivated these men as friends, inviting them to movies or concerts.

Then John planned a party. He invited his new Sierra Club friends and asked them to bring their wives or girlfriends and other friends to the party. This way he had the opportunity to meet many new people and broaden his social contacts.

Shortly after that, John received an invitation to a party given by one of his friends. At the party, John was introduced to more new people, including single women who had been invited by his friend's wife.

This is how John began to meet the type of person he had hoped to meet in bars or through the dating service but never had. He discovered that if you develop friendships among people of the same sex who have similar interests, they tend to be involved with members of the opposite sex who are socially compatible. (This is equally true for women. Their girlfriends usually have husbands or boyfriends who know eligible friends.) This type of social network is the best dating service ever created.

Healthy people have social networks. They have friends who have friends. They go to parties. They invite friends over to the house. Groups of people go out. It's not all couple-bound interactions. They belong to social clubs: ski clubs, chess clubs, surfing clubs. There are all kinds of clubs you can belong to. Junior colleges and educational organizations offer classes which are also opportunities to meet people with similar interests. You might take a course in home-repair or computer skills. Sign up for a poetry workshop or dream analysis.

At club meetings, classes, and social functions, healthy people have casual interactions with a variety of people, men and women. This is how they come in contact with potential partners.

Adrienne met Nick at a party and they talked for a bit. Adrienne enjoyed Nick's sense of humor and found out they shared a love of mystery novels. When the conversation ended, she moved on comfortably to meet more people at the party. Susan introduced her to David, who worked for a publisher, and the three of them talked at length about the current trends in book publishing. By the end of the evening, Adrienne had met several new people, men and women, and had learned something about what she shared in common with them. She liked all of them, but had a special interest in Nick. She would call the hostess and see about inviting him to her holiday open house.

When you have the opportunity to meet several potential partners, you need to ask yourself, as Adrienne did, "Of these people, whom do I like the most?" Then you can choose to spend more time with that person and make plans to do something together.

If you are having trouble meeting eligible potential partners, concentrate on developing a social network, just as John did. Even if you have a group of friends you visit frequently, if they do not bring you in contact with new people, explore other options. Remember, however, that your immediate goal is not to find a partner but to start building a social life around activities that interest you. Make it a point to seek out people, both male and female, who share the same interests. Cultivate them as friends. Put your desire to build a love relationship on the back burner until you have an active social network.

The advantages to building a social network extend beyond finding a romantic partner. Investing time and effort in a circle of friends is a personal investment in yourself. It is a natural way to go about improving your general relationship skills. Basic relating skills apply to all types of relationships: romantic relationships, close friendships, family relationships, and work relationships. The ability to communicate and interact in a meaningful way is a necessary prerequisite to building successful love relationships.

Another advantage to developing friendships is that if you find a partner within your social network, you will probably already have certain friends and interests in common. Although it is no guarantee that a person you meet through mutual friends will turn out to be the partner you want, a socially integrated person is far more likely to be a partner capable of entering into a healthy relationship than a socially isolated person.

CHOICES IN POTENTIAL PARTNERS

When selecting potential partners, it is important to keep in mind what you are looking for in a partner. It is perhaps even more important to identify the types of individuals that do not have the potential to be a quality partner for you.

A quality partner will not try to change or fix you in a fundamental way. Any partner you select must be able to accept you the way you are. This does not mean that your partner will love every detail about you. Everyone has endearing strengths and irritating weaknesses. It does mean, however, that your partner accepts your core characteristics, who you are, your values, your basic life goals. A quality potential partner will not ask you to change your basic nature as a prerequisite for his/her affection or approval.

Similarly, you do not want to select a partner you need to "fix" or "help" in essential ways. If a person demonstrates obvious problems, he or she may be unsafe or simply unable or unwilling to be in a healthy relationship.

Unfortunately, many people are most attracted to a partner with personal problems because they have a fantasy that they can fix this person, or help him/her overcome the problems. These people are not attracted to the individual but to the idea of being needed and useful. Other people tend to be attracted to partners who need to be dominated and controlled.

The problem is, you can't fix your partner or assume responsibility for the way your partner lives. No matter how much time and effort you invest, only your partner can fix his/her problems and assume responsibility for his/her actions. If a potential partner has obvious personal problems or chooses to abdicate his/her responsibility, the chances of his or her becoming a quality partner in a healthy relationship are very low. No matter how sorry you feel for him/her, no matter how much you think you can do for him/her, to get love right you need to abstain from dysfunctional relationships with dysfunctional partners.

THE NEED FOR SAFETY

If you're from a dysfunctional family, finding a potential partner by selecting from the people in your social network may feel strange, even uncomfortable. It is always hard to learn new skills, especially when it involves relearning what we unconsciously learned as children from our caregivers. Yet this is the only way I know to get love right, especially when you've had trouble building satisfying relationships in the past.

For some, the most important feature of this method of relationship building is its emphasis on *safety*. Building a relationship is always risky, even with healthy partners. Relationships make us vulnerable and, like it or not, our partner will from time to time inadvertently hurt us. But unsafe relationships can be devastating, physically, psychologically, and emotionally. It is a sad fact that there are a lot of unhealthy people out there who can hurt you and take advantage of you if you give them the chance. We need to take risks, but we need to know how to self-protect, too.

A second reason to emphasize safety is that the attraction between partners frequently involves strong, irrational feelings that, as a rule, we are not used to controlling. You need to have strong feelings about your partner to make a relationship work—intimate love relationships need passion—but you must have safety, too. You need to know where those strong feelings are coming from and what they are urging you to do. Unless you proceed slowly, practicing what you know about managing feelings, thinking rationally, and acting responsibly, these irrational feelings can put you into yet another dysfunctional, painful relationship.

THE BASIS OF ATTRACTION

Imagine you are at a social gathering and you meet someone who intrigues you. He/she has a certain combination of qualities that seems irresistible. You look around at the other people present and there is no comparison. This person stands out. What's going on?

People in this situation often make the mistake of thinking, "He/She's turning me on!" That's not it. When I'm attracted to you, you're not turning me on, *I'm* turning me on. If there is someone I don't really care to know, he or she is not turning me off, *I'm* turning me off—but I'm not doing it consciously. I am responding to an unconscious program I received from my parents and the culture I live in. This unconscious program is what psychologically attracts us to some people and not to others. There are three dynamics at work here:

1. **Similarities:** I'm attracted to you because you're like me and I can rejoice in my strengths with you.

2. **Complementary differences:** You're different from me and you can cause me to grow in ways that I need to develop.

3. **The need to resolve:** I am drawn to you because you give me the opportunity to resolve past trauma.

When we meet someone, the first thing we do is to look for ways in which this person is similar to us. Unconsciously we think, "Are they like me enough so I can feel comfortable?" We look for something about his/her personality, background, and so on, that causes us to recognize traits we love, respect, and admire in ourselves. If you come from a dysfunctional family, this is a very powerful dynamic, because you probably learned that you are inherently unlovable. When you find your best traits in someone else, however, it becomes safe to love them.

The second basis for the attraction you feel for someone is that he or she has complementary differences: he/she is different from you in intriguing, exciting, and, at times, frustrating ways. Have you noticed how very shy people team up with extroverts? Active people couple with stay-at-homes, and planners with partners who love nothing better than following through and putting on the finishing touches. This seems baffling until we understand that we are programmed to be attracted to somebody who has the power to help us move beyond our own limitations. We are drawn to people who have the very traits we lack.

Then there's the third important psychological attraction: the need to resolve. We are unconsciously programmed to be powerfully attracted to people who have the combined features of the caregivers who traumatized us. This is why when you fall in love it hurts so much. Your unconscious mind needs to resolve your childhood trauma and losses and so your programming draws you to select a partner who has the traits that activate your unresolved memories and feelings, giving you the opportunity to bring these up, resolve them, and move on with your life.

Everyone has some unresolved feelings left over from childhood to work through. We have all been damaged to some extent by our family of origin. Healthy relationships allow us the chance to work through unresolved issues productively by confronting them in a loving, caring environment.

If you come from an extremely dysfunctional family, however, the need to resolve can result in very dysfunctional, painful relationships. It can attract you to partners who are incapable and unwilling to meet your needs. The more dysfunctional you are, the more dysfunctional the people you are going to be attracted to will be. So while this basis of attraction is helpful for people within the normal range of functional families, it presents very serious problems for people from extremely dysfunctional families.

If we come from a dysfunctional family the problem is compounded by the fact that, until we undertake a program of personal recovery, the only skills we have to cope with the trauma are those we learned in our family. We don't have a way of thinking about our problems or the skills to confront and resolve them. What happened when you tried to stretch beyond the programmed limitations of your family? What happened if you tried to break the no-talk rules around the physical, psychological, and sexual abuse that went on? These are the types of issues that come up every time we try to get close to another human being.

This is the trauma that we need to resolve in our lives, and until we do, we will re-create the same relationship patterns time after time. Without careful selection of a partner who has at least the potential to enable you to love yourself, to help you reach beyond your limitations, and to confront your unresolved issues, you stand a very high risk of being hurt and traumatized in the same way again and again.

Once you make the commitment to personal growth and change, you can begin to work through these unresolved issues. By becoming a choice maker and choosing to develop healthy relationship skills, you select a partner capable of helping you to work through past trauma (and whom you are able to help in the same way). You can both choose to refrain from overtly dysfunctional behaviors. When you need to, you can rely on outside help, in the form of therapists and support groups.

As you successfully confront past issues in the context of your relationship, you may find that you and your partner grow apart. People from dysfunctional families seldom get love right in their early relationships because they have many different issues to resolve. This is the value of entering into experimental relationships in which you can learn the skills that can bring you closer each time to the type of healthy relationship you seek.

Aaron, now in his early forties, came from a dysfunctional family. He had spent a lot of time working on his relationships, and he was pleased to see how far he'd come. He told his therapist, "I look back at some of the women I was blindly infatuated with, drawn to with tremendous intensity, and I can't understand how I ever felt that way about them. I realize that I changed as a result of those relationships; they helped me grow beyond where I was, and then I found I didn't need the relationship any longer. Looking back, I'm glad I had those experiences and see that they were necessary. Because of them, I was able to resolve those issues. I don't have to re-create them over and over again."

CHANGING YOUR ATTRACTION PATTERNS

As you work on learning to communicate openly and honestly with your partner, as you learn to make healthier and healthier choices, you will find that you are attracted to healthier and healthier partners. You will find yourself increasingly drawn to people more capable of meeting your healthy relationship needs.

There are two techniques you can use to cause your attraction patterns to change more rapidly. One is to stop living in the rosy memories of the past—which I call euphoric recalls about past partners—and the other is to examine magical expectations about potential partners. The purpose in doing this is to shift your focus from short-term gratification to long-term, healthy gratification.

Euphoric recall occurs when you remember past experiences with a certain partner or type of partner, and you exaggerate all the good times about those experiences while blocking out or minimizing all the pain and problems. People often engage in euphoric recall when they think of breaking up with their partner. This is what makes ending relationships so painful. It's important to remember that euphoric recalls are not based in reality. In reality the pain and the problems outweigh the pleasure, or the relationship would not be ending.

To dismantle your euphoric recall, take your five favorite memories of your partner, the things about him or her you really think you will miss. Write them out, step by step. What actually happened at the time? What was it that you really liked? And then look for the hidden negatives, the aftermath or the consequences.

When you see the romanticized memory of the past in the larger context of a painful, unhealthy relationship, you can begin to see that, in the long run, the bad parts outweigh the good. You can begin to understand that ending the destructive relationship is in your best interest.

You can use a similar technique to reexamine magical expectations about the ideal partner—Mr. or Ms. Right—or how your relationship with your partner might be if you were to get back together again. Notice how you build your fantasy and how you end it. People always cut the fantasy short at the moment of peak pleasure. That way, they never have to think about the real life or long-term consequences of their fantasy.

Jerry came to therapy because of his relationship problems. None of the women he dated turned out to be a suitable partner for him. I asked him if he had thought of changing the way he went about selecting partners.

"I can't give up this kind of woman. They're the only ones who turn me on."

"What is it about them that attracts you? What is your fantasy about them? Tell me the whole thing."

"Well, I imagine I go to the bar and there she'd be. She'd be attractive and sexy. I would go and talk to her and we'd dance, and it would be a real sexy evening. All the feelings would come up. She'd invite me over to her place and we'd make love and have incredible sex."

"Then what would happen?"

"Well, nothing, the fantasy stops there."

"But let's keep it going. Then what would happen?"

"Well, I'd wake up the next morning, I guess."

"How would you feel? What would you say? What would happen then?"

"Well, I'd wake up and then feel kind of uncomfortable, and I'd talk to her, I guess, and . . ."

In the end, when Jerry thought about it, he imagined three possible endings to this fantasy. In the first ending, he would wake up in the morning, feel uncomfortable, and say, "How could I have done this? She isn't what I thought she'd be like at all."

In his second ending, he imagined he would think, "I like what I've done. I want to pursue the relationship." He could also imagine that she might tell him, "Hey buddy, I'm not interested in a relationship, you were just a sexual release." That, he realized, would be very painful.

The third ending was not any better; in fact, it was potentially the worst. He would wake up in the morning, feel he was already committed to this woman to a certain degree, and therefore committed to a high-risk relationship he is scared to death to have.

When Jerry projected the long-term consequences of this fantasy, it took all the fun out of it. He could see how very limited the short-term gratification would be, especially compared to the potential consequences. And what if his partner were unsafe? What if she was emotionally unsafe or infected with the AIDS virus? The consequences could be even more serious.

Try this exercise with your fantasies. As you think about your involvement with your idealized Mr. or Ms. Right, picture all of it, all the way through to the end. You will be able to choose whether the likely consequences of your involvement with this type of person will really provide what you want in your relationship. If not, you can begin conditioning yourself to change your attraction patterns. You can reprogram yourself, when you think about past events, to remember the negative aspects of the relationship rather than the positive. When you reprogram yourself to think of what a relationship with that certain mystery partner might be, the consequences that might result, you stop being attracted to that kind of person.

Doug and Isabel arrived at his apartment at the end of a date and were sitting together on the couch. Doug was thinking to himself how perfect the setting was for a romantic interlude. The fact that he and Isabel had only been seeing each other for three weeks and didn't know much about each other didn't stop him from wanting to create the illusion of the perfect evening.

They sat talking for a time and Doug tried several discreet maneuvers to move into more sexual involvement. Isabel, however, was not complying. Finally Doug asked, "Why are you being so resistant? We can have a fantasy together tonight."

Isabel turned to him in surprise and said, looking him straight in the eye, "I don't want to have a fantasy with you. I want to have a reality with you!"

Ask yourself, "Am I trying to go through my love life creating fantasies or am I trying to create realities?" If you want healthy intimacy, if you want to have your needs met, you need to discard fantasies and wishful thinking.

You can begin to free yourself from fantasies and magical expectations and bring your expectations into line with reality. If you seek a fantasy of a perfect lover or a perfect love, you will be disappointed, because perfection is not in human nature. When your goals for a relationship are realistic, you can find an actual partner that will make this healthy reality come true.

LAYING THE FOUNDATION: THE THREE C'S

In building a relationship, healthy people proceed slowly. They know that finding a compatible partner takes time and that it may take getting to know several potential partners to find one that is truly compatible. They take time to lay a foundation based on what I call the three C's of relationship building: communication, caring, and commitment.

Communication. When healthy people meet a potential partner, their first priority is to find out more about this person. They are curious about his or her values, ideas, feelings, and what he or she does for a living. One of the primary things they want to know is whether this potential partner is a safe person, or if he or she has personal problems that will make him/her dangerous to be involved with. To find the answers to these questions, healthy people know that they need to spend time talking with this person.

Caring. Only through honest communication can you find out enough about your partner so you can learn to care about him/her. Once you have begun to communicate, learned enough about each other to begin to care for one another, you are ready for the third C, **commitment.**

People from dysfunctional families frequently reverse this process. They say, "I can't communicate with somebody unless I care about him/her." These people get into trouble because they invest high-quality caring in people they have never communicated with. Caring emerges out of an in-depth knowledge of who that person is. You care about his or her feelings, experiences, what is important to him/her. But without having spent time with this person, how can you know what these are?

If you have the mistaken belief that you must care before you are able to communicate, you're in a trap, because how can you care about someone you don't know?

Rana came into counseling complaining that she felt as if she didn't know her boyfriend, Max, at all. She said she felt as if she were in love with a stranger. Those were her words. "I thought I knew what he was about, but he keeps surprising me."

When I asked her how much time she and Max spent talking together, she looked puzzled.

"Huh? We seldom talk at all. I have to drag things out of him. He never volunteers anything. It's been that way for our whole relationship."

Yet she cares about him. Can that possibly be rational caring? How can you honestly care about someone who has never told you who he/she is? Who never tells you what he/she is thinking or feeling? How can you rationally care about someone when you don't know what he/she is doing in most areas of his/her life?

The answer is you can't. You can only create the illusion of caring. You can create a delightful fantasy and then project it onto the person you're involved with. In the absence of honest communication you don't have a relationship. All you have is a fantasy.

When you first meet a potential partner, it's healthy to be curious. Curiosity is not caring. When Rana met Max she really liked him. She might have said to herself, "Wow, what a fascinating person. I'd really like to get to know him better." Instead she said, "What a wonderful person he is. I'm in love. I really want to be involved with him. I hope he doesn't reject me." She made the mistake of confusing curiosity with caring.

These three C's are vital to a healthy relationship, and the order in which you place them is very important. If you have been accustomed to selecting your partners solely on the basis of strong sexual attraction or a strong sense of caring and commitment, you need to begin reprogramming yourself. You need to begin thinking rationally about building a relationship on the basis of who your partner really is, what you actually know about him or her, and how well he or she fits what you want in a partner. To do this, you must communicate before you care. You must care before you commit. Without honest communication, honest caring is impossible. Once you care, then you can choose how much you want to commit in a relationship, knowing that the level of commitment is commensurate with the level of caring.

When I say "commitment" in this context, I'm not talking about long-term commitment or marriage; I'm not talking about committing years of your life on the basis of the first or third or fifth date. Commitments start small: "I'll meet you for coffee after the meeting." "I'll call you next week about going to the movie." These are small commitments commensurate with a very low level of caring and based on the amount of communication two people generally exchange in the first days of a relationship. Commitments are made in increments, gradually building over time as the caring between you deepens.

From the very beginning of their acquaintance, healthy partners spend a lot of their time talking. As time goes on, they continue to communicate. They problem-solve together; they self-disclose. They let their partner know what they are thinking, what they are feeling, and what they are about in their lives. Just because you know your partner's shoe size or his or her favorite type of music, you don't stop learning about him or her. Communication is vital in every aspect of a relationship, from beginning to end.

LEVELS OF COMMUNICATION

All communication by definition is a give-and-take situation. It involves "giving"—the process of self-disclosing—and "taking"—the process of listening and responding to somebody else's self-disclosure. When I self-disclose, I go within, find out something about myself and my thoughts, feelings, and urges, and then I tell it to you. You hear what I am saying, formulate a response, and then self-disclose your response to me. I hear what you have said to me, I take it in, I respond to that, and I give you my response. We are now communicating, having a dialogue together.

This is such a basic process that it may seem strange to discuss it in such explicit terms. The fact is that many people do not truly carry out this entire process. Some people are out of touch with their feelings and thoughts. They haven't learned how to communicate them. When their communication is not tied to these inner experiences, they can't communicate honestly or accurately.

Some people have trouble listening to what the other person is saying. They are so involved with their own thoughts and feelings that they are distracted from actively hearing and responding to others.

To have a relationship that works, you need to become a good communicator. This means learning the process of give and take. It also means becoming conscious of the level at which you are self-disclosing and choosing the appropriate time to share different types of information about yourself.

There are four levels of communication: the public self, the personal self, the private self, and the intimate self. Each level has certain categories of information associated with it. You choose the level of communication according to how well you know the other person and the nature of your relationship.

The public level of self-disclosure, or what I call the public self, includes general knowledge about you and your life that you use in casual associations. If you are at a meeting of the local homeowners' association, one of your neighbors might come up to you and ask,

"Are you married?"

If so, you can say, "Yes."

"What's your husband's name?"

"Dan."

"What do you do for a living?"

"I am a computer programmer. Right now I'm working on software to help composers copyright their material electronically straight from a digital master." All of this information is part of the public self. You can then ask your neighbor, "What do you do?" and the conversation can progress from there, staying on the public-information level.

If somebody were to ask, "What's your most favorite thing sexually?" you can say, "I'm sorry. I'm not going to answer that question." Your sex life is part of your private self, not your public self. You will want to have spent a great deal of time with someone before you talk about such private topics, if at all.

Other public-self information you might share includes where you live, the kind of car you drive, where you went to school, and your favorite sports and hobbies.

The second level is the personal self. When you choose to, you can begin communicating about issues that are more personal in nature. This level includes opinions, views, beliefs, convictions. These are topics you have thought through and come to a position on but that are not necessarily anybody else's business until you choose to share them. The personal self is typically reserved for companions who are more than casual acquaintances.

After you have talked with your neighbor for a time, you might feel you know enough about him or her to ask, "What do you think about this new zoning measure we're being asked to vote on?" You are then inviting him or her to begin disclosing on the personal-self level—to share opinions and views on certain topics.

The third level involves the private self. Now safety becomes a factor, because the private self deals with sensitive issues that make you vulnerable. Private-self information includes issues that you feel unsettled about, such as family problems, deciding about a divorce, deciding on a career move, or financial problems. Private information can also include topics that evoke very strong feelings in you that an unsafe person could use to manipulate you, or something that you've done that can be used to discredit you in the view of others. The latter might include having an affair, using drugs, certain tastes in movies and magazines, and so forth.

The fourth level of communication involves the intimate self, intense personal sharing. This is immediate sharing about what I am thinking about you, how I'm feeling about you, and what I want to do with you. It is very immediate I/thou, me to you, person to person. It can be positive: "I really love, care, respect, and admire you." Or it may be negative: "I am really angry at you and embarrassed and ashamed by what you're doing and I feel humiliated by what you do to me."

In conversations, healthy people carefully select the level of their self-disclosure based on what they know about the other person. They generally reserve private-self information for close friends, family members, and romantic love relationships. They are very careful with whom they share on an intimate level.

Being aware of the levels of communication in this way serves as a system of psychological self-defense. If you have been victimized by unsafe partners in the past, you need to learn how to conduct yourself with other people while staying safe. Learning appropriate times and ways to communicate is essential.

When you self-disclose on a personal level in a normal interaction, you can expect the other person to also self-disclose on a personal level. This is a sign that you and the other person are in sync. You are responding equally. If you start disclosing on a personal level and nothing voluntarily comes back from the other person, that's a warning sign. It's a sign to stay at the personal level until you figure out what's going on. Do not go into private issues with someone who is not self-disclosing at least on a personal level. This is an important way to protect yourself.

The first time you disclose on a private-self level with somebody, start with a little issue and see if the sharing is reciprocated. If it isn't—stop, because you're making yourself unnecessarily vulnerable.

Many people have been misled in recent years by well-meaning but misguided self-help books and workshops on relationship training. There has been an overemphasis on making the self vulnerable and taking risks as a key to intimacy. Although risk taking is a key to intimacy with someone you know and trust, it may not be a good idea with a stranger. It is safer to build a relationship by self-disclosing slowly, on the basis of what you honestly know about your partner. It doesn't mean you stop taking risks, but it means you find out who is safe to take risks with and who is not.

The communication you receive from a potential partner will reveal important information about who he/she is. This includes more than just *what* he/she communicates; it also includes *how* he/she communicates: the level of disclosure, the amount and nature of what he or she has to say about himself/herself.

People from dysfunctional families frequently choose to communicate on an all-or-nothing basis. Some want to reveal as much as possible as soon as possible about themselves.

Bruce came to me and said, "I can't understand it. Women will go out with me for the first date, no problem, but they don't ever say yes the second time around. Tell me, why do you think it is?"

I said, "What do you do?"

"Well, on the first date I pick her up and we go out and we have dinner, a nice quiet restaurant all by ourselves so we can talk and get to know each other."

I said, "How does that go?"

"Well, I feel the first thing is I have to be rigorously honest. So here we are at the restaurant, we order, and I say, 'You're aware that I'm a recovering alcoholic, aren't you? Let me tell you my story.' And then I tell her my AA story. I try to be very honest, so I even tell her about how I used to beat my wife."

"What happens then?"

"So then I ask 'Okay, now you know I'm an alcoholic. Do you still want to go out with me?' She usually says, 'That's okay, I understand that. It's okay that you're an alcoholic.' So I tell her about how I was addicted to heroin and sold my body for drug money."

"What happens then?"

"Well, the conversation falls sort of flat, and I usually end up taking her home early. When I call the next time, she won't go out with me. Why is that, do you suppose?"

Bruce's style of premature self-disclosure is typical of people who crave compulsive relationships. It creates intensity, an adrenaline rush, and excitement. But premature disclosure is not really honest communication. It is often a way to set a relationship up to fail before it has a chance to get started. A healthy person takes this kind of communication as a warning signal that something is not right about this person. Even though they may like him or her in other ways, they choose to distance themselves from someone who communicates too much too fast.

Other people from dysfunctional families have apathetic styles of communication. They don't value their partner or the relationship enough to communicate. They don't offer information about themselves to their partner. Instead, they allow him/her to project what he or she wants to about them.

Healthy people communicate because they want to know who their partner is and they want their partner to know who they are. They want openness, but they are careful to choose the appropriate time to share certain types of information. They don't tell the gory details of every indiscretion or every sin they've ever committed, but they do let their partner know the essential nature of who they are and what their past experiences have been.

If I am serious about having a healthy relationship, I value communication with my partner. I want my partner to make a rational decision about being involved with me. I want my partner to have the information necessary to make a rational, nonmanipulative decision about whether to be with me or not.

ME, YOU, AND US AND THE THREE C'S

Communication, caring, and commitment constitute the essential foundation of any healthy relationship. All of them apply to each of the components in the relationship equation: *me, you,* and *us.*

As important as communication is between partners, communication starts with *me.* In order to communicate to others, I have to know within myself what I am thinking and feeling.

Once I know what's going on with me, I have to put that into words and tell my partner about it. As I communicate to my partner, I need to have a deep interest in finding out who my partner is and what my partner is thinking, feeling, and doing in his/her life.

Once I know what I'm about and I've listened to and learned what my partner is about, we can communicate about the relationship, about *us,* who are we as a couple and the kind of relationship we are creating together.

Caring also begins with *me.* First of all I have to care about myself before I'm going to be able to care about anyone else. I have to refuse to put myself into abusive, destructive relationships. Nobody can get me out of a destructive relationship but me, and I have to care about myself strongly enough to get out. I have to make a commitment not to sell my soul in the name of a relationship. I've got to care about me and have a healthy sense of self-love before I can care about anybody else.

Once I care about *me* in a healthy way, next I care about *you,* my partner. I'm genuinely concerned about my partner's well-being and want him or her to grow and prosper and be the best person he or she can. I'm not interested in controlling the relationship. I want for my partner the best of what my partner wants for himself/herself.

When I care about myself as a person and when I care about my partner as a person, I can begin to care about *us.* I can care about the special entity that is being created as a result of our interactions. Caring comes after communication. Without it, you can make the mistake of caring about a relationship that doesn't really exist.

Alicia was sober about three months. She was told by her AA sponsor to abstain from sexual involvement for a year, and Alicia agreed.

Then Alicia saw *him,* Mr. Right, at her regular AA meeting. She was so excited she couldn't even speak to him because she was afraid she'd lose control. For nine months, she never talked to him, but she thought about him constantly and listened to his comments at meetings. She knew she was in love with him. She wouldn't go out or date or get involved with anyone else because she was saving herself for *him.*

Finally, Alicia received her one-year anniversary cake at a big AA gathering at the Alano club. After getting her cake Alicia walked up to the coffee pot and stuck her cup under the spigot just as he stuck his cup under the spigot. Their fingers met. A bolt of electricity jumped through them. He looked her in the eye. She looked him in the eye and said, "Let's go out and get coffee."

They went to his car. She asked, "Can I give you a hug?"

He said, "Certainly."

They hugged each other. They kissed. They took off their clothes. They jumped in the back seat and they made love. Alicia didn't view this as promiscuous. As far as she was concerned she'd been in a relationship with this man for nine months.

Afterward, she said, "When am I going to see you next?"

He looked at her and said, "I don't think it would be a good idea if we ever do this again."

"Why not?"

"Because my wife wouldn't understand."

Alicia was enraged. She jumped out of the car, slammed the door, went to a bar, and blew away her sobriety.

Alicia made the mistake of caring about a relationship that didn't really exist. She thought she truly cared about this man, but in reality, she knew nothing about him and he knew nothing about her. There was no *us* between them.

The ultimate expression of caring is the movement into commitment, and commitment, too, is a three-legged stool. First I need to be committed to myself. No matter what happens in the relationship I'm committed to keep myself well and healthy. If I'm chemically dependent I need to stay sober and work on a recovery program. Any relationship that puts itself between me and my recovery has got to go. In twelve-step language this is a "selfish program." I have to care about myself first. If I lose myself in the process I can't love anybody.

If you are traveling by plane with a young child and there is an emergency requiring the use of oxygen masks, you are instructed to put your own mask on first and then the child's. If you try to put on the child's mask and you pass out you're no good to anybody. You put on your own mask first. That's rational selfishness. If you lose yourself, you can't help anybody.

The second commitment has to be to my partner as a person. I'm going to do whatever I can to support my partner as long as I don't lose myself in the process. If I love my partner I'm not going to enable his/her pathological, self-destructive behaviors. I'm invested in my partner's growth, not in my partner's pathology. I want my partner to be the best he or she can possibly be, but not at the expense of who I am. People who love their partners don't stay married to chronic drinking alcoholics for the rest of their lives. They don't stay in relationships with physically and emotionally abusive people, especially if there are children involved who are being hurt and crippled physically and emotionally because of that.

If you care enough about your partner, you don't tolerate unacceptable behavior from him or her. You draw the line and you self-protect. That's rational caring about your partner.

Finally there's the commitment to us together. The commitment to learning together and growing together. But remember, the commitment to *me* has to come first and the commitment to *you* has to come second. Then comes the commitment to *us*. If I really love you, I have to be willing to give up the relationship if it's in your best interest. If I really love me, I have to be willing to give up the relationship if it's in my best interest.

Graham loved Gladys. They had many things in common, except for one—their fundamental life-styles. Graham was work oriented, loved living in the city, and wanted to advance his career. He needed a partner who wanted a compatible life-style. Gladys was from the Southwest. Her goal was to move back to Arizona, live in a log cabin, and work a twenty- to thirty-hour week to earn enough money to pay the rent. She wanted nothing more than to listen to John Denver music and sit on the front porch reading books or go hiking in the woods. That was Gladys's fundamental nature. A career in the city was Graham's. They both realized that as much as they wanted the relationship to work, it couldn't. It wasn't because they didn't love and care about each other. It was because one of them would have had to compromise too much. The *me* and the *you* came before the *us*.

No relationship is healthy unless all three components are healthy. This is a new concept for many people because this isn't always what we were taught to believe. The Catholic marriage ritual is a perfect example.

The wedding couple walks up to the shrine of the Virgin. There are two lit candles placed before a third candle set on a higher level. The bride takes her candle and the groom takes his candle, and they merge the flames together and light the higher candle. There is *me* and there is *you* and together we can become more than either of us is alone. There is *us*. That's beautiful. But then what does the wedding couple do? *They blow out their own candles.* "And the two shall become one." That's a myth. That is not how it really works. Two never become one. What's more, that is not healthy. As soon as I believe that I can lose myself in you or you need to lose yourself in me, we've got a dysfunctional relationship.

Only by honoring our commitments to *me, you,* and *us* can we lay down a sound foundation for a healthy relationship. Once we have accomplished that, we can begin to build that relationship, level by level.

Self-assessment: Your Partner Profile

I. A Profile of Yourself and Your Past Partners
This assessment will help you to identify the ways in which your unconscious programming has led you to find partners that are (1) similar to you; (2) different from you in complementary ways; and (3) able to bring up unresolved issues from your past.

Go back to your Relationship History and answer the following questions for each partner, beginning with your first relationship.

1. In what ways were this partner and I similar?

2. In what ways were this partner and I different?

3. How did these differences complement my limitations and help me to grow?

4. How did these differences complement my partner's limitations and help him/her to grow?

5. What primary or recurring issues did my partner and I confront in the relationship?

II. Your Ideal Partner Profile

This assessment will help you construct a description of your ideal partner.

Starting with your first partner, answer the following questions about each one, up to your present partner.

1. What did your partner look like? Describe your partner's physical height, general weight and build, hair color, eye color, and other physical traits.

2. What did you look like when you were involved with your partner?

3. What was your partner like as a person? Describe your partner's general personality, mood, temperament, view of life, and the way he or she dealt with other people.

4. What were you like, as a person, when you were involved with this partner?

5. How did your partner treat other people and build relationships?

6. How did you treat other people and build relationships when you were involved with this partner?

7. What did you expect from your partner?

8. What do you think your partner expected from you?

9. What did you believe your partner could do for you that you could not do for yourself?

Take a separate sheet of paper and write "Partner Similarities" at the top of the page. List all of the traits and characteristics your past partners shared with one another.

You will probably begin to see recurrent themes or traits in each of your partners. The result, when you finish this exercise, will be your current ideal partner profile.

III. Your Parental Description

Go back to the questions in the Ideal Partner Profile section and answer each one, substituting your mother and father for your partner. When you complete this exercise, you may be amazed by how many ways your previous partners resemble your parents.

IV. Analyzing Your Relationship Patterns

Some people get involved in the same relationship over and over again, only with different people. They also seem to confront the same issues. They are stuck in a zero growth pattern.

Other people are in a positive growth relationship pattern. Their relationships represent a continuum of ongoing growth: they get involved in a relationship and experience problems but manage to grow as a result of solving them.

It is important to recognize whether you are in a zero growth pattern or a positive growth pattern.

Take another piece of paper and write at the top "Lessons Learned/Issues Resolved" on one side and "Unresolved Issues" on the other side. Then, going back to your relationships, try to determine whether the key issues and problems confronting you in each relationship carried over into the next or seemed to be resolved. When you have finished, notice which column has more entries: the "Lessons Learned" or "Unresolved Issues."

CHANGING YOUR PARTNER PROFILE

Once you have completed your Ideal Partner Profile, you can decide if you want to continue to follow these relationship patterns or if you want to change them. Is the person in your Ideal Partner Profile the type of person you can have a healthy, meaningful relationship with? If the answer is no, the first step is to abstain from getting involved with this type of partner. You will need to make up your mind to experiment with dating and become involved with people who have the potential for a healthy relationship.

As you grow and develop, your Ideal Partner Profile will gradually shift. Being aware of what your high-risk partner profile is can help you avoid destructive relationships that can slow your growth.

Chapter 7

BUILDING THE RELATIONSHIP: *US*

PRINCIPAL CHOICES
- The type of relationship you want to establish.
- The level of commitment you want to make to your partner.
- How deeply you want to bond with your partner.

When Jamey and Wendy met they each thought they had found the perfect mate. They shared an interest in political activism and were sexually compatible. They began to spend a great deal of time together. Two months later, they took a ten-day vacation to Spain. It turned out terribly for both of them. Away from their common interest, they found they had little to talk about. They wanted to do different things, and each was constantly frustrated trying to accommodate the other. They couldn't agree on how their money should be spent. In the end, they realized how little they knew about each other and how little they had in common. When Jamey and Wendy returned home, they ended the relationship.

Jamey and Wendy didn't realize that creating a healthy relationship—creating the *us* from the *me* and the *you*—is a process that evolves over time and incorporates many different aspects of our lives. Jamey and Wendy's brief acquaintance, while intense, had not allowed them to share the variety of experiences or to develop the trust necessary for the level of intimacy they expected of their relationship.

People from functional families who experienced healthy intimacy as children honor this relationship-building process and follow it naturally, even unconsciously. These individuals tend to have large social networks that include acquaintances, companions, friends, and intimate friends as well as their partner. They find it relatively easy to initiate, deepen, and maintain or terminate relationships. They know that intimate relationships build slowly, stage by stage, as the partners learn more about each other and emotionally bond together.

To those who had little or no experience with healthy intimacy as children in their family of origin building a healthy relationship may seem a mysterious, frightening, or even impossible task. Their lack of knowledge may lead to one of two problems in their relationships. The first problem occurs when one or both partners demand rapid, high-intensity intimacy that the relationship is unable to support. Jamey and Wendy were expecting levels of friendship and companionship that they had not established. The second problem arises when one or both partners expect the relationship to progress so slowly and cautiously that the relationship cannot develop sufficiently to meet their own or their partner's needs.

When Jane and Walt began dating, Jane explained that she wanted the relationship to develop slowly. For the first few dates, she insisted that they go with friends and she refused to see Walt alone. Walt was sympathetic to her desire to allow the relationship to develop at a moderate pace. They spent a lot of time talking and getting to know one another. Walt expressed his attraction to Jane and his desire to become more sensually involved. Jane refused, saying she needed more time to get to know him.

Finally after nine dates, Walt called Jane and said that he was sorry but he felt he needed to end the relationship. Jane was dismayed. He said, "I don't think you really like me very much at all. Every time I try to do more than give you a brief kiss, you turn away and say 'not yet.' I don't understand that. I guess we want different things."

Jane thought to herself, "Well, that's men. They always push too fast and too far for what they want."

In reality, Walt simply had reasonable expectations of how quickly a relationship should progress. He respected Jane's desire to allow the relationship to build slowly and enjoyed getting to know her before he acted on his sexual attraction to her, but she was overly cautious. He was right to recognize that they had different expectations.

To avoid these problems it is important to know how healthy relationships develop, the stages through which they progress, and the skills couples can use to enhance their relationship at each stage. Many people have trouble developing healthy relationships because they have not learned that relationships exist on a continuum, with a series of predictable stages. These stages create a sequence so that one builds on the other, incorporating prior elements, expanding on them and developing new ones.

BLUEPRINTS FOR A RELATIONSHIP

For this reason, it is useful to think of building relationships in terms of building a house. The two processes are similar in several important ways. For example, the first step in deciding to build a house is to decide what kind of a house you want to build, based on your needs, wants, and resources. You make a similar decision when you determine the type of relationship you want at this time in your life: short term or long term, experimental, transitional, or an intimate encounter.

Next, you need somewhere to build the house, a space large enough to accommodate the type of structure you want. In relationship building, this means preparing a space in your life large enough to accommodate the type of relationship you want. You clear the land. When you undertake a program of personal growth and development, you are making such a place. Abstaining from dead-end relationships and dysfunctional behaviors leaves room in your life for healthy relationships.

After you have cleared the land, you need to invest in the materials. If you want a quality house, you invest in quality materials. For a quality relationship, you invest the time and effort necessary to find a potential partner you believe is capable of contributing to the type of quality relationship you are trying to build.

At this point, you have done what you can to prepare the *me* and the *you* components of the relationship equation. As we saw in the last chapter, you then need to lay the foundation for the relationship through communication, caring, and commitment. Then you can begin building on a sturdy foundation of increasing knowledge and trust in your partner that will support the relationship.

At each stage in the building process, you continue to communicate and care enough about your partner to honor your commitments, which are commensurate with the particular level of relationship at which you currently find yourself. You don't commit all at once, but gradually, step by step.

Relationship Levels
1. Acquaintanceship
2. Companionship
3. Friendship
4. Romantic Love
5. Committed Love

Then, you are ready to put in the time and effort to build the type of relationship you want. Healthy relationships unfold on five levels. The first level is *acquaintanceship,* casual communication, where you communicate on a public-self level. This level of relating involves the social courtesy we need to extend to each other so that we can coexist in a crowded world; all relationships, no matter how intimate, need casual communication. The second level is *companionship,* in which we share mutually enjoyable activities with our partner. The third level is *friendship,* in which we share our experiences, values, feelings, and thoughts with one another in a unique way, valuing our partner as a person different from other people. The next level is *romantic love,* in which we enhance our friendship through sensuality, sexuality, and passion. Finally there is *committed love,* in which we make a decision that the relationship we have is so valuable we want to make our partner an integral part of our day-to-day life, accepting the responsibility for our relationship in its social, legal, and personal dimensions.

Each of these five levels is important and each has its unique place in your life. When you master one level in a relationship you retain the skills you learned in that level and keep using them, even as you are gaining new skills in the next level. You keep building level by level, just as the second story of a house is built on the first, the third on the second, and so forth. Without a solid first story, the other stories cannot stand.

If you're starting a new relationship, these levels can guide you in building healthy intimacy by showing you how to establish and structure the relationship. If you're already in a relationship, these levels can help you assess your strengths and weaknesses as a couple, and help you find areas that you can work on to improve your intimacy with your partner.

Level 1: Acquaintanceship/Casual Contact

Acquaintanceship, or casual contact occurs when people interact in a superficial but courteous manner with little or no commitment to one another. If you work in a large office building or for a large company, you have casual contact every day with people you know virtually nothing about: they may be secretaries, mail-room workers, or people in another department. If you attend conferences or workshops, you meet many people with whom you carry on polite, easy chitchat. These are comfortable, superficial interactions. They are appropriate to the situation and make it a positive, friendly experience. There is no expectation that the relationship is more than that. We are not obligated to take care of these people or to be their friend. They are not obligated to be ours. Most casual contacts never develop beyond this superficial stage. You might go to the same dentist for twenty-five years and never talk about anything more personal than sports and the benefits of dental hygiene.

If you are interested in building a relationship, you will want to establish a whole range of casual contacts within your social network so that you meet a variety of people, some of whom may turn out to be potential partners. You communicate with acquaintances first on a public-self level and then, if you feel good about it, on a personal-self level. On the basis of what you learn about this person, you may become curious to know more. You use your thoughts and feelings to decide if you like him or her well enough to want to know him or her better.

If you are already in a relationship, you need to know how to establish and maintain effective casual contact with your partner.

Casual contact skills are very important. Many relationships get into trouble not because of big glaring differences between partners but because they don't know how to share a bathroom together. They don't know how to handle household chores. Much of life is superficial and routine. If we want to share our life with another person, we must learn how to share the superficial routines as well as the intense and glorious moments.

If you want to rebuild a troubled relationship, you can start out by attending to casual, productive communication with your partner. Don't begin with the big issues. Build some comfortable time together that can act as a foundation for trust and caring. Learn how to communicate with each other with dignity and respect in the little moments of life.

Jimmy and Natalie had been married for three years. In many respects, they had a good marriage. They communicated well about the important issues but day-to-day issues kept them in constant conflict. In therapy we talked about the importance of basic courtesy because each partner felt that the other was often discourteous and rude. Together we established rules for courtesy, such as saying "thank you" when the other had done something nice. Then I asked them to think through their daily routine together and pinpoint the trouble spots. The first problem they mentioned involved the routine household chores, particularly the grocery shopping and kitchen clean-up. I helped them to make up a schedule in which they would do these activities together. Their second problem was a sense of isolation from one another. We set up another daily ritual in which Jimmy and Natalie would sit together for fifteen minutes every evening and review the sequence of the day, just talking about what happened and how they felt about it.

Initially, these changes were difficult, because these were new routines, but as they practiced them, their life became easier. These simple changes effectively ended the petty conflicts that had seriously compromised their ability to live together. Jimmy and Natalie began feeling much better about each other and themselves. They felt more appreciated, more comfortable, and discovered they could get along on a daily basis without feeling oppressed.

People who crave love and attention don't feel comfortable with casual contact. They experience love either as intense and all-consuming or as abandonment. They do not like superficial relationships with casual people in their life. They feel upset when their intimate relationship ebbs into a period of casual contact. Their emotional hunger makes them want to drive each moment for intense interaction. At best, they call these casual moments boring. At worst, they find them terrifying.

This nonstop drive for intensity does not allow the normal cycle of contentment and comfort to exist in a relationship. Without superficial contact, a relationship will not be able to flow through the quiet, gentle moments that constitute the foundation of long-term love. Like Jimmy and Natalie, we begin to feel out of touch with our partner, unappreciated and unacknowledged. If you are used to all-or-nothing intensity in your relationships, the concepts of comfort, security, casualness, and feeling good while feeling safe are foreign to you. You may not even believe these feelings can possibly convey intimate, romantic love.

Eileen and Richard spent their weekends together, usually at Richard's house. When Richard's friends called, he talked with them for a while. Eileen was furious. "You don't care about me!" she accused him one day. "I just sit here while you talk to your friends on the phone. You're abandoning me!" Eileen couldn't see that Richard's affection didn't change just because he was talking on the telephone with a friend.

In working to overcome these feelings of abandonment, Eileen learned to understand that she was still loved even when their relationship was not intense, or when Richard's full attention was not focused on her. She saw that when Richard went out with his friends for the evening, he wasn't abandoning her but meeting his own needs for time with his friends. She began to use her time away from Richard to meet her own needs for time with her friends and family.

Casual contact with your partner or close friends is not abandonment. Simply because your partner wants to turn down the intensity for a period of time doesn't mean that he or she is abandoning you. Healthy relationships don't require intense involvement all the time. Healthy partners know they are still loved even when they are casually communicating, doing something else, or temporarily separated or detached from their partner.

Level 2: Companionship

Companions do things together. They share interests and activities. At the companionship level *what* you do takes precedence over *whom* you do it with. Perhaps you have tickets for a play or a baseball game; you think about asking someone to go with you, and that someone might be any one of a number of different people.

Most people have several friends with whom they interact on a regular basis at the companionship level. Coworkers are often companions. If you want to go out to lunch at work and one coworker can't make it, you might keep asking until you find someone who can. Healthy people have many relationships that stay at the companionship stage and never develop into deeper or more intense relationships. These relationships bring interest and variety into our lives without our needing them to be more.

When I want to see a movie, I have several people I know I can call. First I call the person I'd most like to see the movie with. I know my friend Alan enjoys action movies, so I call and say, "Alan, I want to see this new Charles Bronson movie that's been so highly reviewed. Would you like to go with me?"

Alan might say, "Gee, I've already seen the movie. Why don't you come over to my place and we'll spend the evening watching television?"

If I have my heart set on seeing the movie, I tell him, "Thank you, Alan, but I want to see the movie. We'll get together another time."

Then I call the next person on my list. "Do you want to go see a movie with me?" and so on down the list.

People from dysfunctional families frequently have trouble with the concept of choosing an activity over a person. They feel they need to be intensely focused on the person. In response to Alan's invitation to watch television, they might be tempted to say, "Okay, Alan. I guess I can see the movie another time. I'll be over at seven." As they learn to practice healthy intimacy, however, they will learn that even the most compatible couples will put an activity before their partner from time to time.

If you are developing a new relationship, your casual communication with a potential partner will probably have uncovered certain areas of interest you have in common. You might find you both like hiking, listening to music, or that you have mutual friends. You can now choose to invite this potential partner to join you in these activities or to go out to dinner with your mutual friends.

There is limited commitment or involvement at the companionship stage. If you have had trouble with compulsive or painful relationships in the past, the companionship level is especially important in the building of a safe and healthy relationship. It allows you to spend time getting to know your partner in a safe way, because you are not yet sexually involved or intensely sharing.

The safest first date is a movie or a dinner party, both of which are structured situations with other people where there is limited opportunity for intense time alone. In this setting, you can safely observe the other person, see how he or she interacts with others. Does he or she act appropriately? Ask yourself how you feel about this person. If you don't feel good about him or her, you can end the relationship at this stage, without becoming involved or hurt by it. Or you can decide to keep the relationship on the companionship level without expecting it to be more.

Once you invite your partner to share an activity in your world, he or she will reciprocate and invite you into his or hers. Ted invited Mary on their first date to attend a symphony concert. A week later, Mary called to invite Ted to a friend's party. Each of them communicated to the other that they were interested in doing things together. There is an unspoken understanding that your invitation will be followed by your partner's. If you don't get a reciprocal invitation right away, it may be that the person is shy or unsure about asking you. If you believe this might be the case, invite him or her to share another activity. If, however, you still do not receive a reciprocal invitation, that's a warning sign. If your partner doesn't invite you into his or her world, it may be that he or she doesn't have a world to invite you into because he or she has few, if any, interests and doesn't have a social network. If so, he or she probably also lacks important social skills. A second reason might be that he or she is hiding something from you, perhaps even a wife or a husband.

A third possibility exists. If your partner doesn't invite you into his/her world, it may be that he or she simply does not like you well enough, for whatever reason, to invite you there. It is an unpleasant fact that when you begin dating and building relationships, you are going to get rejected by some people. The whole process of dating involves meeting new people, getting to know them, and finding out if you like them enough to invite them into your life, and if they like you well enough to do the same. Simply because somebody wants to be involved with you doesn't mean you want to be involved with him or her. And just because you want somebody to be involved with you doesn't mean he or she has to want to be involved with you. All we can do is invite, and sometimes the other person will say no, thank you. When that happens, deal with the rejection without anger and without blame by simply understanding that you are two different people.

If you are from a dysfunctional family, you may have to curb your tendency to overcommit in relationships. Don't rush the relationship. Even if you like a person, you can stay at the companionship level, where there is minimal commitment, until you are ready for the next level, friendship.

If you are already in a relationship and you want to improve it, you can pretend you're starting all over again with your partner at the companionship level. Begin planning mutually enjoyable activities together so you can reopen the communication process. Many people in long-term relationships fail to communicate often or deeply enough to let their partner know who they are or the changes they are experiencing. This is how couples grow apart. It doesn't matter how much you loved each other six years ago but how you feel here and now. You need to spend time getting reacquainted with who you are today, so that caring can emerge in the new context of who you are at this stage of your life. This means that people in long-term relationships have to start dating again. "Let's do something special this Saturday night." By doing things together that both you and your partner can enjoy, you can rebuild a foundation of trust and sharing good experiences together.

Level 3: Friendship

In a friendship, you spend time together with an individual sharing and enjoying his or her company. The *person* becomes more important than the *activity*. In this way friendships are the reverse of companionships.

If Paula hasn't seen her friend Diane for a few weeks, she makes a point of calling her to arrange to spend time together.

"What about getting together Saturday afternoon?"

"Sure, what did you have in mind?"

"Well, I'm open for suggestions. What about lunch?"

"Actually, I think I'd like to take advantage of the good weather. What about a bike ride?"

"Sounds good. Afterward we can pick up a pizza and have dinner at my place. Okay?"

Paula doesn't really care what she and Diane do. She knows they share a lot of the same interests and they almost always have a good time together. They've known each other for a long time and feel comfortable together.

When you turn someone into a friend it doesn't mean you stop being companions or interacting casually. Instead, you've now got three modes of operation. You can shift back and forth.

"Hello, how are you? What about this weather?" (casual contact).

"I want to go to a movie. Will you go with me?" (companionship).

"I want to spend time with you. I'm interested in how you're feeling and what's going on in your life. Would you be my friend this afternoon?"

In a friendship we share who we are, what we're thinking, what we're feeling. We communicate our opinions and may share some private information about conflicts we feel or decisions we need to make. We value friends for the people they are, the unique combination of qualities and strengths they have. When we find a partner with whom we enjoy doing a variety of activities and sharing our thoughts and feelings, it is a good sign that we are compatible.

In a new relationship, as you and your partner spend more time together as companions learning more about each other, you naturally begin to care more about each other. When you choose to, you can invite your partner to become your friend. At this point, you begin spending more unstructured time together, time just to talk and be with one another, going out to dinner, or spending an evening watching television. As you get to know this person better and you continue to feel good being with him or her, you can feel increasingly safe, and gradually take more and more risks in sharing who you are. How does he or she respond to your disclosures? Does he or she validate and affirm your feelings? Again, watch to see if your partner reciprocates with similar information.

In rebuilding a troubled relationship, affirmation and validation are very important. Often both people feel their partner doesn't hear them or take them seriously. To reestablish a relationship at the friendship level, I suggest that partners forget everything they know about their partner and pretend they are meeting one another for the first time. They begin asking their partner basic things about themselves that they may in fact already know: "Who are you?" "What are you interested in?" "What do you feel about so and so issues," "What do you like and dislike?" This gives you a chance to share information, open up, and talk about these subjects. This enables you to invite your partner to share aspects of himself/herself that he or she would want a friend to know.

This exercise encourages couples to talk about value issues. They begin sharing their personal self with their partner and asking him or her questions about his or her personal self. Then, when they listen to their partner's response, they make sure to affirm it, value it, and appreciate it, using basic communication skills.

Level 4: Romantic Love

In a healthy relationship, romantic love is a natural progression from companionship and friendship. After a couple has spent time together building trust, mutual respect, and enjoyment of one another, they then deepen their relationship through intense sensual and sexual experiences. It is important to remember that romantic love is far more than a feeling of passion. It's possible to experience passion and sexuality in the context of a superficial relationship, as in the case of one-night stands.

You can only have romantic love with a friend. You can only have a friend who is at times a companion. And you can only have a successful companionship if it's based on the ability to interact casually with each other effectively. Romantic lovers are sexy friends, but the friendship comes first.

Unfortunately, this is not how most people go about relationship building. Many people confuse infatuation with romantic love when, in fact, there is no correlation. They have sexual encounters with people they don't know well, perhaps don't even know at all. Having casual sex does not mean you have a love relationship. You're having sex with a stranger. It can be exciting, but it can also be very dangerous.

If you have had a history of dysfunctional relationships and have built past relationships primarily on sexuality, my advice is to go slowly and wait to have sex with your partner until you have shared a variety of experiences and developed a companionship and a friendship. Wait to disclose on the private or intimate levels. Spending time in a nonintense way with your partner is the only way to know if your partner is safe, either physically or psychologically.

If you come from a functional family or have progressed in your relationship skills to the point that you have developed the ability to determine who is trustworthy and who isn't, you can move into higher levels of sexuality and intimacy more rapidly. As you practice relationship skills and learn about healthy intimacy, your judgment about people and your ability to set boundaries will increase dramatically. People who have these capacities are able to communicate and get down to intimate issues very quickly, but these are skills most people need to acquire consciously.

Relationships built primarily on sexuality frequently don't last and often will lead you into a dysfunctional relationship—that is, a compulsive relationship that has intense passion and sexuality with no basis of shared values or substantial experiences.

Romantic love is based on a clear, conscious knowledge of your partner. There are powerful sexual feelings, but these occur within the context of a solid and trustworthy friendship. You know your feelings and thoughts about your partner and you have made a decision to act on them.

In a new relationship, when you reach the level of romantic love, you need to be honest with your partner and share your feelings about sexuality and sensuality with him or her. You need to communicate and ask questions so that you know what sex means to your partner. Some people engage in sexuality with relatively little feeling of commitment; for others, becoming sexually involved carries with it a great deal of commitment.

Some people feel that committed love should come before sexual involvement. If that's your sense of morality, be sure to communicate it to your partner.

In rebuilding a troubled relationship, couples need to practice what Harville Hendrix refers to as "reromanticizing the relationship." You consciously think back to the activities you used to enjoy together that created romantic and passionate feelings during courtship. You invite your partner to engage in those activities with you all over again in a new setting. Then you also begin thinking about what kind of activities could create the same mood or ambience.

Another technique is to have the couple engage in active fantasy together. "What would you consider an extremely romantic, sexy date? What could we do to create that together?" Some people have a dress-up night out. I've known couples who take separate cars to the same nightclub. The woman arrives first, and the man goes in and picks her up. The important point is to have fun and enjoy one another. In the midst of day-to-day living, do what you need to keep the spark and preserve the romance.

Level 5: Committed Love

As romantic love develops, it leads naturally into committed love, which for many people means marriage. In committed love, we say that we value the relationship so much that we want to become a permanent part of each other's life and build a substantial reality based on the *us* of our relationship. We make commitments in the real world to meet each other's physical, emotional, and social needs. Our commitment means that when things get tough, we don't walk out. We stay and work them through. We live together, share expenses, combine our resources, perhaps marry and have a family together.

Commitments on this level are reserved for long-term relationships. In short-term relationships, our commitment is less. If we choose to have an intimate encounter, it may involve virtually no commitment; we are together with a partner for a short time for the purpose of having an intense relationship outside the normal context of our lives. That's it. We may not choose to develop it into anything more. In experimental and transitional relationships, some couples never get beyond the companionship stage; others build level by level up to romantic love. Then, for one reason or another, the relationship ends. We do not want or expect these short-term relationships to go any further. We are not obligated to go to the next stage of commitment. A long-term relationship is different.

The horrible truth is that committed romantic love relationships either grow or die. In long-term relationships, once you and your partner are involved at the romantic love level, sooner or later you need to make a decision about whether you are going to end the relationship or go further to create a working partnership, with all of the obligations and responsibilities that entails.

Certain things cannot happen in an intimate relationship without a commitment. There are certain levels of trust that are impossible, certain levels of intimate sharing and life planning that cannot occur. Can you responsibly agree to have a child if you're not committed to another person for the duration of the parenting process? Without a commitment from your partner, it is foolish to invest a major portion of your life, your energy, or your resources. You need to realize that if you want certain experiences, you must commit to a long-term relationship.

Many people spend their entire lives at lower levels of relationship. They communicate, they care, and make short-term commitments. They move through casual contact, companionship, friendship, dabble with romantic love, and then, as soon as the word "commitment" comes up, they run. They go back and start all over again with somebody else, moving the relationship through the same levels and then they balk again. Every time they get to a difficult part in their relationship, they run.

At some point they may begin to recognize that they are never going to grow beyond this unless they choose to make the commitment even though they are scared.

Rob had dated Marcie for a year and a half when Marcie began asking Rob to make a commitment. Either they were going to move in together and live together or the relationship was going to end. "It was a cold winter day in Milwaukee," Rob told me. "I remember walking the streets and realizing that at that moment the relationship was either going to grow or die. I was absolutely terrified of making the commitment, but I didn't want the relationship to die. So I decided to do it anyway. I realized that if I wanted to experience love, I would have to act in spite of the fear."

There is nothing wrong with being afraid of commitment: a commitment is a terrifying responsibility. Everybody has that moment of fear. Whenever you make the commitment to anything—to buy a new house, change your job—no matter how good, you realize that by making this commitment you are giving up other options. If you come from a dysfunctional family, the fear is going to be worse, and it becomes harder to make the choice to love, to make the choice to commit.

It is hard to accept that there is nothing you can do to force your partner to make a commitment. All you can do is extend the invitation. Marcie asked Rob for a commitment, but only he could make the decision to commit. If your partner cannot make a commitment, there is nothing you can do to change that. You can only be responsible for your own choices. You need to ask yourself, "Do I want to continue to commit to someone who won't commit to me?"

When you build a relationship level by level, you are prepared to make a sound and healthy commitment. You don't have to guess about your partner, because you know him or her intimately. You know how you feel and think about him/her, and how he/she feels and thinks about you. You know how you act around one another. You can make a decision based on this in-depth knowledge of this person in a variety of situations.

You may still be scared of the commitment, but when you examine your choices, you will be able to say, "We really do have a good positive relationship, good sex, and passion. We can be together intimately and it feels good. This person is my friend. Even if we never had sex again, we are still friends. We enjoy doing things together. We can structure time together. We live together on a day-to-day basis and comfortably coexist. I am committed to this person already in a variety of little ways because I care about him/her and we communicate effectively. We don't engage in dysfunctional behavior with each other. So even if I'm afraid, I know it is a good choice."

Remember that commitment is not all or nothing. We make little commitments all the time. In a relationship, initially we make small commitments to each other that then grow in a gradual and healthy way. We begin by saying to each other, "Yes, I'll spend Friday evening with you." "Yes, I'll share recreational activities with you." "Yes, I'll listen to your personal problems and share my feelings with you." "Yes, I'll make love with you." "Yes, I'll stay and talk it out if we have a fight." "Yes, I'll have a monogamous relationship with you." "Yes, I'll put up with your bad habits." "Yes, I'll live with you." "Yes, I'll invest money with you." "Yes, I'll marry you." "Yes, we'll have children together and make a commitment to raise them together." When you build a relationship safely and slowly, one commitment grows upon the other as the relationship grows. Just because you make a commitment at one level you are not obligated to move to the next.

There are, of course, no guarantees and no absolute standards of right and wrong, compatibility, or intimacy. You need to make your commitment to your partner based on your own judgment of the strengths and weaknesses of the relationship. All relationships involve risk, but healthy partners prefer to take risks in which the odds are in their favor.

FLEXIBILITY

Healthy relationships operate on a continuum of levels. This flexibility allows you to have your needs met and to meet your partner's needs in the context of the relationship. It allows you to handle the concrete details of daily life—such as holding down a job and maintaining the household—and at other times to be intense and intimate with your partner.

To achieve this flexibility, however, you must communicate your needs to your partner. Without this communication, misunderstandings may occur.

Cindy was feeling lonely and wanted to spend some high-quality time with her husband, Mark. When he called her from work and asked if she would like to see a movie that night, she was pleased that Mark wanted to spend time with her.

She said, "I'd love to spend the evening with you, but I really don't want to go to a movie. Let's do something else together."

Mark said, "Oh, gee, I really wanted to see that movie. I've been waiting for it to come out for months. I know my friend Dick wants to see it. You're welcome to come along with us, but I can understand your not wanting to see it. I'll be home about eleven."

Cindy was devastated, outraged. She felt dumped. She couldn't tell Mark what she was feeling because initially she wasn't aware of it herself. When Mark got home, her anger had escalated to rage and they had a violent argument. What happened?

Mark was inviting Cindy as a companion to see a movie he had been waiting for months to see, and Cindy was inviting Mark to spend time together, sharing their feelings and communicating on a friendship basis. Mark did not understand Cindy's invitation and Cindy did not understand Mark's invitation.

If Mark and Cindy had been aware of the dynamics of the various relationship levels, their conversation might have had a different outcome.

Cindy might have responded to Mark's invitation by saying, "Mark, I'm having a rough day and I really need to be with you as a friend tonight. Will you stay home with me and talk? Then we can go to see the movie tomorrow night."

Mark then would have had the option to agree to Cindy's suggestion or to decline. If he felt strongly that he needed the night out, he might have explained his feelings, as Cindy did, and tried to find a solution that would meet both needs. He might have said, "Cindy, I'm sorry you're having a rough day. But I am tired, too, and I need to unwind. I know I won't be able to be a good listener for you tonight. I really want to see that movie. Tell you what— why don't I go to the early show, and that way I'll get home around nine-thirty and we can talk for a while before we go to bed?"

Although Cindy probably would still be disappointed, she wouldn't be as angry because she would realize from Mark's response that he really did care about her feelings. She would also understand that although Mark's needs, at that moment, were in conflict with her own, he still loved and cared about her. If she agreed to his alternate suggestion, she might say, "All right. I'm still disappointed, but I can wait to see you. In the meantime, maybe I'll call one of my girlfriends and talk with her for a while. Maybe that will help me unwind a bit and we can just relax when you get home."

Our wants and needs within a relationship change hour by hour, and it is important to communicate these changes clearly to our partner. We need to express our need for closeness as well as our need for time alone, and to remain open to his or her needs. Healthy relationships allow us the flexibility to do this. In a healthy love relationship there is a constant flow or shifting from one level to the next, as we go about the business of our daily lives. We do not need to be intensely involved all the time, only when we want to be.

ENHANCING THE RELATIONSHIP

Emotional bonding is a term used to describe the strong feelings of union that occur between two people. In the friendship, romantic love, and committed love relationships, we are building these feelings and strengthening this bond.

According to the *McGill Report on Male Intimacy,* five primary elements determine how well two people will emotionally bond: time together, shared experiences, depth of interpersonal exchange, exclusivity, and collective concern. As you build your relationship, you may want to explore ways to deepen the quality of the bond between you and your partner. You can do so by examining these areas in your present relationship.

Primary Elements of Emotional Bonding
1. Time together
2. Shared experiences
3. Depth of interpersonal exchange
4. Exclusivity
5. Collective concern

Time together. Intimacy grows over time as a couple builds a history together. This time can be measured in three ways: the length of the relationship and the frequency and duration of each contact.

The primary formula in evaluating the effect of time together upon intimacy is summed up in the equation Proximity + Time = Intimacy.

Shared experiences. To be intimate, we must be willing to share our thoughts, feelings, and experiences honestly with our partner. Develop the habit of relating information about a broad variety of your experiences with your partner. It is important to share real-life experiences, too; and the more meaningful these experiences are to us, the more conducive they are to intimacy.

Depth of interpersonal communication. We share our personal and private self with close friends and intimate partners. With them, we discuss our values and attitudes toward work, money, relationships, and the functional issues of life. We disclose more of our values and our feelings than we do with acquaintances and companions. We share with our partner the essence of who we are. This is the ultimate test of intimacy. Can you let your partner know who you really are and feel that you will be listened to, understood, taken seriously, and affirmed as a person?

Exclusivity. When you invite another person to be intimate with you, you are, in essence, saying that this person is important in your life. You are making a commitment to share something with that person that you do not typically share with other people in more casual relationships. You let him or her see a part of you or your experience that you hold private from others. You're making a decision to make this person special.

Collective concern. This sense of we-ness is vital to intimacy. In essence, we say, "I am important, you are important, and the relationship we are creating together is also important."

Normally, collective concern grows as you begin to spend time together, share experiences, disclose on an in-depth interpersonal level, and develop exclusivity by sharing your lives with one another in a unique and special way.

THE INTANGIBLE CALLED LOVE

The information in this chapter, like all the information in this book, is not designed to tell you what you want or how to design your relationships. Its purpose is to give you basic information about relationships and healthy intimacy so that you can make the choices to bring about the consequences you want. As you seek to build or enhance your relationship, knowing the levels and appropriate activities and communication of each can help you achieve your goals.

It is important to realize that relationships are more than logical sequences and behaviors. They include also an intangible called love. Some call it eros, primal passion, or chemistry. Whatever you call it, it is the unpredictable element upon which successful intimate relationships are based. If you and your partner have that quality, knowing the levels of relationship will enhance it and keep it alive. If it's missing, this information will not create it for you.

I have known many couples who have worked hard to spend time together, share experiences, exchange in-depth, interpersonal communication, and to share exclusively and develop a sense of we-ness, yet love never blossomed for them. It is possible to do all the right things with a particular partner and never get love right because the basic chemistry, the magical feeling of attraction, is just not there.

It is true also that one of the saddest situations occurs when a person feels deep, genuine love for a partner who cannot return that love. You may want to love your partner, you may do everything possible to try to make yourself love him or her, but this unpredictable intangible exists outside our conscious choice. The control we have to exercise over it lies in our choice as to how we act on it.

The Snake and the Snakette

A number of years ago, I was in Nevada to deliver a workshop lecture. There I met a couple who shared with me the story of their relationship. Their pet names for each other, they said, were Snake and Snakette. Each had a wedding band in the shape of two intertwined snakes. Here is what they told me.

One evening, both of them were sitting at an AA meeting, when *bong!* The attraction between them was immediately apparent. Snakette, however, had listened to a tape of my lecture about the levels involved in building healthy intimacy. She didn't know what to do because her head and her feelings were in conflict. She could hear her conscious brain saying, "No, don't. Walk in the other direction! Run!" But the unconscious was saying, "It's Him! It's Him!"

So Snake and Snakette sat down and Snakette clearly explained her position. She said, "I can't go out with you. You're a snake." This didn't deter the man at all. He said, "What do you mean, I'm a snake?" So they went out to her car and listened to the tape with the story about the man walking in the woods who found the poisonous snake. Now that they both understood about dysfunctional relationships and the dangers of casual sex, they set about trying to figure out what to do.

Finally, they decided that since the unconscious attraction was so strong, they would do everything possible to build their relationship in a safe and rational way. They were going to follow the instructions on building healthy relationships to the letter.

First, they were only going to see each other in the Alano Club with other people present sitting at a table drinking coffee. All other contact was forbidden because, Snakette explained, "We're now at the casual contact level. We should not have sex at this level because we both have very destructive relationship histories. So we'll become companions by drinking coffee and talking about this marvelous tape. Then we can move on to the third level, friendship, at which point we will feel free to begin experimenting with the romantic feelings that are there. We're going to be really safe because we have moved from casual contact into a companionship, into a friendship, and now we can begin getting romantic. Then, once we find out we're romantically compatible, we will be able to consider whether or not we want to make commitments and get married."

They had this all planned out. They knew this was the right way to proceed. They were going to act upon it, they agreed to act upon it, and they did. Five weeks later they were married.

Snake and Snakette weren't following the "rules" of relationship levels and progressive intimacy, although they pretended they were. Serious committed relationships require time to deepen and mature. Snake and Snakette's attraction for one another was so strong, they allowed their sexuality to override what their logical minds told them to do. In acting on their sexuality before taking the time to really get to know one another, they took a chance that the friendship and companionship would develop later.

Snake and Snakette's successful relationship is the exception, not the rule. They took a gamble that their relationship could work despite the odds—and they won. Many more couples who act spontaneously on their sexuality before building a foundation of companionship and friendship come to regret it later. Snake and Snakette differed from the majority of these couples, however, because they knew about the levels of relationship, the possible consequences of having sex with a stranger, and made the choice to take the risk anyway. In this, they were exercising a basic principle of getting love right.

Where love and relationships are concerned, little can be guaranteed. You can follow all the rules and not achieve what you want; you can break the rules and get what you want. The important difference in choosing to get love right is that you take responsibility not only for your actions but the consequences of those actions. You have realistic expectations of what a relationship can be and do; and what it cannot be and do. Healthy intimacy is a process of communicating and learning about yourself, your partner, and your relationship: *me, you,* and *us.* The more you know, the better equipped you will be to make the best choices possible.

Self-assessment

This questionnaire is designed to help you evaluate your relationship-building skills and degree of emotional bonding with your partner. If you are not presently in a relationship, complete the answers on the basis of past relationships. If you have a partner, set up a meeting and compare your answers with your partner's, if possible.

Acquaintanceship Skills

1. **How skilled is your partner at meeting your needs for casual, friendly interaction?**

____a. very skilled   ____b. skilled   ____c. not very skilled
Explain your answer:

_____

_____

_____

2. **How skilled are you at meeting your partner's needs for casual, friendly interaction?**

____a. very skilled   ____b. skilled   ____c. not very skilled
Explain your answer:

_____

_____

_____

Companionship Skills

3. **How many of your preferred leisure activities does your partner enjoy sharing with you?**

____a. many   ____b. some   ____c. very few
Explain your answer:

_____

_____

_____

4. How many of your partner's preferred leisure activities do you enjoy sharing with him or her?

____a. many   ____b. some   ____c. very few

Explain your answer:

_____

_____

_____

Friendship Skills

5. How skilled is your partner at telling you that he or she likes, respects, and admires you as a person?

____a. very skilled   ____b. skilled   ____c. not very skilled

Explain your answer:

_____

_____

_____

6. How skilled are you at telling your partner that you like, respect, and admire him or her as a person?

____a. very skilled   ____b. skilled   ____c. not very skilled

Explain your answer:

_____

_____

_____

Romantic Love

7. How strongly in love are you with your partner?

____a. very strongly   ____b. strongly   ____c. not very strongly

Explain your answer:

_____

_____

_____

8. How strongly in love is your partner with you?

____a. very strongly   ____b. strongly   ____c. not very strongly

Explain your answer:

_____

_____

_____

Committed Love

9. **How committed are you to staying in this relationship and making it work?**

____a. very committed   ____b. committed

____c. not very committed

Explain your answer:

_____

_____

_____

10. **How committed do you believe your partner is to staying in this relationship and making it work?**

____a. very committed   ____b. committed

____c. not very committed

Explain your answer:

_____

_____

_____

Emotional Bonding Questionnaire

1. **My partner and I are both committed to building a relationship of long duration.**

____ True   ____ False

2. **My partner and I have frequent contact with one another, both in person and by telephone.**

____ True   ____ False

3. **My partner and I spend at least two hours of high-quality communication time per week.**

____ True   ____ False

4. **My partner and I discuss a variety of issues that affect our lives.**

____ True   ____ False

5. **My partner and I share a variety of experiences together and we discuss what these experiences mean to us after they are finished.**

____ True   ____ False

6. My partner and I enjoy sharing our public selves with one another.
____ True ____ False

7. My partner and I enjoy sharing our private selves (our attitudes about work, money, and life-style preferences).
____ True ____ False

8. My partner and I share our personal selves with one another by discussing our private-self concept and issues that leave us feeling scared and vulnerable.
____ True ____ False

9. My partner and I share special experiences or special parts of ourselves that we do not share with other people.
____ True ____ False

10. As a result of our relationship, my partner and I share a feeling of uniqueness or specialness. We know that we are important, in a very special way, to each other.
____ True ____ False

11. My partner and I share a strong joint identity, as a couple.
____ True ____ False

Chapter 8

SEXUALITY IN RELATIONSHIPS

PRINCIPAL CHOICES
• To accept fully your natural sexual drives and preferences.
• To take responsibility for your sexual feelings, behaviors, and consequences.
• To communicate fully to your partner about your sexual history and the value you place on various sexual activities.
• To teach your partner how to meet your sexual needs and to become willing to learn from your partner how to meet his or her needs.

Miniskirts were in fashion when I sat in the first session of Stan Martindale's psychology class. The professor was a stocky man in his mid-fifties, with a marine crew cut. He wore khaki military coveralls, smoked a pipe, and carried an armful of books.

Shortly after he entered the classroom, Stan told us that we were going to discuss the psychological issues that cause many students to drop out of college. He said the first issue was sexuality.

"We need to start with the basics," he said as he picked up a piece of chalk and turned to the blackboard. He drew a huge penis and testicles and turned back to the class.

We were shocked. The women were trying to pull their miniskirts down over their knees and the men were giggling nervously.

Stan puffed on his pipe, pulled it out of his mouth, looked at the class and, pointing at the blackboard, asked, "Who knows what that is?"

The class sat in stunned silence. Stan let the silence settle in and then said, "Hmmm, you're worse off than I thought."

With that introduction, Stan began a comprehensive lesson on sexuality—the basics, as he said. My professional training and experience since that time have confirmed for me the value of the principles to which Stan Martindale first introduced me.

Human sexuality, Stan stressed, is a normal and natural part of life. In mature, healthy relationships, sexuality is more than sexual release or gratification. It is the physical expression of a psychological, emotional, and spiritual bond with our partner. In essence, we tell our partner, "I love and cherish who you are physically, psychologically, emotionally, and spiritually. I trust you with my body and the most vulnerable aspects of my mind and spirit."

Healthy partners know that there is nothing inherently wrong, dirty, or evil about sexuality. They fully accept their sexual drives and preferences and know that they and their relationships benefit when they act upon their sexual preferences responsibly, without shame or guilt. There is a wide range of "normal" sexual behavior. Aside from certain extreme behaviors, such as sadomasochism or self-mutilation, Stan taught, a person should honor his or her sexual preferences and communicate them to his or her partner.

In a healthy relationship, both partners enjoy sex, rejoice in it, and are fulfilled by it. Sexuality is a powerful force that can forge a strong bond between partners. Yet sexuality also carries with it very important responsibilities and obligations.

"It's the difference between playing with tinker toys and parachuting from airplanes," explained Professor Martindale. "When you're playing with tinker toys, you don't have to be too careful, because it's difficult to get hurt. When you're parachuting from airplanes, you need to know what you're doing. You need reliable information about the risks involved and the safeguards you need to ensure your safety."

HEALTHY PASSION VS. INFATUATION

The key for people who want to get love right is to learn how to tell the real thing—sexual passion that exists in the context of a healthy love relationship—from short-term infatuation that will fizzle rapidly and die. Although there are no hard and fast rules, healthy passion is multidimensional and involves a combination of factors, each of which plays a part in the quality of the whole. The more compatible we are with our partner in each of these areas, the more intense our sexual experiences will be, and the better chance the relationship has of standing the test of time.

The Components of Healthy Passion
1. Physical Preferences
2. Psychological Factors
3. Sexual Compatibility
4. Shared Sense of Spirituality

Physical preferences. Professor Martindale came into class one day and asked, "Have you ever tried to figure out why you feel a strong sexual chemistry with some people while with others the spark just isn't there? And no matter how hard you try with these other people you can't get the same level of intensity? I want to show you an experiment."

He passed out slips of litmus paper. "I want you to go around the room one by one, put this paper in your mouth, suck on it for a moment, and tell us what it tastes like."

So I put the paper in my mouth and tasted nothing. The person next to me tried it and tasted nothing. The third person tried and said, "Yuck, I can't stand it! What an awful, bitter taste."

After we had all tried it, we found that about two thirds of the class tasted nothing and one third of the class tasted an intense bitterness. Yet the same chemical was on every sheet of paper. The secret behind this difference is that only about 30 percent of the general population have the right taste receptors on their tongue to taste this chemical. The other 70 percent taste nothing because they lack these receptors.

Physical attraction is a process analogous to tasting the litmus paper. When you look at somebody, if his or her physical appearance—the color of their skin, the color of their hair, the general shape and features of their face and their body—fits an innately encoded preference system, bang, something fires off.

Then if you get close to that person, and talk with him or her, and the voice matches an innately encoded preference for the sound of a voice, bang, something else goes off. Then if you reach out and touch his or her hand and you like the feel of the skin and it feels absolutely right, bang, something else goes off. Then if you get close enough to smell what the person smells like and it's the right smell, you're halfway to heaven. And then when you kiss, and he or she tastes right, too—that's it. That's magic.

Imagine you were to conduct a survey to learn the number of people in each of three categories: those who fit your ideal physical preference profile 100 percent; those who have some features of your physical preference profile, but not all; and those who completely lack any of these features. I believe you would find very few people would fall into either the first or third categories. Most people fit somewhere in the middle. They meet enough of your preferences so that, when other factors are right, they can be compatible partners and create with you a satisfying sexual relationship. So while many people believe that there is one Mr. Right or Ms. Right, the fact is many people will fit your sensual profile to a certain extent.

The process of matching a particular person to our criteria of physical attraction is largely an unconscious process. We do not choose which traits we find attractive and exciting. Because of this, we often make the mistake of believing that our sexuality is beyond our control, when, in fact, it is not. When we sense something about another person that appeals to us, we allow ourselves to feel attracted to that person. We turn ourselves on.

"That's crazy," Doug told his therapist. "I'm not turning myself on. Jane's doing it to me."

The therapist suggested that on his next date with Jane, Doug carefully observe on a minute-to-minute basis his level of sexual arousal.

"I was amazed," Doug reported during his next session. "I remembered being turned on by Jane all of the time, but that wasn't true."

What Doug discovered is that his level of sexual attraction rose and fell. Our partner's behavior alternately turns us on and turns us off. If we have decided, consciously or unconsciously, to be sexually turned on to this person, we focus on what attracts us and block our perception of what repels us. The opposite is also true.

If we have decided to be turned off by someone, we focus on the things they do that repel us while we block out what attracts us. Since we do this automatically and unconsciously, we're generally not aware of it and may believe we're not responsible for it.

Like Doug, many people do not believe that the locus of control for sexual impulse rests within them, especially people who are naturally prone to compulsive behavior. They don't say, "I'm turning myself on by how I'm thinking about or envisioning this person." They say, "He/she's turning me on. And if he/she's turning me on, what can I do about it?"

This is how we set ourselves up for Big Bang relationships: We allow our emotions and sexuality to overrun our rational mind and we become sexually involved with a person purely on the strength of this physical attraction. When you become a victim of your own sexual urges, you are placing yourself at risk of a dysfunctional or even a dangerous relationship, especially if you have had problems in the past.

You can choose to accept responsibility for your feelings and refuse to act impulsively before weighing the possible consequences. Once you do, you will be more in control of your relationships and better able to find a healthy and safe partner who can give you what you want. You will have the power to choose whether or not to act on your sexual feelings. When you feel turned on, you can ask yourself, "Is this a safe person? Is this the right time and place for sexual involvement?" If the answer is "no," you have the power to turn yourself off and move on. If the answer is "yes," you can give yourself more fully to the moment and act on your sexuality in a safe environment.

Psychological factors. We discussed the psychological bases for attraction in chapter 6. The law of *similarities* attracts us to a partner who is similar enough to ourselves to make us feel safe. The law of *complementary differences* attracts us to a partner because he or she has characteristics that challenge and excite us. The *need to resolve* causes us unconsciously to seek out a partner who triggers unresolved pain and motivates us to resolve it. When all three factors are present, we feel a strong psychological attraction to this person.

Sexual compatibility. Sensual preferences attract us to our partner, but it is our shared sexual preferences that create intense sexuality. Everyone has sexual turn-ons and turn-offs.

Sexual turn-ons are things that we enjoy sexually. Some of these are active. We may enjoy doing certain things to our partner, like kissing or stroking his/her body. Others are passive. We may enjoy having our partner do these things to us.

"Our lovemaking was incredible," says Jack. "When I did what I really wanted to do with Sarah, she loved it. I could surrender to my sexuality. I could let my primitive sexual impulses take over and let go. And, the more I let go, the more Sarah loved it."

"It was the same way for me," said Sarah. "I was amazed at how Jack could intuitively touch me just the way I needed to be touched. I could see that, in surrendering to his pleasure, he gave me pleasure. And when I did what I enjoyed, he loved it. Making love was a shared experience. I could surrender totally to Jack because he naturally and instinctively did things that I loved. Jack was the first man I ever met to whom I could surrender completely. I didn't feel self-conscious. I didn't feel a need to think about or evaluate what I was doing. I could just let myself go and we both loved it."

What Jack and Sarah are describing is healthy sexual passion. This intense form of love is the natural culmination of the sensual attraction we experience when we first meet our partner. Although this combination of sensuality and sexuality initially attracts and bonds many couples, not all couples find their sexual relations problem free.

The height of sexual passion is reached in surrendering to the sexual experience. In order to surrender, we must share a common set of turn-ons and turn-offs with our partner. When I do what turns me on, you get turned on. When you do what turns you on, I get turned on.

Sexual turn-offs are things that we find offensive, disgusting, or frightening. For example, some people enjoy oral sex. Others don't. Doing something that is a sexual turn-off can lower or destroy your sexual arousal.

When Jack and Sarah met, they were both excited and turned on by each other. Their first several sexual encounters were exciting and satisfying for both of them. Then, as Jack became more comfortable, he began to ask Sarah to do things that she found offensive.

"It's not that I'm a prude," said Sarah, "there are just certain things that I don't like, and when he tries to do those things it turns me off."

When one partner has a sexual turn-on that his or her partner experiences as a sexual turn-off, it creates a conflict. He or she may feel deprived to not experience this pleasure. The other may feel persecuted or abused because he or she is expected to do what he or she dislikes.

With open communication, however, most couples can negotiate a satisfying sexual relationship in spite of some differences in their sexual preferences. But sexual passion alone is not enough to make a relationship work in the long run.

Shared sense of spirituality. Jack and Sarah had been married one year. When I asked Jack to describe his feelings toward their lovemaking, he had difficulty putting his thoughts into words. He said, "So much is represented by our lovemaking that it's difficult to describe. I feel a sense of completeness. It's a new experience. I connect with old memories and the joy of new horizons opening before me. I find peace and serenity."

In essence, Jack finds spiritual meaning in the physical act of love that he shares with Sarah. This is because they have learned to share more than just physical sexuality. They have learned to share their most important values, experiences, and feelings. Each has learned to risk letting the other know who he/she really is. Jack and Sarah have learned that they can feel complete with each other.

The essence of sexuality is a search for the spiritual. We are seeking union, within ourselves, through union with our partner. Through healthy sexuality, we can share an intense sense of our most important values, and, in the process, temporarily transcend the limits of our loneliness and isolation.

The sense of spiritual gratification is a reflection of two phenomena, one physical and the other psychological. On a physical level, healthy sex can create a powerful altered state of consciousness. When we fully surrender to our sexuality, powerful changes occur in our brain chemistry. These changes create a wonderful feeling of release. At times, the feeling is so intense that we seem to explode out of ourselves and feel as if we are merging with the universe. At other times, this altered state is more peaceful, manifesting itself as a deep sense of serenity and peace.

Psychologically, we temporarily merge with our partner and become lost in each other. For a moment, it seems as if we are one. We feel complete and deeply affirmed. In the aftermath of lovemaking, many people find a renewed sense of meaning and purpose in life.

In order for this intense spiritual experience to unfold, you must be able to surrender and totally abandon yourself to your sexuality and the sexuality of your partner. To do this you must develop a deep acceptance of yourself, and your physical and psychological drives and preferences. Then you must develop and nurture a deep physical, psychological, and emotional bond with your partner.

THE RISKS OF SEXUAL INVOLVEMENT

Some people have different sexual relationship goals. They don't want to have a sexy friend. They want a sexual partner. Their goal is not deep intimacy, it is sexual contact. As long as both partners are responsible, consenting adults and both are seeking the same level of relationship, it is possible that this type of relationship will meet their mutual needs.

It is important for you to evaluate your sexual needs and wants in a relationship. Are you looking for a friend, a casual lover, or a committed love relationship? Once you know the answer to this question, you will be able to communicate that clearly to your partner and find out what kind of relationship your partner wants.

The most serious problems in sexual relationships originate from a common source: people don't communicate about sex. In my experience in counseling, conducting workshops, and talking with people in group therapy, I have learned that most of the time people go to bed with their partner and nobody even asks the other one if they want to. There is no discussion of sexuality or what it means or where it's going. There is no discussion of birth control. There is no discussion of disease prevention. There is no discussion of past sexual history. Most people engage their hormones and leave their rational minds behind. In this day and age, this can be a dangerous practice. Your partner may be infected with a contagious disease, such as AIDS, or he or she may be physically or psychologically dangerous.

If you decide to have sex with somebody it should be because you have thought about it and rationally determined it to be a safe, exciting thing to do, and you have decided that you are willing to pay the consequences of doing so. Sexual involvement always has consequences. It's always a risk because you never know what's going to happen—and the less you know your partner the higher the risk.

It is difficult to judge the safety of someone you do not know well. If you have had trouble in the past, the most important advice anyone can give you is to go slowly. In addition, keep in mind the following guidelines:

• Never have sex with someone because you feel guilty.

• Never have sex with someone because you feel obligated.

• Never have sex with someone because you think it will change them.

• Never, never have sex with someone unless you feel safe.

SPECIAL ISSUES OF CHILDHOOD ABUSE

It is estimated that between 30 and 40 percent of all women and between 10 and 20 percent of all men have been sexually abused before the age of sixteen. Sexuality for these individuals poses a special risk. If you come from a dysfunctional family, you may find that as you begin to be intimate with your partner, the intimacy and the sexuality bring up memories of past physical and sexual abuse. When someone becomes intimate with your body, that is going to create very strong reminders of times when somebody was abusive to your body. When you become sexually involved, if it becomes frightening or terrifying or generates very powerful memories, you need to get into therapy to explore these issues.

If you do seek therapy because you are a sexual-abuse survivor, it's very important to involve your partner in the counseling process. The whole issue of disclosing past sexual abuse, whether you are a man or woman, has powerful ramifications for your sexual partner. He or she is going to have a lot of feelings and issues that need to be professionally facilitated. If the therapist does not want to involve your partner in your therapy, you need to insist that he or she do so, or you need to find a therapist who will.

LEVELS OF SENSUAL AND SEXUAL INVOLVEMENT

Many people don't understand why sexual love relationships are so different from other relationships. This is because, in addition to the unconscious attraction we feel toward a potential partner, sexual relationships involve a different set of needs and different levels of activities. Just as relationships unfold gradually on a continuum of levels, so sensual and sexual involvement between people similarly progresses through four stages.

The Levels of Sensual/Sexual Involvement
1. Attraction
2. Flirtation
3. Sensual Involvement
4. Sexual Involvement

Attraction

Attraction is initially based on physical and psychological factors. When people feel a sexual attraction to someone, they have a choice. They can either move toward sexual involvement or they can recognize the feeling and decide not to act upon it. They can choose to turn off the feelings of attraction.

Many people feel sexually attracted to others but never act on it. They are aware of their feeling, recognize it for what it is, but don't translate it into behaviors or signals to the other person. If they choose, however, they can express their attraction through flirtation.

Flirtation

Flirting is an active expression of sexual energy that communicates to the other person that you think he or she is sexually attractive and desirable. Much of this communication is nonverbal: the way you look at the person, the tone of your voice, your body language, and the way you make subtle physical contact with him or her.

Many interactions proceed from attraction to flirtation, but stop there. The couple may recognize the sexual energy they share, engage in sexual signaling, and may even tease, taunt, and joke with one another about it, but one or both partners make the decision to stop the relationship there. They set a clear boundary.

Flirtations can be destructive when one partner flirts but does not intend to follow through on it. This puts the other person in a difficult position. Allen was enjoying flirting with Betsy. He was in a good mood at the party and felt especially outgoing. Betsy, too, was enjoying their flirtatious conversation and believed that Allen was interested in doing more than talking. When Betsy tried to move closer to Allen and take his hand, however, he quickly removed it with a frown. Betsy felt rejected and confused.

Flirtation can operate on a continuum from subtle flirting to seduction. Subtle flirting is simply a nonverbal message to someone that you find them sexually attractive. Seduction is a very strong nonverbal message that you want to be sexually involved with them. Seduction can be open and direct or subtle and manipulative.

Sensual Involvement

Sensual involvement occurs when you begin to make physical contact with your partner. As the flirtation builds and you communicate with each other more, you and your partner may begin to make physical contact. Casual physical contact progresses to sensual involvement. A casual touch of the elbow becomes a caress, an arm around the waist becomes an embrace. A handshake becomes holding hands, and eye contact turns into long gazes.

The progression into sensuality is often slow and subtle, but there are definite sequences of behavior. Some people feel that sensual involvement is acceptable in its own right, and have no intention of progressing into more overt sexual behaviors. At this point in your relationship, it is important to know what you want and what your partner wants, and to establish clear expectations and limits.

Sexual Involvement

Most people believe that the line between physical affection and sexuality is easily understood. In college, I conducted a survey on this issue for a research class and discovered that this was not the case. For my survey, I created a list of common sensual and sexual behaviors and asked the question: "Which of these behaviors, if you shared them with a partner, would cause you to conclude that you had had sex with him or her?"

The list started with holding hands, walking arm in arm, hugging, kissing on the cheek, kissing on the mouth, French kissing, sexual petting while fully clothed, sexual petting with clothes open but not removed, sexual petting without clothes on, sexual arousal to orgasm manually, sexual arousal to orgasm orally, and sexual arousal through intercourse.

I was amazed at the variety of answers I received to the question. Some people said they considered French kissing and heavy petting sexual involvement, while others did not consider oral sex to be sexual involvement.

This establishes a very important point about sexuality. There is no one definition of sexual activity. Everyone defines it for himself or herself. This means you have to communicate to your partner your feelings, expectations, and needs and learn about his or her feelings, expectations, and needs. You need to know your partner's feelings about sensual and sexual involvement and reach an agreement about what you want to do and how far you want to go.

After dating for a short time, Randy and Simone engaged in heavy petting and French kissing. They were both satisfied with this level of sensuality and sexuality but placed different values on these activities. Because Randy defined sexual relations as oral sex and intercourse, heavy petting and French kissing were not sex. Simone, however, felt differently. She believed that both of these were sexual activities, and her willingness to participate in them represented a high level of personal commitment. Later, when Simone asked Randy for a greater commitment in the relationship, this misunderstanding caused both much confusion and unhappiness.

In addition to the value you place on various sensual and sexual activities, you and your partner also need to communicate about what you want sexually from one another. To be a good lover, you need to teach your partner what to do to arouse your sexual desire. No one is going to know instinctively what to do to arouse you. In many respects, good lovers can be defined as people who learn to satisfy their partner's sensual and sexual needs and who teach their partner to satisfy their own needs and wants.

Another area of frequent misunderstanding and conflict between partners is how to go about asking your partner for sex. Many people believe that it is rude or vulgar to ask their partner to make love with them. They believe their partner should know automatically and spontaneously when they're feeling sexually turned on, that their partner should sense their sexual needs and respond to them spontaneously. This is unrealistic. If you want your partner to know you want to have sex, you have to tell him or her. Conversely, you need to know how to respond to your partner's request for sex.

No matter how much we love our partner or how much we value our lovemaking with him or her, there will be times when we do not want to be sexual. You need to know how to refuse your partner's invitation for sex gently and sensitively. There is a skill to saying no that can convey the message, "No, I don't want to make love to you right now. I love you and care about you, and I love to make love to you. I'm looking forward to when we do again, but just not now." Similarly, there will be times you will have to deal with rejection. Not everybody wants to meet your sexual needs all the time.

Yet another misunderstanding may arise between partners when we are not sure what it is we want from our partner. Many people think they want to have sex, when they really want their partner to meet another need. A man might come home from work and

say, "Make love to me," but is really saying, "Tell me I'm important and powerful." Others ask for sex when they are bored and
want to do something interesting. Many women say "Have sex
with me," when they're really saying, "Make me feel whole and
complete." Many women also ask for sex when they really want
physical affection and cuddling.

So you need to ask yourself, "What do I really want?" You must
challenge yourself to separate your sexual needs from other needs
that may masquerade as sexual requests. If you are trying to get
other needs met through sex, you'll never perceive the sex as
satisfying. It can be the best sex in the world, but the original need
you felt will remain unmet.

SEXUALITY IN RELATIONSHIP BUILDING

Frank met Marian at a party. They immediately liked each other,
so Frank invited Marian to attend a play with a group of his friends.
As their acquaintanceship grew, they became more attracted to
each other and began to flirt with one another. Both Frank and

Levels of Relationship	Progression of Sensual/Sexual Involvement
1. Acquaintanceship	1. Attraction
	2. Flirtation
2. Companionship	3. Sensual Involvement
3. Friendship	
4. Romantic Love	4. Sexual Involvement
5. Committed Love	

Marian had been involved previously in painful love relationships.
They wanted to avoid making the same mistakes, so they decided
to build their relationship slowly. Over a period of several weeks,
they shared a number of companionship activities together, usually
with other friends and occasionally as a couple. As their compan-

ionship grew, they held hands often, and hugged and kissed each other to express their mutual affection. Over the following months, their friendship deepened and they moved slowly into more explicitly sexual behaviors, such as petting and, eventually, intercourse. The fact that they had gradually introduced sensual and sexual activities allowed them to build a strong, solid friendship first. As their relationship moved into a romantic love, they decided to share an apartment and began to combine their money in some purchases that neither could afford alone. They also made a commitment to be monogamous and to do their best to meet each other's social, psychological, and sexual needs.

Notice the progression. As Frank and Marian's relationship grew through levels and stages, their sensual and sexual involvement kept pace, developing simultaneously. This is the safest way to build a relationship. If you have a history of dysfunctional relationships, I strongly recommend that you proceed in this way.

There is an additional benefit to building your sensual and sexual involvement with your partner slowly. When you have built a strong friendship before you choose to act on your sexual desire for one another, the intensity of your lovemaking will be extraordinary because you will not be acting solely on the strength of your hormones. You will be acting on the strength of a strong feeling of love and caring for the person. You have passion and safety combined. You can surrender to the sexual experience without the fear that something awful or terrible is going to happen to you.

Not all healthy relationships unfold this way. Other relationships begin with intense passion and then, after the sexual infatuation dies down, the partners begin to get to know each other as people and develop their friendship. This type of progression works well for individuals who recognize the risks involved and are prepared to accept the adverse consequences, if any. When you begin a relationship in this way, there is no guarantee that it will develop into anything more than a sexual relationship. It is important that both partners realize this. Sharing sex does not mean intimacy. Partners in these relationships must be very clear about their expectations to avoid disappointment later.

A third way couples integrate sensual and sexual aspects into their relationship is to build the relationship first, becoming close friends before the sexual elements of the relationship slowly begin to surface.

Tony and Mary met each other in college. They liked each other and got along well together. They attended study groups and would often spend evenings studying together. Occasionally, they would go out socially, but it was usually with groups to do such things as attend a party or go to a movie.

Mary was comfortable with their relationship and considered Tony a close personal friend. As they spent more time together, however, her feelings began to change. They began to engage in more activities as a couple and both became aware that they were becoming sexually attracted to one another.

THE ART OF SEDUCTION

Elly, a patient of mine, came in to her session very distraught one day because of an incident with a coworker. She had known Barry for over ten years and knew his wife and their children. Yet all of a sudden, "for no reason at all" she said, he had tried to French kiss her. She was very distressed by what she saw as inappropriate behavior and a breach of faith. When I asked her to explain how this all came about, she told me this story.

Elly and Barry were assigned by their firm to attend the same out-of-town conference. This is the first time this had happened. Barry came over to her and said, "You know, we're both assigned to the same conference. It would really be great to get to spend some time with you in a different environment than work."

"I think it would be great to spend time with you, too," Elly replied.

Barry said, "So then you won't mind if I look you up at the conference?"

She said, "Absolutely not, I'd enjoy it."

When Elly arrived at the hotel there was a message for her from Barry. She called him on the phone.

Barry said, "I'm glad you could make it. Would you like to have dinner tonight?"

"That would be very nice," Elly said.

"Would you like to eat here, where there'll be a lot of other conference people to interrupt, or would you like to go out to a private place where it will be quiet and we could talk?"

She said, "Let's go somewhere private."

The restaurant was a quiet, romantic little place. Barry and Elly talked and shared experiences. About halfway through dinner Barry reached over, squeezed her hand, and said, "I've really enjoyed this evening, Elly, and I'm feeling really close to you."

"I've enjoyed it also and I feel really close to you, too, Barry."

After dinner, on the way to the car, Barry said, "Would you like to go back to the hotel, or would you like to take a walk? Around the back of the hotel there's a wooded area."

"I don't know, what would you like to do?"

"I'd like to take a walk."

"That's fine." As they walked, he reached up and put his hand on her elbow. Elly didn't respond. Then he put his arm around her waist and she didn't say anything. Soon they were walking hand in hand around the building and talking.

When they returned to the hotel, Barry said, "I've really enjoyed being with you. I'd like to keep talking. Would you like to keep talking?"

She said, "Yes, I would."

He said, "I've got some soft drinks up in my room, would you like to come up and have a soft drink?" She said yes, and so they went up to his room. She took off her shoes and sat on the bed.

He asked, "Would you mind if I took off my shoes?"

She said no, so he sat down on the bed next to her and they opened their soft drinks. As they sat there talking, he looked into her eyes, she looked into his eyes, and he tried to French kiss her "for no reason at all."

As we discussed it, Elly could see that what had appeared to her to be an unwelcome sexual advance had been preceded by an entire sequence of sexual signaling. At each step of the way Barry asked for and received Elly's consent before going further. Elly, however, completely failed to recognize this nonverbal limit testing. Barry had taken Elly's responses to mean that she, also, felt an attraction and wanted to engage in sensual activities. In the end, what Elly thought of as "no reason at all" Barry had read as a very definite invitation to be sexually intimate.

Unfortunately, this is a very common scenario. People who choose to remain unaware of sexual signaling can find themselves in situations they do not want to be in and for which they are unprepared. The sad fact is that many women in Elly's situation become victims of date rape. It is vitally important that you recognize this sequence of verbal and nonverbal signaling so that at each level you can consciously choose whether or not you want to continue to the next level and then be able to communicate that decision to your partner.

When a woman recognizes that her partner is asking for a greater level of physical contact, she should have the capacity to turn her partner down subtly but very quickly before it progresses. Most men, if they receive no encouragement from their partner, will not attempt to go any further. Their egos are too fragile.

The situation is different when men receive what they perceive to be a series of "go" signals only to then have the woman abruptly say "no." By this point, they are ego-invested and their manhood is at stake. The risk of their becoming very aggressive is much higher, especially if they've been drinking.

Seduction should be a conscious, mutually agreed-upon experience, not something that happens unconsciously or because one partner wishes it. Mature adults play the game consciously and take full responsibility for what they do. If you are a man, and you choose to move into flirtation and seduction, you should be aware that you are making the decision to do this and take responsibility for it rather than blame your partner.

The same is true for women, but there is an additional caveat. Women are often victimized because they play the seduction game with part of them knowing that they're being seduced and another part of them saying, "No, he really doesn't mean it. I can't hurt his feelings by telling him to stop." By not taking conscious responsibility for their part in the seduction, they are allowing themselves to venture into dangerous situations that can easily result in date rape.

This does not mean the woman is responsible for rape. When

you're walking down an unlit street in a high-crime neighborhood and somebody knocks you out and steals your purse, you've still been robbed. The robber has still committed a crime and is fully responsible for the consequences. But you have put yourself in a situation where your risk of being robbed is much greater. In the same way, when a woman is the victim of date rape, she is not responsible for her partner's actions; sole responsibility rests with him. But if you don't want to be victimized, you need to avoid situations that increase your risk.

The first precaution you can take is to recognize the sexual signaling when it starts. Know how to give nonverbal cues that you are choosing not to participate. When somebody touches your arm, you can subtly turn away and break off the contact, letting your partner know in no uncertain terms that that's not acceptable to you. If somebody tries to put his arm around you, you can subtly turn in a way that breaks the contact and communicates the definite message that you do not want him to do that.

Then you need to deal with the situation verbally with very basic communications:

"Excuse me, I don't like your arm around my waist."

"Would you please not touch my arm that way."

"Excuse me, I don't want to hold hands with you. Please don't try that again."

Make very direct statements and then change the subject. If your partner persists in his physical contact, break the contact at once and get away from him as quickly as possible, because he's looking for trouble.

A colleague of mine has a sign in her office that says "What part of 'No' don't you understand?" If you want to say no to sexual involvement, use the word "No."

"No, I don't want you to touch me that way."

"No, I do not want to have sex with you."

"No, I will not go to bed with you."

Another important fact for women to know is that there is substantial research that shows that physical and sexual aggression in men is amplified, intensified, and magnified by alcohol. Men who normally are not aggressive can become aggressive or even violent when drinking heavily. If you are going to take precautions for your safety, realize that when you're with a man who is drinking, if you don't want to be intimate with him, you don't want to be alone with him. This is true especially if you don't know him. But even if you do know him, or think you do, remember that date rape by definition is perpetrated by someone you know.

SEXUALITY IN ESTABLISHED RELATIONSHIPS

"I don't understand why sex is such a big deal to you," Nora said. "We've been married for five years and there are so many other good things about our relationship. Why do you have to keep blowing our sex life out of proportion?"

"I'm not blowing it out of proportion," said Nick. "Sex is important to me. I want our sex life to be like it used to be. Don't you remember how passionate and fulfilled we were the first year or so that we were together? We've lost that and I want it back!"

"Nick, we can't go back in time. I'd like it to be the way it was too. But it isn't. I don't think life works that way. It's normal and natural for the passion to drain out of a relationship. Isn't it?"

Therapists answer this question in different ways. Some say that it is possible to have constant, high-intensity sex if you learn how to do it. These therapists often specialize in teaching techniques that promote intense sexual gratification. Many of these therapists overvalue sexuality and make it the main or central focus of the relationship, while devaluing other aspects of the relationship.

At the other extreme, some therapists say that it is unrealistic to expect sexual intensity to survive in a long-term relationship. The theory is that anything we do routinely becomes routine. These therapists tend to undervalue the role of sexuality in a relationship and minimize its importance.

I believe in the middle ground. I believe it is possible to maintain sexual passion in a relationship, but the passion ebbs and flows. It may reach intense peaks and then subside only to rise again as the long-term relationship moves to a new level. The passion in healthy relationships is not purely sexual. It is emotional and spiritual. The intensity continues to rise out of an ever closer union with a partner you love and cherish.

Given time, healthy sexuality grows through four stages: infatuation and risk taking, the power struggle, safety and comfort seeking, and the ebb and flow of love.

During the *infatuation and risk-taking* stage, sexuality is viewed as the most important part of the relationship and the entire relationship becomes organized around it.

After a while, the infatuation begins to subside and both partners feel threatened by the loss. As they strive to keep the infatuation going, the relationship enters the *power-struggle* stage. The partners begin to make both sexual and nonsexual demands on each other. They communicate the unspoken plea, "Please make it as good as it was."

In a healthy relationship, the resolution of this power struggle results in the mature realization that sexuality is only one component of the relationship. Since we still love each other, even though the driving sexual infatuation is no longer present, we're able to abandon the power struggle and experience each other without constantly demanding high-intensity sex or concessions that will make us feel loved.

This marks the beginning of the *safety and comfort-seeking* stage of sexual love. We're able to surrender our demand for constant, high-intensity sex and trade it in for the comfort of emotional intimacy.

As we grow closer, we inevitably discover a new aspect or dimension of our partner that excites us. Our former sense of passion is reignited. High-intensity sexuality returns. This is the beginning of the fourth phase of mature sexuality, *the ebb and flow of love*.

In a healthy sexual relationship we keep falling in love with our partner over and over again. The infatuation flares again and the sex is really great. The infatuation tapers off and we begin to move apart. But because we are committed to our partner and our relationship, we work through any problems until we fall in love with them all over again.

INTIMATE ENCOUNTERS AS EXTRAMARITAL AND EXTRARELATIONSHIP AFFAIRS

The Kinsey report tells us that approximately one third of all people in committed relationships will have an intimate encounter with someone other than their partner during the course of their lives. Although many people may disapprove, intimate encounters in the form of extramarital or extrarelationship affairs are fairly common. Therefore, it is important to understand what these relationships are, and the options people have in coping with them.

There are two ways to approach the issue of these types of intimate encounters. The first and most common is to take a moralistic viewpoint: when a person is in a committed relationship with another, intimate encounters are wrong. It is dishonest to have an affair, and doing so constitutes a violation of trust.

The problem with this approach is that people who are drawn to intimate encounters typically feel compelled to engage in them, even though they know they are wrong. Many of my patients who have struggled with the issue of whether or not to have an affair have told me plainly, "I know it's wrong, but I still feel a need to do it."

The second approach is a rational, reality-testing approach. I help people explore the options of going ahead with the intimate encounter to determine their motives and what they have to gain. What is the best thing that could happen? What is the worst thing? What is the most likely outcome? By exploring the range of possible consequences, the person is better equipped to make a decision about the consequences they are risking.

I next ask clients to evaluate their motives for the intimate encounter. What are they trying to accomplish? Are they seeking a relationship that would magically fix them? Are they seeking an escape from some inadequacy, real or imagined, in their current relationship? Are they looking for a unique or novel experience that isn't available to them in the context of their current relationship? Many of these issues needed to be addressed.

The next issue is to explore the options they have for dealing with their current partner. Many therapists tell their patients they must be totally honest with their partner about their desire.

Ideally, this honesty will help the partners communicate about what is lacking in the relationship so they can correct those deficiencies. As a result the desire to have the intimate encounter will disappear. The problem is that this approach doesn't always work.

Many people who decide to be totally honest with their partners about their desire to have an affair have found that it permanently damaged their relationship. Trust was shattered, and the couple was unable to recover. This was especially problematic for several clients who, after discussing the issue with their partner, decided to go ahead and have the intimate encounter anyway.

The general rule is that total honesty can be risky. To disclose the desire to have an intimate encounter or the fact that you have had one or are about to have one will generally put your relationship at risk. No one can be sure that the couple will be able to weather this storm and survive the stress the intimate encounter places on the relationship.

Maggie had had an affair and was totally guilt ridden. We talked about it in her therapy session and she made the decision to tell her husband, Ned, because she believed Ned was open minded and loving enough to understand. We decided she would do it in a couple's counseling session. When the time came, she self-disclosed the fact of her affair to him, very nervously. Ned accepted it perfectly, and said, "You know, I can understand that because I had an affair, too." Maggie immediately became enraged and, after a few choice words, stormed out of the office. Three weeks later, she filed for divorce.

If you do not believe total honesty is the best choice in your situation, what other options do you have? One obvious answer is to engage in the intimate encounter and not disclose the fact to your partner. Many people choose this option. In some cases, the intimate encounter was short-lived and instructional. The person realized very quickly that the intimate encounter was not going to meet his or her needs, caused higher stress, and did not have the magical outcome that he or she expected. He/she quickly ended the affair and returned to his/her established relationship with a renewed commitment.

In other cases, the results are very different. The partners engaging in the intimate encounter found that it whetted their appetite for experiences that were not available in their current relationship. This prompted them to end the relationship and re-negotiate a different life-style.

Others have intimate encounters on a regular basis throughout the course of their long-term relationships. It is common for people to have regular extramarital partners. These arrangements often produce stress and dysfunction, but at other times the partners report that they work within the context and limitations of their current relationship.

I do not endorse the policy of having extramarital or extrarela-tionship affairs. I do, however, see value in exploring all possible options to help people thinking of such intimate encounters deter-mine the benefits and disadvantages of each alternative. Telling others what they can or cannot do generally doesn't work.

If a person is in a committed relationship and is having difficulty, I strongly discourage engaging in any form of intimate encounter. In this context, the affair serves to detract from the issues of the relationship and create extraneous problems that distract the cou-ple from confronting the issues that they need to resolve.

SEXUALITY IN THE 1990S WITH THE RISK OF AIDS

Whether we like it or not, the presence of the AIDS epidemic in America today requires us to change many aspects of the way in which we conduct our sexual relationships. Everybody needs to be concerned about AIDS and other sexually transmitted diseases and take action to address these concerns.

There can be no "casual" sex when every sexual act can be a life-threatening encounter. If you are thinking of having a random sexual encounter, don't do it. Consider sexual involvement only with someone you are truly attracted to and when you believe it will be meaningful to you and your partner in a significant way.

There is no such thing as safe sex, there are only safe partners. You can do anything sexually with a person who is not infected with HIV (or other venereal disease), and it's perfectly safe. There are varying risk factors with various sexual activities with someone who is infected.

The major concern, therefore, must be that you have a safe partner. Increasingly, AIDS is spreading into the heterosexual community. Attractive, healthy, vibrant people contract the disease, as Magic Johnson's example illustrates. You need to know your partner well enough to know that he or she has a sexual history that puts him or her in a low-risk category.

The highest-risk partners are intravenous drug users; those who have had homosexual experiences, particularly those who have practiced anal sex and have been anal receptive; people who have frequented prostitutes; people who have had blood transfusions; and people who have had multiple sexual partners, especially those who have been highly promiscuous.

If you learn that your partner fits one of these high-risk patterns, I urge you to sit down with him or her and say, "I'd really like to get sexually involved with you, but you have a high-risk background. I need to have some evidence that you're not infected." Then have the person get an HIV test and show you the results.

A negative result from a test, however, is not proof that the individual is not infected with the AIDS virus or that he or she cannot transmit AIDS to a sexual partner. Once a person is infected, it takes the body anywhere from three to six months to develop sufficient antibodies against the virus to register positive results on a test. If your partner has been infected within the last three to six months, he or she may still have a negative AIDS test and yet have the disease and be able to infect others.

It is important to realize that you can never be 100 percent certain that your current partner is safe. Even if you have been married to one person for the last twenty years, there is still the possibility that he or she has had an affair that you don't know about. Most experts recommend that when you have sex with anyone, even if you believe him or her to be a perfectly safe partner, you practice safe sex. That means using a condom. In the 1990s, sexual partners have to become comfortable introducing condoms into the process of foreplay and sex. If you're not comfortable with your body, you're probably not going to be a good lover. If you're not comfortable with the idea of condoms, you're probably not going to be a safe lover.

A survey conducted by *New Woman* magazine revealed that 86

percent of the women surveyed knew that AIDS was a dangerous disease and that the use of condoms could prevent transmission of AIDS. Only 22 percent of the women reported changing their sexual behavior by insisting that the men wear condoms when they went to bed with them. When the others were asked why they had not changed their behavior, it came down once again to a lack of basic communication skills. They didn't know how to ask their partner to use a condom. They didn't know how to say, "No, that's dangerous. I will not put myself at risk of getting a fatal disease."

Partners need to talk openly about their sexual histories. If your partner says, "Oh, that's not important, I don't want to talk about that," you must assume that he or she has a high-risk history. If your partner is uncomfortable or unwilling to talk about it with you, then he or she is unwilling to talk about it with anybody. That means he or she may have been involved with high-risk partners and not know it.

I asked a single friend of mine how he is responding to the risk of AIDS. He replied that he is very careful in screening his partners for unsafe sexual practices. I asked if he used a condom.

He said, "My belief is if you have a safe partner, you don't need a condom."

"Bill, what if your partner's lying to you?"

"Well, I screen them for integrity. If I feel she is a low-integrity person, I won't have sex with her."

"Bill, have you ever lied to a woman about your sexual history?"

"Well, yes. Years ago I did, but I wouldn't do it now."

"What if your partner is in the same place you were ten years ago?"

"Well, I'm good enough at judging character so that won't happen."

None of us is an open book. Are you willing to bet your life on your ability to "read" another person?

"I have another question, Bill." I said. "Even if you were able to accurately judge the integrity of your partner, how do you know that she didn't have sex with an unsafe partner? Statistics show that most adults today have had multiple sex partners. In terms of disease transmission, you're not just having sex with your current partner. You're having sex with every one of that person's previous sexual partners, too. How can you know for certain?"

The bottom line is, Bill can't know for certain that any of his partners are safe. No one can know for certain about any given partner. It is entirely possible that a woman has sex with a man who has been sexually abstinent for six years. Yet six and a half years ago, that man had a short experimental period with homosexuality and contracted the AIDS virus. And he passes it on to his sexual partner. Anytime you have sex with someone, your chances of contracting a sexually transmitted disease are the same as if you had had sex with every person with whom that man or woman has had sexual contact.

CHOOSING HEALTHY SEXUALITY

Today it is more important than ever to identify your sexual choices. Today more than ever healthy sexuality requires you to take full responsibility for who you are and what you do. The primary choice is self-responsibility. Are you going to take responsibility for who you are, what your values are, what you do, and the consequences of what you do? Or are you going to abdicate your responsibility and blame someone else for your sexuality and your actions?

Healthy, lasting relationships involve a shared sense of intense passion and sexuality, but the passion and sexuality are not the key or central aspects of the relationship. The relationship revolves around a variety of shared values, life-style preferences, and mutually respected traits. Each partner knows who the other really is. Each loves and cares about the real essence of the other. The sexuality enhances this core of mutual respect and admiration.

To have a healthy, vibrant sex life is a matter of choice. Healthy people make the choice consciously and they act upon it responsibly. In doing so, they create a safe environment in which to act out the kinds of sexual behavior that truly excite them and give them fulfillment, without putting them at undue risk. They maximize the excitement and minimize the risk of adverse consequences.

An important part of being alive and being a sexual human being is to find another human being with whom you can fully express your sexuality. This means owning your own physical and psychological sexual drives and finding a partner who honors and is excited by that part of you and whose sexuality you can honor. Together you can go about setting up an environment in which you can express your sexuality safely and responsibly.

The Sexual Love Questionnaire

The following questionnaire is designed to help you evaluate the sexual dimension of your love relationships. If you are not presently in a relationship, complete the answers on the basis of past relationships. If you have a partner, set up a meeting and compare your answers with your partner's. Discussing your answers with your partner can surface painful issues. In discussing your views of your partner's sexuality, it is important to be gentle and supportive.

Sensual Preferences

1. How well does your partner meet your sensual preferences in the following areas? (Circle the appropriate number on the scale next to it. A "10" means that preference is fully met. A "0" means that preference is not met at all.)

a. Physical appearance

    10..9..8..7..6..5..4..3..2..1..0

b. Tone of voice

    10..9..8..7..6..5..4..3..2..1..0

c. Feel of his or her skin

    10..9..8..7..6..5..4..3..2..1..0

d. Natural body scent

    10..9..8..7..6..5..4..3..2..1..0

e. Taste of his or her body

    10..9..8..7..6..5..4..3..2..1..0

2. How well do you believe you meet your partner's sensual preferences in the following areas?

a. Physical appearance

    10..9..8..7..6..5..4..3..2..1..0

b. Tone of voice

10..9..8..7..6..5..4..3..2..1..0

c. Feel of his or her skin

10..9..8..7..6..5..4..3..2..1..0

d. Natural body scent

10..9..8..7..6..5..4..3..2..1..0

e. Taste of his or her body

10..9..8..7..6..5..4..3..2..1..0

Psychological Similarities

3. Describe three major ways in which you believe you and your partner are psychologically similar (that is, you share common values, attitudes, beliefs, emotional response, and so on):

a. _____

_____

b. _____

_____

c. _____

_____

Complementary Differences

4. Describe three differences between you and your partner that you find exciting, beneficial, or attractive:

a. _____

_____

b. _____

_____

c. _____

_____

Antagonistic Differences

5. Describe three differences between you and your partner that you find unattractive, frustrating, painful, anger provoking, or difficult to deal with:

a. _____

_____

b. _____

_____

c. _____
_____

The Opportunity to Resolve

6. Describe three ways in which your partner treats you as you were treated by your parents:

a. _____
_____

b. _____
_____

c. _____
_____

7. Describe three ways in which you treat your partner as he or she was treated by his or her parents:

a. _____
_____

b. _____
_____

c. _____
_____

Shared Spirituality

8. How strongly are your higher values affirmed through sexual involvement with your partner?

____a. very strongly ____b. strongly ____c. not very strongly

9. How strongly do you experience an altered state of consciousness that gives your life a sense of renewed meaning through sexual involvement with your partner?

____a. very strongly ____b. strongly ____c. not very strongly

Sexual Turn-ons

10. List your three most exciting sexual turn-ons:

a. _____
_____

b. _____
_____

c. _____
_____

11. List what you believe to be your partner's three most exciting sexual turn-ons:

a. _____
_____

b. _____
_____

c. _____
_____

12. How willing are you to experiment with new sexual behaviors in order to discover new sexual turn-ons?

____a. very willing   ____b. willing   ____c. not very willing

13. How willing is your partner to experiment with new sexual behaviors in order to discover new sexual turn-ons?

____a. very willing   ____b. willing   ____c. not very willing

Sexual Turn-offs

14. List three of your most important sexual turn-offs:

a. _____
_____

b. _____
_____

c. _____
_____

15. List what you believe to be three of your partner's most important sexual turn-offs:

a. _____
_____

b. _____
_____

c. _____
_____

16. How much do your partner's sexual turn-offs inhibit the expression of your sexuality?

____a. not at all   ____b. a little   ____c. a lot

17. How much do your sexual turn-offs inhibit the expression of your partner's sexuality?

____a. not at all   ____b. a little   ____c. a lot

Knowing How to Ask for Sex

18. How skilled are you in asking your partner to meet your sexual needs?

____a. very skilled   ____b. skilled   ____c. not very skilled

19. How skilled is your partner in asking you to meet his or her sexual needs?

____a. very skilled   ____b. skilled   ____c. not very skilled

Knowing What You Are Asking For

20. Which of the following questions are you most likely to confuse with the request for shared sexuality?

____a. Will you make me feel loved?

____b. Will you make me feel important?

____c. Will you make me feel powerful?

____d. Will you make me feel excited?

____e. Will you make me feel complete or whole?

____f. Will you make me feel better or different than I do?

____g. Will you give me attention?

____h. Will you give me affection?

21. Which of the following questions is your partner most likely to confuse with the request for shared sexuality?

____a. Will you make me feel loved?

____b. Will you make me feel important?

____c. Will you make me feel powerful?

____d. Will you make me feel excited?

____e. Will you make me feel complete or whole?

____f. Will you make me feel better or different than I do?

____g. Will you give me attention?

____h. Will you give me affection?

Saying "No" to Sexual Requests

22. How skilled are you at saying "No" to sexual requests in a manner that is supportive of your partner?

___a. very skilled ___b. skilled ___c. not very skilled

23. How skilled is your partner at saying "No" to your sexual requests in a manner that is supportive of you?

___a. very skilled ___b. skilled ___c. not very skilled

Dealing with Sexual Rejection

24. How skilled are you at accepting sexual rejection without criticizing yourself or your partner?

___a. very skilled ___b. skilled ___c. not very skilled

25. How skilled is your partner at accepting sexual rejection without criticizing himself (herself) or you?

___a. very skilled ___b. skilled ___c. not very skilled

Overall Sexual Fulfillment

26. Overall, how sexually fulfilled are you in your current relationship?

___a. very fulfilled ___b. fulfilled ___c. not very fulfilled

27. Overall, how sexually fulfilled do you believe your partner is in your current relationship?

___a. very fulfilled ___b. fulfilled ___c. not very fulfilled

Safe Sex

28. How comfortable are you in using condoms and other safe-sex procedures in lovemaking? How comfortable is your partner?

___Very comfortable and we've integrated into our lovemaking

___Uncomfortable, but we do it anyway

___Uncomfortable, which means sometimes we do it and sometimes we don't

___Openly resistant: we don't do it, ever

29. How comfortable are you in screening your partner for the risk of AIDS and other sexually transmitted diseases?

___Very comfortable, and I always do it

___Uncomfortable, but I do it anyway

____Uncomfortable, which means sometimes I do it and sometimes I don't

____Openly resistant: I don't do it

30. How comfortable are you in responding to your partner's questions about your sexual history?

____Very comfortable; I can talk freely and honestly about it

____Uncomfortable, but I am able to talk honestly about it

____Openly resistant; I choose not to talk about it

III
LEARNING
TO
CHANGE

Chapter 9

COUNTERDEPENDENTS AND CODEPENDENTS: THE ROLE OF PERSONALITY STYLES IN RELATIONSHIPS

PRINCIPAL CHOICES
• To identify counterdependent or codependent traits in your personality.
• To recognize whether these traits are causing problems in your relationships.
• To choose a healthier balance by embracing and integrating your shadow self.

"**I** really thought Mitch was a great guy," Shelly told her sister. "He was so strong and competent, and ready to take care of me. I just surrendered myself totally to him. The next thing I know, I'm taking care of him. He doesn't even appreciate the things I do for him. I want to get out of this relationship, but I can't. When I think about leaving him, I get scared and panicky. I realize that he's the best thing I ever had in my life."

"When I met Shelly," Mitch said to his friend Ray, "she was so soft, warm, and receptive to me. She was so understanding and caring. Then I got involved with her and she stopped appreciating me. She turned into a nag; suddenly she was dissatisfied with everything I did. No matter what I gave, it wasn't enough. No matter what I did, she wanted more. I'm just sick and tired of her. But when I think of leaving her, I just can't. We fight all the time, we argue constantly. I feel chained to her and can't get out."

Opposites attract, the old saying goes, and this is especially true in the case of compulsive relationships. Mitch and Shelly were as different as night and day. Mitch was strong, independent, and self-assured. He liked to take charge and needed to have things his own way. Mitch had all the traits of the *counterdependent* personality.

Shelly, on the other hand, was insecure and always depended on others, particularly the men in her life. Although her many skills earned her praise at work, Shelly was never really comfortable without someone stronger to reassure and guide her. She fit the profile of the *codependent* personality.*

"God makes 'em, God matches 'em," my grandmother used to say. As polar opposites, the counterdependent and codependent personalities fit together like a lock and a key. Each partner depends upon the other to provide the psychological elements he/she needs but cannot express. It is a twofold dynamic. Counterdependents, like Mitch, who need to act strong and control others, sense in codependents a vulnerability that they can't allow themselves to experience. They also see a partner who won't challenge their strength or resist their efforts to control. Codependents, like Shelly, who need to act weak and care for others, see strengths in counterdependents that they can't allow themselves to experience. They also see a partner who will act as a powerful protector and won't force them to connect with their strengths or take responsibility for their behavior.

The law of complementary differences creates a powerful attraction between these two personalities. Their extreme imbalance makes the counterdependent and codependent feel incomplete by themselves. When a counterdependent and a codependent come together, they feel they have discovered their missing half. The attraction has little to do with their partner, however, because the missing half lies deep within themselves in the unexpressed weakness and insecurity of the counterdependent and the unexpressed strength and grandiosity of the codependent.

Shelly and Mitch are unhappy in their relationship but feel powerless to get out. They want to work to make things better, but

* The terms *counterdependent* and *codependent* have been variously used by authors and speakers in different contexts. For the purpose of this discussion, these terms relate specifically to the personality structures outlined here; they have no correlation with chemical dependence. Both counterdependent and codependent personalities may develop a chemical addiction if other contributing factors are present.

they don't know how. Shelly blames Mitch for all that is wrong in the relationship, and Mitch blames Shelly. They don't see how their own character traits are hooked into their partner's or how these traits trap them in a dysfunctional relationship. Nor do they see that the only way to free themselves of the psychological chains and locks that hold them is to embrace and integrate these unexpressed selves and move toward a healthy balance of traits. The only key that will open these locks is personal change; only when the *me* and the *you* have achieved a healthy balance can the deadlock of *us* be broken.

Understanding the traits of the counterdependent and codependent personalities and learning to recognize them within our own personality and that of our partner, therefore, constitute an important first step in strengthening a relationship.

THE COUNTERDEPENDENT

Counterdependents outwardly appear secure and independent, able to cope with everything. In the movies, we celebrate this macho hero, the man of steel, in such characters as James Bond, Rambo, and Dirty Harry. Not all counterdependents are men— many women are just as counterdependent as their male counterparts. Look at television character Murphy Brown, for example. Male or female, the counterdependent never reveals his or her vulnerability but practices being strong all of the time—and the stronger the better.

Counterdependents learned that the only way to survive, to be loved and accepted—or to keep from being hurt or destroyed— was to become as strong as possible.

When Mitch was in the third grade he joined a Little League softball team. One day Mitch tripped and fell while trying to catch a fly ball. He skinned his knees and hands as he skidded to a stop face down on the field.

Mitch's father was the team's coach. When Mitch didn't get up immediately, his father ran out to him and asked him what was wrong. Mitch was trying to hold back his tears as he told his father that he hurt his hands and knees. His father quickly examined them and told him to stop crying. "Don't be a sissy," his father ordered.

"Those are just minor bruises. They don't hurt!" When Mitch continued to cry his father got an angry look on his face and said in a hard whisper, "Stop crying right now, or when we get home I'll really give you something to cry about!"

In this instance and countless others like it, Mitch learned that if you let others see that you are hurt they will only hurt you more. To survive, you have to hide your pain and pretend you feel strong even when you don't. Most counterdependents have childhood memories in which they were hurt, expressed their pain, and were punished for it.

Healthy families teach children to incorporate a wide range of behaviors that they can use to meet their needs depending on the situation. Children in these families learn to respond adaptively by expressing strength and independence at appropriate times and dependence and neediness at other times. They learn that they will be accepted and loved no matter what feeling or behavior they demonstrate.

Children from dysfunctional families learn to behave in the world according to mandates and injunctions. The primary mandate and injunction counterdependents learn are:

• You must always act strong or you will die.

• You must never reveal your weaknesses to anyone at any time, or you will die.

Counterdependents have internalized these messages through automatic thoughts and behaviors. As a result, in their adult relationships, they lack the flexibility necessary to make constructive relationship choices about how best to meet their own needs or the needs of their partner.

Maria told me that she had trouble with her relationships because her partners complained that she was too controlling, that everything had to be done her way. When I asked if she thought this were true and why she did this, she quickly replied, "Because if I let them handle things they would mess it up!"

"How do you know that?" I asked.

"Because it's always been that way!" Maria explained. She then told me how she had to take care of her brothers and sisters from the time she was very young. Her mother was a manic depressive who would swing from being severely depressed to being extremely agitated and excited. Because of her mother's mental illness, Maria couldn't rely on her to do anything. Her father, who was rarely home, left the responsibility for the house and care of her siblings to Maria. When things were not done well, her father would yell at Maria and criticize her. She learned very early to do everything herself so that it was done right.

As an adult, Maria continued to find she couldn't rely on others. It was a self-fulfilling prophecy. Subconsciously, Maria looked for relationships with partners who would reinforce her need to be strong. She only felt attracted to men who were weak and helpless. Strong men did not excite her. Then when her partner failed, she'd blame him and say, "See, I told you so." If her partner began to assert himself or show independence, she'd lose interest in him.

Maria cursed her bad luck with men. She never saw that it was her own personality that led her to choose this particular type of partner again and again. It was only when Maria began to confront those personality qualities and to recognize her unexpressed character traits that she was able to find more balanced partners and build healthy relationships.

THE CODEPENDENT

Codependents define themselves by their weakness and their passivity. Outwardly, codependents are insecure and dependent upon others. They do such a good job of hiding their strength they convince themselves that they are inadequate and incapable when in fact they are not. As a result, they need the strength of the counterdependent to feel whole. Like the counterdependent, the codependent can be either male or female.

Codependents, too, learned their essential character traits as children. While the counterdependent learned to act strong, the codependent learned to survive by passively accepting whatever crisis occurred in his/her dysfunctional family environment.

Shelly's father was an alcoholic who would terrorize Shelly and her mother whenever he got drunk. Shelly's mother never fought back, nor did she attempt to get out of the situation.

One day Shelly's father got drunk and tore the house apart. Her mother took her into one of the bedrooms and closed the door.

They sat huddled together on the bed as they listened to her father stumble around breaking dishes and lamps and overturning the furniture.

"Why don't you make him stop?" Shelly screamed at her mother when she couldn't stand the fear anymore. "Why don't you do something?"

Shelly's mother took her in her arms and soothed her by teaching her how to survive a lion attack. "There's only one way to survive if a lion attacks," her mother whispered quietly in her ear. "Remember, lions are stronger and faster than we are. If we would try to fight back or run away, the lion would kill us. The only way to survive a lion attack is for us to lie down and pretend that we're dead so the lion will get bored with us and eventually leave us alone." She finished her story by telling Shelly that her father was like a wild lion when he was drunk, and if she could just turn off her feelings and act as if nothing was wrong, he would eventually stop and everything would be all right.

The primary mandate and injunction of the codependent are mirror images of the counterdependent's. The codependent learns:

• You must always act weak and helpless, or you will die.
• You must never reveal your strengths to anyone at any time, or you will die.

Counterdependent Mandate/Injunction	Codependent Mandate/Injunction
1. I must act strong.	1. I must act weak.
2. I must never show weakness.	2. I must never show strength.

Underneath their outward facade, however, codependents are very strong. Think how much strength and energy it takes to put up with a drunk for years, to put up with the abuse and never act out the anger. The problem is, all of their strength is directed into lying down and playing dead.

A woman came to me in counseling. "I can't do anything in my life," she told me. "I'm so weak and so helpless, nothing ever goes right."

I said, "Tell me about your life."

"Well, I'm married to a guy who's a cocaine, alcohol, and heroin addict. He hasn't worked a day in his life for the last eighteen years. I work three jobs just to support him. I also raise four kids. I'm working sixteen to eighteen hours a day. I make $42,000 a year and that bastard spends it all on drugs. There's nothing I can do to stop him."

I said, "Why do you stay with him?"

She looked shocked, "How would I support myself without him?"

I said, "It seems to me you can earn a living."

"I could not. What are you accusing me of? You'd think I'd stay with somebody like him if I were able to earn a living?"

"Aren't you earning $42,000 a year?"

"Yes, but that's only because—" and she had a string of "reasons" why she could not survive without him. She was locked into her role as a helpless victim, incapable of action. Without a willingness to recognize and acknowledge the formidable strength she already exercised in her life, nothing I could say would change that self-perception.

THE MIRROR EFFECT

The relationship of the counterdependent and the codependent to one another can be understood best by thinking about mirrors. For every tendency the counterdependent displays, the codependent displays its mirror image. These are the psychological locks that bind counterdependents and codependents together. There are four primary traits:

Counterdependents and Codependents
The Interlocking Traits

Counterdependents:		Codependents:
1. Grandiosity	←→	1. Insecurity
2. Independence	←→	2. Dependence
3. Self-centered	←→	3. Other-centered
4. Intrusiveness	←→	4. Lack of boundaries

Counterdependents are grandiose, independent, self-centered, and intrusive. Codependents are insecure, dependent, other-centered, and receptive.

Grandiosity/Insecurity

Grandiosity	Insecurity
Mandate/Injunction	Mandate/Injunction
I must be more than;	I must be less than;
I must not be less than.	I must not be equal to or
	more than.

Counterdependents follow the mandate/injunction: "I must be more than everyone else; I must never be less than anyone else." They hypnotize themselves with fantasies of power: "If I can get to be big enough, strong enough, and secure enough, I can be okay." The problem is, every time they get bigger and better and stronger, it's not enough. No matter how many bench presses they can do, how secure they are, or how much they have, underneath they're scared. They can't accept this about themselves, however, so they repress the feeling and even their awareness of it. They cling to their codependent partner who can make them feel powerful.

Codependents are insecure. The mandate/injunction construct codependents follow is: "I must be less than others; I must not be equal to or more than others." They may be extremely competent but, unless they have someone powerful to pat them on the head and affirm them, they are terrified to act on their own. This is why codependents are so often exploited at work. The only way codependents can acknowledge their competence and power is to work for others. They run the organization for their counterdependent bosses who take all the credit and pay them minimum salaries.

Counterdependent people feel a sense of entitlement. "I am entitled to have what I want, when I want, where I want, and how I want." Codependents feel very deprived. "I don't really have a right to anything. I'm just grateful for what I can get." With minimal expectations, they make few demands and receive little from life or their relationships.

Independence/Dependence

Independence Mandate/Injunction	Dependence Mandate/Injunction
I must rely on myself;	I must rely on others;
I must not rely on others.	I must not rely on myself.

Counterdependents are independent. "I must rely on myself," they learn. "I can't rely on others." Codependents learn the opposite mandate and injunction: "I must rely on others; I can't rely on myself." Both are reflex actions backed up by automatic thinking.

A counterdependent man married to a codependent woman gets up in the morning and can't find his wallet. "I couldn't have lost it," he thinks. "She put it somewhere." So he storms into the room and says, "What did you do with my wallet?"

She hasn't seen his wallet, but she says, "I must have put it somewhere. Let me look." She thinks, "If his wallet is lost it must somehow be my fault. I didn't put it away right for him. It must be something wrong with me." Anytime anything goes wrong, the counterdependent will blame somebody else. Anytime anything goes wrong, the codependent will blame himself or herself. If anything goes right, the counterdependent will take credit for it. Codependents tend to give away credit when anything goes right. If they took credit for it, it would be an admission of strength.

Counterdependents are demanding and praise-seeking. Codependent people are complying and approval seeking; their need for approval is a primary driving force in their lives.

Self-centered/Other-centered

Self-centered Mandate/Injunction	Other-centered Mandate/Injunction
I must focus on self; I must not focus on others.	I must focus on others; I must not focus on self.

Counterdependents are self-centered and insensitive. "I must focus on myself," they believe. "I must not focus on others." Counterdependents don't know what other people feel and most genuinely don't care. They are exploitative and use others. The tendency of the counterdependents to depersonalize others and view them as objects locks into the tendency of codependents to depersonalize themselves and think of themselves as objects.

"Don't worry about a cab," Diane told her coworkers when they arrived at the airport at 12:45 A.M., too late for the last bus downtown. "I'll just call Dick and have him come get us. Dick won't mind."

Codependents are overly sensitive to others. "I must focus on others; I must never focus on myself," they think. They are so other-focused, they can anticipate another person's feelings and wants without his or her having to say anything. "I can always tell what kind of a day Ralph had," Mary told her friend proudly, "just by the way he opens the door."

Codependents are altruistic. Their need for approval and affirmation from their partner is so great, they often fail to protect themselves. "All right, so I take some punishment, but that's okay.

I'm willing to sacrifice myself for this relationship." As a result, they are very nurturing to everyone but themselves.

Intrusive/Receptive

Intrusive Mandate/Injunction	Receptive Mandate/Injunction
I must control others; I must not let others control me.	I must allow others to control me; I must not control others.

Counterdependents are controlling and intrusive. They think, "I must control others; I must not let others control me." They frequently invade the privacy of others without thinking about it. They believe they are entitled to special access that others are not. At the same time, they themselves set up very rigid personal boundaries and are expert at keeping other people away.

Codependents are very poorly defended and as a result are receptive to the intrusiveness of others. "I must let others control me," they believe. "I must not control others." They don't know how to stand up for themselves and so make easy victims. What codependents and their partners don't realize is how passively controlling codependents can be.

These four interlocking traits bind counterdependents and codependents together. The more extreme the two styles are, the more of a death grip the partners find themselves in. They are trapped in a compulsive relationship.

CHANGING PARTNERS

In acting out their fixed roles, the counterdependent and codependent create a mutual scapegoat system. When troubles develop in the relationship, each partner feels victimized by the other. They don't think about how their behavior hurts their partner or the relationship, but only how their partner has hurt them. They blame the problems in the relationship on the qualities of their partner, without recognizing the part they themselves play.

The counterdependent, the controlling personality in the relationship, is the overt villain. "The more I can control, the more I can manipulate, the stronger I can be, the more I can get my partner to do what I want." Counterdependents control by creating a crisis, while codependents are passively lying down and playing dead, surviving the crisis their partner creates.

Rob, a typical counterdependent, decided he wanted to have a party. He asked his girlfriend Sally to help him with it, and she agreed. "Here's what I'd like," Rob said. "I'd like to have a party, nice and simple. I want to just go out and buy platters of food at the delicatessen and do everything really simply."

Sally, in a manner typical of codependents, said, "No, no, no. If you're going to have a party, we're going to have to do it right. And I'll be able to help you with it. I'll get a caterer and I'll hire your housecleaner to really get the house clean. You won't have to worry about a thing; I'll take care of it all."

"I don't want to go to all that work. I just want a bunch of friends over. It seems like you're making it harder than it needs to be. Let's just keep it simple."

"No, don't worry, I'll take care of it. You won't have to work harder, but it's important that we impress your friends."

Rob replied, "Okay, as long as you'll take care of it, I'll turn the whole thing over to you."

As time got closer to the party, Sally hadn't done anything. Rob asked her about it. "Don't worry, I'll take care of everything," Sally said with a smile. Privately she grimaced and said to herself, "What a selfish, inconsiderate person! Can't he see how much I have to do? Can't he see how much work this party's going to be? The least he could have done is offer to help. But if I said anything, he'd just get mad and he wouldn't do it anyway, so why bother? If I don't take care of him, he'll never take care of himself."

On the day of the party, Sally got up at 5 A.M. to clean the house and cook a fancy dinner. Rob slept in until 9 A.M. and came downstairs. Sally was angry and storming around the house. When Rob asked her was was wrong, Sally said, "I just thought you'd get up early and help me with all this work. After all, it is your party."

Rob got angry with her. "I told you to keep it simple! You should have listened to me. I'm not bailing you out of this one. You said you would handle it, handle it. See you later, at the party." And he left the house.

Sally took care of everything, and of course it was a wonderful party, except that Sally was so tired and so burned out that she couldn't have a good time. She spent the evening telling all her friends how unreasonable her boyfriend was and how she did him a big favor producing this party and he just didn't appreciate it.

As the top dog, the counterdependent gets the blame for the conflict in the relationship. What neither partner realizes is that the top dog is not in control, the under dog is. The codependent is using tyranny of the weak to manipulate the situation. The codependent partner can't show strength or overtly control his/her partner, so he/she manipulates behind the scenes, saying *yes* while meaning *no*. Far from being a helpless victim, the codependent in fact controls the relationship through his/her weakness and passivity.

When you're standing on somebody, you appear to be on top, but in fact the person under you is holding you up. If he or she chooses not to support you, you fall down. Controllers, that is, counterdependents, need to have a victim—the codependent—so they can't afford to have their victim leave them or they will lose their power. Neither realizes that both partners are equally responsible for the problems in the relationship.

The codependent complains, "The relationship would be so good if you weren't so strong and domineering and didn't push me around so much."

The counterdependent responds, "What do you mean? If I didn't take charge of this relationship, you'd never do anything right. You're so insecure, you can't get anything done. You're always trying to tear me down. Sometimes I wonder why I married somebody like you."

When the pain and the frustration each partner feels with the other reach the breaking point, they usually end the relationship and look for new partners. So when counterdependents leave their codependent partner for someone new, with whom do they fall in love? Another codependent. Different size, different shape, different career, but the same underlying psychological dynamics and personality.

Similarly, when codependents tire of their counterdependent partner's efforts to control, use, and manipulate them, they, too, get rid of their partner. And what do codependents rush out and find? Another counterdependent.

Without understanding the dynamics at work in their failed relationship, the partners are doomed to re-create the same problems in the next relationship—and the next and the next. If you continue to act out your extreme codependent or counterdependent personality traits, you have no choice but to connect with someone with the complementary traits you need to feel complete. As relationship counselor Earnie Larsen has observed, "If you refuse to change your personality, you'll find that no matter where you go . . . there you are."

The problems experienced by counterdependent and codependent partners are not simply *us* problems or *you* problems. When it comes to personality styles, the problems have to do with *me*. The steel trap in which these individuals find themselves lies within as they act out the self-defeating mandates and injunctions that keep them from healthy intimacy.

Until we begin to address the problems within ourselves, therefore, nothing our partner does can fix us. Because, as Earnie Larsen also said, "If nothing changes, nothing changes."

THE SHADOW SELF

The ironic truth about counterdependent and codependent personalities is that the very qualities they seek so desperately in their partners are in fact the specific traits they already possess. They can't consciously know it, however, because we have been taught all their lives to repress these qualities. Psychologists call the repressed side of a person's personality the shadow self. It is this denial of a vital part of ourselves that makes us feel incomplete.

The most important step in developing a balanced personality is to recognize the presence of our shadow self. The counterdependent must recognize that he/she secretly harbors a codependent shadow self that feels pain and vulnerability and needs to be loved and nurtured. The codependent needs to see that deep within himself/herself exists a counterdependent shadow self—a strong and competent person, capable of taking care of himself/herself, regardless what others think.

The counterdependent and the codependent are so evenly balanced in their traits that, from time to time, when either one briefly acts out his or her shadow self, the other also does. Each blames the other for this unaccountable behavior.

Angela told Todd one evening, "It's your brother's birthday in two weeks. What are you going to get him?"

"I don't know," Todd replied. "I haven't thought about it."

"Well, I'm tired of buying all the presents for your relatives. You never think about mine; you never even think about your own relatives. You always leave it to me. The least you can do is buy a lousy birthday present for your brother."

"Don't worry; I'll get the present."

The next evening Todd brought home a mystery novel.

"What's this for?" asked Angela.

"It's the present I got for my brother."

"Well, that's not very nice. He doesn't even like to read. Why would you get something like that? I meant get something he'd like." Todd lost his temper and began yelling. At first Angela sat quietly, but then, when Todd continued to berate her, accusing her of nagging and criticizing, she grew angry and lashed out at him, accusing him of being selfish and uncaring. Todd recognized that there was a degree of truth in what Angela said and suddenly felt guilty and ashamed.

Both Angela and Todd first acted out their inherent personality traits as codependent and counterdependent. Angela issued an unconscious invitation to Todd to exhibit his natural counterdependent traits: "Don't worry, I'll handle it!" She then proceeded to manipulate the situation by her criticism. When Todd lost his temper and began to victimize Angela, her counterdependent shadow self lashed out, causing Todd to connect to his weak and vulnerable shadow self. Each blamed the situation on the other: "If he hadn't been yelling at me, I never would have said those things. He lost his temper first." Angela explained.

"I only feel weak and hopeless because Angela tore me down," Todd thought.

The pathway to healthy flexibility lies in making peace with our shadow self, accepting and integrating its qualities into our everyday behaviors. The trouble is, the first few times we consciously try to express the traits of this shadow self, we experience anxiety, fear, guilt, and shame—the emotions our family of origin used to make us act the way they needed us to act. As a result, coming to terms the shadow self is often very difficult and painful. It requires us to violate the image of ourselves that we learned as children.

BEGINNING TO CHANGE

People can begin to discover their shadow selves by discussing their perceptions of their strengths and weaknesses with others and asking for feedback. Often people find this process requires the help of a trained psychotherapist.

During this process, many people find out things about themselves that they don't like. As they begin discovering their shadow selves, painful memories from childhood usually begin to emerge. People need to examine these memories, express the feelings they arouse, and figure out what they mean. This allows them to integrate the memories into their conscious identity as adults.

Sheila always saw herself as dependent, helpless, and victimized by others. Her self-evaluation taught her that a part of her was also strong and capable. Her first reaction was to judge herself harshly. "I'm a bitch just like my mother was," she said to her group one night. "I hate her and yet I turned out just like her!" As the group asked her to explain what she meant, a flood of long-forgotten and painful memories streamed through her mind. She saw images of her mother criticizing her, her father insulting her, and her brothers making fun of her.

As she talked about these memories and struggled with what they meant, Sheila began to see how she was taught to believe that being strong was wrong and dangerous. Because her mother, father, and brothers had used their strength to hurt her, she believed that if she were strong she would inevitably hurt others in the same way and this would make her a bad person. She mistakenly equated strength with being bad.

This is a common problem with people who were victimized as children. They come to believe that there are only two roles they can play in life—victim and victimizer. Healthy families teach children positive ways to get their needs met and flexibility in dealing with others so that no one is either victim or victimizer. Dysfunctional families, in their extreme all-or-nothing view of the world, teach their children to survive in extreme ways—to become either the victim and allow others to hurt them, or the victimizer and hurt others.

To free ourselves from this trap, we must accept responsibility for our actions and the consequences of these actions. When the counterdependent can recognize and acknowledge the victim in himself/herself, and the codependent can recognize the victimizer within himself/herself, a fundamental shift occurs. With effort, Sheila learned to accept her personal power and take responsibility for directing that power and energy in positive ways. This included acting in her own behalf so that she could choose to be powerful or vulnerable as she needed, to live the way she chose and build the healthy relationships she wanted.

ACHIEVING A HEALTHY BALANCE

Accepting our shadow self gives us the power of choice. When we incorporate our repressed traits into our self-image we can begin to choose from a range of behaviors that allow us to meet our needs more comfortably. We begin to express balance in our personality and our life-style and are no longer compelled to seek what we need from our partner in the context of a dysfunctional relationship. We know who we are and can accept ourselves as whole and complete human beings, with all our gifts and flaws. If counterdependent, we can learn that when we are tired, we can rest. When we are hurt or sad, we can cry. When we need love and caring, we can cuddle up with someone and ask for comfort. When we need self-protection, we can insulate ourselves from others. We can do all of these things without feeling ashamed and embarrassed.

If codependent, when we are angry, we can express it without shame or guilt. When we are threatened, we can set limits. When we are attacked, we can defend ourselves and openly fight back.

The balanced personality is characterized by four traits that constitute a middle ground between the extremes of the interlocking counterdependent and codependent personality traits.

The Pathway to Change

Counterdependent ⟶ Healthy ⟵ Codependent

1. Grandiose	⟶ Secure	⟵ 1. Insecure
2. Independent	⟶ Interdependent	⟵ 2. Dependent
3. Self-centered	⟶ Socially Interested	⟵ 3. Other-centered
4. Intrusive	⟶ Responsive	⟵ 4. Receptive

The first trait of a balanced personality is *security*. Rather than being grandiose or insecure, healthy people are secure in themselves. This sense of security is based upon a strong sense of self-esteem. Healthy people are positive and self-confident. They know they can meet the challenges of life with the help of others. They believe in their self-worth and their right to enjoy the good things that life has to offer.

The second trait of the healthy personality is *interdependence*. Healthy people can look within, contact their own strength, and act on that strength without asking anyone's permission. They are capable of contacting their weaknesses and dependence, too, and in a healthy, straightforward way communicate that dependence and receive the help they need from others.

One day thirteen-year-old Josh was trying to cut the lawn, but his lawn mower kept hitting a large rock embedded in the ground. Josh tried everything he could think of to move the rock. He pushed on it, pulled at it, dug a hole around it, and tried to pry it out with a stick and shovel. Nothing worked. Finally, in desperation, he went to his father.

"Dad," Josh said, "I give up. I've done everything I can but I can't move the rock."

His father said "Son, you haven't tried everything. There is one more thing you can try to get that rock moved."

"What's that?" Josh asked.

"You can ask for help. You don't have to do everything yourself."

Healthy people are *socially interested*. They are aware of their own needs and take appropriate actions to meet them. Because they are secure enough in themselves, they can be also concerned about the needs of others. They often choose to provide support and assistance to others. They are not willing, however, to give of themselves to such an extent that their own well-being suffers. Barring major catastrophes and emergencies, they will not sacrifice themselves to others.

The fourth trait of the balanced personality is *responsiveness*. Healthy people have a variety of ways to deal with others. They maintain flexible boundaries capable of affording them both safety and intimacy. The knowledge that they can protect themselves against unwanted intrusion when they need to makes it possible for them to open up and allow others to become close. If someone starts to exploit them, they can be assertive, even aggressive, in protecting themselves. This flexibility makes healthy intimate relationships possible.

LEARNING TO CHANGE

Changing from a counter- or codependent personality style requires time and patience, but if you are firm in your commitment to personal growth, you will see positive results.

Walter was cochair of the committee for a large fund-raising event to benefit the local high school. As the date of the program drew closer, Keri, Walter's cochair, called to tell him that the other committee members had agreed that he would not be included in the evening's program but was assigned to ticket collection and handling the reporters covering the event.

At first, Walter felt insulted at being left off the evening's agenda. He had worked very hard to bring the event about and felt that the committee had no right to relegate him to such a menial role.

His first urge was to lash out at Keri, his natural tendency as a counterdependent. He considered the biting words he could say and the accusations he could make to Keri and others on the committee. His next thought was that he knew the consequences of doing that. It would make him feel very good in the short run but very guilty later on. It would lead to bad feelings among everyone involved and perhaps compromise the event itself. Walter decided against it. Instead he said, "I understand what you're saying. I can't pretend I'm not disappointed. I'll have to think about this. I'll get back to you tomorrow."

When threatened, Walter still felt the impulse to respond in a characteristically counterdependent manner—but he could choose whether to act on it or not. He relied on his ability to recognize what he was thinking, how he was feeling, the urge to action, and the probable consequences of that action. This process helped him to choose a way of dealing with the situation that he could feel much better about in the long run.

THE PROCESS OF CHANGE

Even if you are trapped in a dysfunctional relationship, you can work toward establishing a healthy relationship. Change is possible, although it is not easy.

Personal growth and development progress through a series of four predictable stages: First there is the **recognition** that there is a relationship problem. This generally happens when one partner confronts the other about some specific aspects of relationship. As the partners face the difficulty in resolving these problems for themselves, they are motivated to go to the next stage and **to obtain outside help** in the form of objective information about their problems and their solutions.

The third stage involves completing an **intensive personal inventory and an inventory of your relationship.** You have to compare your relationship to known standards of healthy and dysfunctional relationships. In the fourth stage you must be willing to take what you've learned and apply it to **change** your relationship.

Relationship Change Requires
1. *Recognition* that there is a problem
2. *Outside help* in the form of information and techniques
3. *A personal and relationship inventory*
4. *Changing* unhealthy patterns to healthy patterns

Mitch and Shelly began to bottom out in their relationship. It happened as a result of Shelly's getting involved with ACOA groups. She realized that there were many things about Mitch and the relationship that she didn't like. One day, feeling particularly discouraged, she sat down and wrote out a list. Immediately, she suffered a panic attack. Her automatic thinking went off. "There's no way I can tell Mitch what I have just written."

Although she kept her list secret for months, the act of writing it had changed her. Shelly now became more aware of the problems in the relationship and when something happened that hurt her or made her unhappy, she knew it.

"It's not as bad as it could be," she told herself. "It could be worse. As far as men go, Mitch is really a pretty good catch." She knew she was lying to herself and it bothered her.

Mitch wasn't satisfied with the relationship, either, but he didn't know why. Shelly was meeting all of his needs, sort of. If he was honest, he wasn't really happy. The high-powered sex tapered off after about six or seven months. Shelly was still available to have sex with him, but he just couldn't get the highs he used to. Part of him blamed Shelly, but part of him blamed himself.

Mitch saw something else that disturbed him. "It seems like Shelly is on a different wavelength." The things that excited him seemed to mean very little to her. For his part, Mitch didn't enjoy the things that Shelly did and didn't understand why Shelly enjoyed them. Mitch felt that Shelly wasn't really being honest with him.

"If she would just grow up and be honest, she'd be able to give me what I want. That's her job." He felt she was playing a game or just going along to please him. He began to feel like he really didn't know her at all.

Then it happened. One evening Shelly told Mitch there was something she wanted to tell him. She took a deep breath, sat down, and read the list to him. Shelley began by telling him she thought he was a workaholic and that his work was more important to him than she was. "I feel like a second fiddle. You're working all the time. You never have time for me except when you want to have sex. And sometimes I wonder if you love me or you just want to have sex with me."

Shelly went on to tell him she often didn't enjoy their lovemaking. "I know you enjoy it, so I do the best I can to please you, but you're rough, you're too controlling, and you're too intense. It seems all you want is your own pleasure and you don't really care about mine."

Shelly also told him she was tired of listening to him and building up his ego all the time. "Sometimes I think you're self-centered," she said. "You brag about yourself all the time. You make grandiose, unrealistic plans. You often make a fool of yourself by bragging about yourself to our friends and I get embarrassed. I sometimes don't feel like you need me. You're so independent there isn't room for me."

She capped the whole thing off by telling Mitch she thought he was intrusive, insensitive, and didn't really care about her. "I sometimes feel used. It feels like you're only interested in me when I can tell you what you want to hear and do what you want me to do. That's no longer acceptable to me."

Mitch was devastated, although he couldn't show it. "I can't believe she's saying this." He thought they had a perfect relationship, but Shelly was telling him something different. "What's wrong with me?" he thought. "I feel like I'm going crazy."

It took Mitch several weeks to get his responses together. Then he wrote out a list and presented it to Shelly.

"I was really upset with the list you read to me, Shelly. As a matter of fact, it devastated me and it really hurt that you didn't see my pain. I couldn't believe what I was hearing and I couldn't believe you could be so cold and so callous in telling me about it."

Shelly sat rigidly in her chair. Inside she was scared to death. She expected Mitch to hit her or leave. Instead, he went on, "You criticize me for being grandiose. I have to be grandiose. You're so insecure you never plan anything. If I don't take charge, nothing ever happens. It seems like you are afraid to take a risk or do anything out of the ordinary without my making the decision."

Shelly winced because part of her deep inside said, "That's true. I won't do anything without this guy's endorsement." So he went on. "You say you want to be independent but I don't believe it. You depend on me a lot. When I try and tell you to be more independent you get mad. I don't include you in things because it feels like you're trying to smother me. When you do get involved, you end up criticizing my way of doing things. It's never good enough. You want to change it. It seems like you've made it your job in life to do a makeover on me and my personality. And I resent it. I thought you loved me."

Shelly was now ready to cry but she held it back. She wanted to hear what Mitch was saying. "He's not hitting me!" she thought in amazement. "He's not leaving me. He's not going crazy. He's talking to me." It was the last thing in the world she expected— that Mitch would actually talk to her about a problem.

Mitch continued. "I get confused. I love you and I want you to be happy. I want our relationship to work, but it seems that when I am being me, when I am acting the way I really want to act, when I'm doing the things that really make me feel alive and excited, it seems that those times you don't really like me. It seems like you're scared of me and that those things turn you off. I feel like I have to be something I'm not in order to make you happy and I'm just not willing to do that.

"Shelly, you give me mixed messages all the time. You look unhappy and I ask you about it, but you say everything is fine. I know you're lying but I don't know what to do about it because the more I pressure you, the more closed off you get."

Mitch continued. "You tell me I'm too aggressive sexually. You always act as if you enjoy it. You've always told me I'm a good lover and now all of a sudden I'm an insensitive monster in bed. Why didn't you tell me? How can I be responsible for your reactions when you act like everything's fine when it really isn't?"

He then told Shelly that he felt she became overly involved with people. "It seems like you sacrifice yourself to others. Your friends take advantage of you. Then you get angry with me when I tell you to stand up for yourself." At this point, Mitch started feeling like crying. He was really hurting on the inside. He felt very much alone. He felt very exposed. He wanted to get close to Shelly but he didn't know how, and, at this point, he didn't trust her. He felt that if he opened up and got close she'd clobber him. "It really hurts to think that you just put up with me," he told her. "I thought we had a good thing and now you tell me you just tolerate the things I do. And I'm having a real hard time with that."

Notice these complaints to Shelly. He felt Shelly was insecure, overdependent, other-centered to the point of being a martyr, and receptive to the point of pretending that she liked things that she really didn't like. All of these are codependent traits.

Now they had it on the table. They both knew that something was wrong and both were willing to try and fix it. Mitch knew his self-centeredness was a problem and he decided to change it. Mitch said, "I'll just stop being self-centered," but every time he tried he felt a sense of panic. His heart started pounding, he got very scared. Shelly had a similar problem. As a codependent Shelly was always focused on others and she realized she had lost herself in Mitch and decided to try and change that. She tried to focus on herself instead of Mitch and present aspects of herself to Mitch that she felt good about. But thinking about herself was terrifying. She was amazed at how caretaking Mitch could turn the fear off very quickly.

They both tried everything they could think of to address their problems, but nothing worked. They tried to talk it out and they ended up arguing. The relationship didn't get any better; in fact, it got worse. They began to feel hopeless. They didn't want the relationship to end, but they didn't know what else to do about it.

Fixing a troubled relationship is a tough process. Most of the time, we can't do it alone, so we need to get some outside help. The first form of help we need is new and accurate information that can give us a new way of thinking about the problem. Relatives and friends may be very willing to give advice and support but they are usually little help. They may mean well, but they're not experts in relationships.

I had an electrical problem in my house so I called my brother-in-law, a professional bricklayer, to fix the problem. He came over and worked on the problem for over six hours. In the end, he couldn't fix it. He told me, "There's no way to fix it. The lights will never work right." I wasn't satisfied, so I then called a professional electrician. The professional electrician came over, looked at the problem, worked on it for thirty-five minutes, and fixed it. As an expert electrician and not a bricklayer, he had accurate information and professional skills. He knew what to do and he did it.

You can begin to get the expert advice you need at the library or a bookstore. There are many good books as well as audio and video tapes on relationship problems and how to fix them. You can start the process by taking responsibility to learn new information and gain new insights about relationships.

The second form of help you need is objective feedback. You need somebody who can come into your relationship, look at what you're both doing, and honestly tell you what's going on. For many people professional counseling can be a lifesaver. Marriage and family counselors (designated M.F.C.C.) are trained to help couples communicate more effectively and to work together as a team. Counselors are knowledgeable about common relationship problems; they also know how to listen and how to give objective, unbiased feedback. They can also give you techniques to deflate the resistance that inevitably comes up when dealing with entrenched relationship issues. With professional counseling you can learn the fastest and easiest ways to resolve your relationship problems.

How do you know if you need professional counseling? Sit down with your partner and try to work out your problems by yourselves. If you end up running around in circles and not getting anywhere, you need a referee. Most couples do initially. Relationship problems are typically caused by unconscious habits that we blindly repeat over and over again. We're both so close to the problem, we can't see how we prevent its solution.

The third step in relationship change is to clarify the problem by means of an inventory of ourselves and our relationship. Mitch and Shelly worked together to inventory their problems. They used three categories: my problems, your problems, and our problems together. Of course, they both had a number of problems, but their goal was to identify the two major problems in each category. Mitch identified self-centeredness and extreme independence. Shelly identified insecurity and other-centeredness.

Then they both sat down together and said, "What are the biggest problems in our relationship?" They said they both expected the relationship to provide instant gratification. Mitch wanted instant excitement and intense sexuality. Shelly wanted to feel affirmed, complete, and secure. With new information, they realized their relationship was not a drug and shouldn't be used as one. And they both had a tendency to lose their boundaries. They would get overinvolved with each other to the exclusion of everyone and everything else. They wrote down these problem lists.

They were ready now for the fourth stage, which is change. They had to start doing things differently. This was the most difficult and scary of all, but they made a commitment and stuck to it.

MAKING AMENDS

The first change we have to make is to acknowledge that our current personality style has caused us problems and has hurt our partner. Before we can change, we must accept responsibility for the pain we have caused and apologize to our partner for hurting him/her. It's called making amends.

Mitch and Shelly sat down and began to talk about their problems. Mitch started the process. "Shelly," he said, "I love you. I really do! I know I've done things that hurt you. I know I've caused you pain and I'm sorry. I thought I was helping. Now I can see that I wasn't. The truth is I'm not always in control of what I do. When I get scared or feel weak and helpless I go on automatic pilot. My grandiosity and self-centeredness flare up. It seems like I have to invade your space and criticize you. I can see it's a problem. I know it hurts you. I'm sorry and I want to work at changing it."

Shelly then said, "Mitch, I'm part of the problem. I'm afraid to tell you how I feel. I'm intimidated by you. I always blamed my fear on you and used you as an excuse for not being honest and telling you things that I knew you needed to hear. My passivity has hurt you and it's hurt our relationship. I'm sorry and I'm willing to work with you to change it."

This amends process sets the stage for change. It allowed both Mitch and Shelly to put the past behind them, forgive, talk honestly, and resolve unfinished past experiences. The process gave them hope that their love was still alive. It helped them see that they both created the problem and that together they could resolve it. It affirmed to both of them that they were willing to work at this together.

The next step in changing our personality is to practice the traits of the personality style opposite to our own. Counterdependent partners have to stop exaggerating their strengths and learn how to accept and communicate their weakness and insecurity. They must learn to recognize when they're being self-centered and consciously try to focus their attention on their partners. They need to stop being the overt controller of the relationship and allow the relationship to become a partnership. They also need to realize that their grandiosity is a cover-up for fear and insecurity. They need to start telling their partners about their fears and feelings of weakness. They need to become aware of their extreme independence and learn how to depend upon their partners and give their partners credit for helping them. Finally, counterdependent partners have to recognize their tendency to be intrusive. They have to back off and stop intimidating their partners and stop invading their partner's privacy.

Codependents need to recognize that they use their feelings of insecurity and weakness as an excuse to avoid recognizing and taking responsibility for their strengths and capabilities. They need to stop seeking to manipulate their partner and exercising the tyranny of the weak. Instead, they have to learn to recognize and act upon their strengths. They need to recognize when they are insecure and learn how to challenge themselves: "Am I really unable to do this or am I just scaring myself out of trying?" They need to learn how to act in spite of the fear.

THE OUTCOMES OF HEALTHY CHANGES

The best way to address a troubled relationship in which counter-dependent and codependent personality traits are interfering with our ability to get love right is to involve our partner in the process of growth and change, as Mitch and Shelly did. If, however, this is not possible, you can decide to work on your own development separate from your partner. This approach is more difficult and puts the relationship at greater risk of dissolution.

It is important to keep in mind that counterdependents and co-dependents come together to establish a psychological balance. The relationship survives only so long as both partners maintain the equilibrium. If you grow and change and your partner does not, an imbalance occurs. The more you move toward a healthy balance of traits, the less you will support and reinforce extreme personality styles in your partner.

With all good intentions, people say, "I'm going to stop meeting my partner's pathological needs. I'm not going to fall back into my old, unbalanced patterns." They are then bewildered when their partner becomes angry and upset. They don't realize that by changing the *me*, they have upset the balance of *us*, the relationship. Of course their partner is angry.

As you begin to embrace your shadow self and start to change who you are, your partner will be confronted with a choice. He or she will either also change and work with you to find a healthier balance or he or she will leave.

You need to realize that your actions will alter the relationship, whether for better or worse. Discuss your intentions with your partner. You can say, "We're going to need to renegotiate this relationship because I am no longer willing to act out in ways that our arrangement says I have to. I'm no longer willing to care for you in pathological ways. I am no longer willing to put up with your unacceptable behaviors."

Personal growth and change is a very powerful process. At the outset, it is impossible to know where you're going to come out on the other side. You need to make a commitment to that process and let your partner know what you're doing in as caring and sensitive a way as you can.

"You'll be affected by my changes because as I change I won't be the same person you originally got involved with. I'm going to become fundamentally different and you don't know who I really am. Right now I don't know who I really am. We have to take the risk together that maybe at the end of this process of discovering who I really am, I may become somebody that's unacceptable to you. And you may become somebody that's unacceptable to me."

Breaking out of your counterdependent or codependent personality takes courage. It is a difficult task, and at times, downright terrifying. With effort, however, you can achieve a healthy balance. In doing so, you will have acquired the ability to be true to yourself while being intimately involved with your partner. You can become secure in who you are and what you need and want from others. You will be secure enough, too, to be able to give to others what they ask of you. Your interdependence will enable you to follow the direction of others, knowing that you are also capable of leading.

When you are socially interested, you can interact freely with others without imposing your identity on them or allowing them to intrude on you. When you are responsive, you are flexible enough to be truly intimate in a relationship that can offer you both passion and safety.

Relationship growth and change mean you can become a true choice maker, with the freedom to do and have what you want in life. In particular, you can choose your partner on the basis of who he or she really is, who you really are, and the type of relationship you want to have, because you will no longer need to satisfy your own imbalance and inner emptiness.

Addictive Relationship Trait Questionnaire

Part I: Self-evaluation

Instructions: The following questionnaire is designed to help you determine whether you tend to be counterdependent or codependent in your relationship style. It is rare to find someone who is totally codependent or totally counterdependent. Most of us have a balance of both traits with a definite tendency toward one style more than the other. Each statement asks you to choose between two different answers. Select the answer that best fits you most of the time.

When in an intimate relationship I am most likely to feel

____1. A. powerful B. ineffectual

____2. A. self-confident B. uncertain

____3. A. self-important B. insignificant

____4. A. entitled to special treatment from my partner B. unable to get what I need from my partner

____5. A. special B. ordinary

When in an intimate relationship and a problem develops, I tend to

____6. A. trust my own ability to solve it. B. trust my partner's ability to solve it.

____7. A. distrust my partner's ability to solve it. B. distrust my own ability to solve it.

____8. A. blame my partner for causing the problem. B. blame myself for causing the problem.

When I think about myself, I generally

____9. A. overidentify with my strengths. B. overidentify with my weaknesses.

____10. A. deny my weaknesses. B. deny my strengths.

In a relationship I am more likely to

____11. A. make demands of my partner. B. expect my partner to make demands of me.

If my partner could give me only one of the following things, I would like to get more

____12. A. praise for what I have done. B. approval that tells me I am okay.

I feel most fulfilled in a relationship when I can

____13. A. relax and not have to pay attention to my partner's needs. B. intuitively sense my partner's needs and meet those needs without being asked.

If my partner and I had legitimate conflicting needs I feel that the right thing to do would be to

____14. A. take care of my needs first.   B. take care of my partner's needs first.

I feel better when my partner

____15. A. takes care of me.   B. allows me to take care of him or her.

In relationships I tend to

____16. A. get close to my partner while keeping myself safe.   B. get close to my partner by making myself vulnerable.

____17. A. not tell my partner things that could hurt me later.   B. tell my partner everything even if he or she might hurt me because of it.

____18. A. directly ask my partner for what I want.   B. wait for my partner to give me what I want.

Part II: Partner Evaluation

Instructions: The following questionnaire is designed to help you to determine whether your partner tends to be counterdependent or codependent in his/her relationship style. Remember, this is your impression of your partner. Ask your partner to complete a self-evaluation (Part I of this questionnaire) and then compare his or her answers with yours. Select the answer that best fits your partner most of the time.

When I am in an intimate relationship my partner is most likely to feel

____1. A. powerful   B. ineffectual

____2. A. self-confident   B. uncertain

____3. A. self-important   B. insignificant

____4. A. entitled to special treatment from me   B. unable to get what he/she really needs from me

____5. A. special   B. ordinary

When I am in an intimate relationship and a problem develops my partner tends to

___6. A. trust his or her   B. trust my ability to solve it.
     own ability to solve it.

___7. A. distrust his or her   B. distrust my ability to solve
     ability to solve it.   it.

___8. A. blame me for caus-   B. blame self for causing the
     ing the problem.   problem

When my partner talks about self he or she generally

___9. A. overidentifies with   B. overidentifies with weak-
     strengths.   nesses.

___10. A. denies weak-   B. denies strengths.
     nesses.

In our relationship my partner is more likely to

___11. A. make demands of   B. expect me to make demands
     me.   of him or her.

**If I could give my partner only one of the following things, he or
she would like me to give more**

___12. A. praise for what he/   B. approval that tells him/her
     she has done.   he/she is okay.

**My partner seems to feel most fulfilled in a relationship when he
or she can**

___13. A. relax and not have   B. intuitively sense what my
     to pay attention to my   needs are and meet those
     needs.   needs without being asked.

**If my partner and I had legitimate conflicting needs, my partner
would probably feel that the right thing to do would be to**

___14. A. take care of his or   B. take care of my needs first.
     her own needs first.

My partner seems to feel better when I

___15. A. take care of him or   B. allow him or her to take care
     her.   of me.

In our relationship, my partner tends to

___16. A. get close to me   B. get close fast even if he or
     while keeping self   she gets hurt.
     safe.

___**17.** A. not tell me things that could hurt him or her later.   B. tell me everything even if I could use it later to hurt him or her.

___**18.** A. directly ask for what he or she wants.   B. wait for me to give what he or she wants.

Relationship Trait Questionnaire
Scoring Sheet

Part I: Self-evaluation:

1. A = ___   B = ___
2. A = ___   B = ___
3. A = ___   B = ___
4. A = ___   B = ___
5. A = ___   B = ___

Subtotal 1:   A = ___   B = ___

6. A = ___   B = ___
7. A = ___   B = ___
8. A = ___   B = ___
9. A = ___   B = ___
10. A = ___   B = ___
11. A = ___   B = ___
12. A = ___   B = ___

Subtotal 2:   A = ___   B = ___

13. A = ___   B = ___
14. A = ___   B = ___
15. A = ___   B = ___

Subtotal 3:   A = ___   B = ___

16. A = ___   B = ___
17. A = ___   B = ___
18. A = ___   B = ___

Subtotal 4:   A = ___   B = ___

Grand Total for Myself: A = ___   B = ___

Relationship Trait Questionnaire
Scoring Sheet

Part II: Partner Evaluation:

1. A = ___ B = ___
2. A = ___ B = ___
3. A = ___ B = ___
4. A = ___ B = ___
5. A = ___ B = ___

Subtotal 5: A = ___ B = ___

6. A = ___ B = ___
7. A = ___ B = ___
8. A = ___ B = ___
9. A = ___ B = ___
10. A = ___ B = ___
11. A = ___ B = ___
12. A = ___ B = ___

Subtotal 6: A = ___ B = ___

13. A = ___ B = ___
14. A = ___ B = ___
15. A = ___ B = ___

Subtotal 7: A = ___ B = ___

16. A = ___ B = ___
17. A = ___ B = ___
18. A = ___ B = ___

Subtotal 8: A = ___ B = ___

Grand Total for My Partner: A = ___ B = ___

Interpretation

Part I of this questionnaire measures your preference for either counterdependent or codependent behaviors in a relationship. It does not measure the degree to which those behaviors and preferences create dysfunction in your relationship.

1. Grandiosity and Insecurity

Subtotal 1 indicates your tendency toward either grandiosity or insecurity in a relationship. If you selected three or more answers of A, you tend toward grandiosity. If you selected three or more answers of B, you tend toward insecurity.

A. According to this questionnaire, I tend to be:

_____1. grandiose   _____2. insecure

B. I____with what the questionnaire indicates.

_____1. strongly agree   _____3. disagree
_____2. agree   _____4. strongly disagree

2. Independence and Dependence

Subtotal 2 indicates your tendency toward either independence or dependence in a relationship. If you selected four or more answers of A, you tend toward independence. If you selected two or more answers of B, you tend toward dependence.

A. According to this questionnaire, I tend to be:

_____1. independent   _____2. dependent

B. I____with what the questionnaire indicates.

_____1. strongly agree   _____3. disagree
_____2. agree   _____4. strongly disagree

3. Self-centered and Other-centered

Subtotal 3 indicates your tendency to be either self-centered or other-centered in a relationship. If you selected two or more answers of A, you tend to be self-centered. If you selected two or more answers of B, you tend to be other-centered.

A. According to this questionnaire, I tend to be:

_____1. self-centered   _____2. other-centered

B. I____with what the questionnaire indicates.

_____1. strongly agree   _____3. disagree
_____2. agree   _____4. strongly disagree

4. Intrusive and Receptive

Subtotal 4 indicates your tendency to be either intrusive or receptive in a relationship. If you selected two or more answers of A, you tend to be intrusive. If you selected two or more answers of B, you tend to be receptive.

A. According to this questionnaire, I tend to be:

___1. intrusive   ___2. receptive

B. I___with what the questionnaire indicates

___1. strongly agree   ___3. disagree

___2. agree   ___4. strongly disagree

5. Counterdependent and Codependent

Grand Total 1 indicates your tendency to be either counterdependent or codependent in your overall relationship style. If you selected nine or more answers of A, your overall relationship style tends to be counterdependent. If you selected nine or more answers of B, your overall relationship style tends to be codependent.

A. According to this questionnaire I tend to be:

___1. counterdependent   ___2. codependent

B. I___with what the questionnaire indicates.

___1. strongly agree   ___3. disagree

___2. agree   ___4. strongly disagree

Interpretation of Part II
1. Grandiosity and Insecurity

Subtotal 5 indicates your perception of your partner's tendency toward either grandiosity or insecurity in the relationship. If you selected three or more answers of A, you tend to see your partner as being grandiose. If you selected three or more answers of B, you tend to see your partner as being insecure.

A. According to this questionnaire, I tend to see my partner as:

___1. grandiose   ___2. insecure

B. I___with what the questionnaire indicates.

___1. strongly agree   ___3. disagree

___2. agree   ___4. strongly disagree

2. Independence and Dependence

Subtotal 6 indicates your perception of your partner's tendency toward either independence or dependence in a relationship. If you selected four or more answers of A, you tend toward independence. If you selected two or more answers of B, you tend toward dependence.

A. According to this questionnaire, you tend to see you partner as:

_____1. independent   _____2. dependent

B. I_____with what the questionnaire indicates.

_____1. strongly agree   _____3. disagree
_____2. agree   _____4. strongly disagree

3. Self-centered and Other-centered

Subtotal 7 indicates your perception of your partner's tendency to be either self-centered or other-centered in the relationship. If you selected two or more answers of A, you probably see your partner as self-centered. If you selected two or more answers of B, you probably see your partner as other-centered.

A. According to this questionnaire, my partner tends to be:

_____1. self-centered   _____2. other-centered

B. I_____with what the questionnaire indicates.

_____1. strongly agree   _____3. disagree
_____2. agree   _____4. strongly disagree

4. Intrusive and Receptive

Subtotal 8 indicates your perception of your partner's tendency to be either intrusive or receptive in the relationship. If you selected two or more answers of A, you probably see your partner as intrusive. If you selected two or more answers of B, you probably see your partner as receptive.

A. According to this questionnaire, I tend to see my partner as:

_____1. intrusive   _____2. receptive

B. I_____with what the questionnaire indicates.

_____1. strongly agree   _____3. disagree
_____2. agree   _____4. strongly disagree

5. Counterdependent and Codependent

Grand Total 2 indicates your perception of your partner's tendency to be either counterdependent or codependent in his/her overall relationship style. If you selected nine or more answers of A, your partner's overall relationship style tends to be counterdependent. If you selected nine or more answers of B, your partner's overall relationship style tends to be codependent.

A. According to this questionnaire, my partner tends to be:

_____1. counterdependent   _____2. codependent

B. I_____with what the questionnaire indicates.

_____1. strongly agree   _____3. disagree

_____2. agree   _____4. strongly disagree

Chapter 10

INTIMATE COMMUNICATION:
THE BEGINNING OF CHANGE

PRINCIPAL CHOICES
• To learn and practice healthy communication skills.
• To recognize the unfinished issues that activate your need to resolve.
• To learn to distinguish between emotional process issues and practical issues in relationships.
• To learn to listen to, understand, take seriously, and affirm your partner's point of view when dealing with emotional, process level issues.
• To practice problem-solving on practical issues.

"**J**oyce and I just can't communicate," Steve said to his friend Joe. "We get into these arguments that go nowhere. Sometimes I think it's hopeless!"

Joyce was talking with her friend Mary. "It happened again last night," Joyce said. "I wanted to talk with Steve about how much he's working. He's burning himself out and I'm getting worried. I made up my mind that I wouldn't overreact, but once he got started, I just couldn't stop myself. We argued for about an hour and got no place. Sometimes I think he does it deliberately."

Communication is an ongoing problem for many couples. When they try to work through a problem, the communication breaks down and they go around and around in endless circles. Often it seems the harder they try, the more useless it becomes.

Most couples lack the skills necessary to communicate effectively in a way that validates and affirms their partner. This is especially true with emotionally charged subjects. When they are angry, they want to express their anger right then; they overreact and drop emotional bombs. Or when they feel accused of wrongdoing by their partner, they want to defend themselves at all costs, to prove they are right and their partner is wrong. In these situations, neither partner listens to the other because both are intent on meeting their own needs. Tempers flare and another pointless argument ensues.

To avoid these "go nowhere" arguments, couples must master a range of healthy communication skills. First, we need to learn how to express ourselves completely and to listen carefully. Many problems occur between couples simply because of unclear communication. Healthy partners talk *and* listen in a meaningful way.

Second, when we encounter a situation that generates strong feelings, particularly negative emotions, we need to learn how to recognize the source of those feelings. What's really going on? Are we angry because of something our partner has done, or because something in the present situation has triggered emotions left over from previous experiences? We are drawn to our partner in part because of our need to resolve past trauma. When we become intimate with our partner, something about this person activates the unresolved issues we carry with us from previous experiences, especially our childhood. Reexperiencing this trauma allows us to feel the emotions and work them through. We can do this, however, only if we recognize these feelings for what they are. We must develop the ability to separate the here-and-now issues from past unfinished business.

We then need to bring these issues to our partner in a rational dialogue that enables both of us to be heard and understood in a safe environment. Talking through painful feelings with our partner helps us resolve the issue and bring closure to it in a way that enhances our understanding of ourselves and our partner.

Finally, couples need a basic problem-solving process they can use to find the best solution to the practical issues they inevitably encounter. This involves understanding what aspects of the situation are my problems, which are your problems, and which are our problems, identifying the options available, and choosing the best one.

COMMUNICATION 101

When a couple comes into therapy with the goal to improve their relationship, I begin with the basics. I teach them a simple formula to develop fundamental communication skills. Many couples discover that using this formula has a profound effect on their relationship.

Communication is a two-part process. One person originates the communication and the other receives it. Unfortunately, we often reduce this two-part process by half. We talk but we don't listen. We engage in sequential monologues: I talk, you talk, I talk, you talk, and neither of us really listens to the other.

To communicate effectively, we must change this pattern so that when our partner talks, we engage in *active listening*. When we actively listen, we are fully focused on what the other person is saying to us. We are not thinking of our own needs or what we are going to say next. When he or she is finished, we *paraphrase* what we have heard. That is, after the other person tells us something, we repeat in our own words what we heard: "What I hear you saying is . . ." Then we do an accuracy check by asking, "Am I right?"

This exercise is very valuable for couples, especially if they have been together for a long time and have fallen into poor communication habits. They may have become so used to their partner—the way he/she thinks, the way he/she typically responds to certain situations—that they come to think they don't have to listen to what is being said. They've heard it before. Instead, they practice mind-reading; they know what their partner is going to say before he/she says it. They don't bother to find out if they are right or not. Other times, they "know better" than to believe what their partner says: "He says it's all right if we go to the movies instead of watching the football game, but I know he doesn't mean it. He really wants to stay home. That's how selfish he is!"

Begin using this formula on a regular basis with simple issues that have no emotional content.

Bob took care of the family's two cars. He was in charge of their routine maintenance and for taking them to the garage when necessary. Tuesday evening after dinner Bob said, "Laura, I've scheduled your car for a tune-up at the garage Thursday morning at nine. You can take my car to work that day and I'll drive yours to the garage. I can walk to work from there."

Laura told Bob, "What I'm hearing you say is that you've scheduled my car for a tune-up at the garage on Thursday morning. You'll lend me your car to take to work while you take mine to the garage, since you can walk to work from there. Is that right?"

"Yes, it is."

"That's fine, Bob. Don't forget that Thursday afternoons I have my meeting downtown and then I usually end up driving my co-workers home. I hate to worry about having enough gas. Can you make sure your car has enough gas? Can you stop by the gas station Wednesday for a fill-up?"

"What I'm hearing you say is that on Thursday afternoons you have your meeting downtown and then drive your coworkers home. You hate to worry about whether you'll have enough gas, so you are asking me to fill up the tank on Wednesday. Is that right?"

"Yes, it is. Can you do it?"

"Yes, I can do it; I'll be happy to. I'll stop on my way home from work Wednesday afternoon."

"You're saying you'll stop to get gas on your way home from work Wednesday afternoon. Thank you, that's fine."

Practicing this process can also help you evaluate the effectiveness of your present communication habits. Do you or your partner have difficulty paraphrasing your partner's communication? Do you or your partner need to state your meaning more than once before the other can accurately paraphrase it?

This formula is simple, but the benefits of using it can be profound. The reason is that this way of relating to our partner satisfies a very basic human need. We all need to be heard, taken seriously, and understood. When our partner takes the time and effort to actively listen and to verify what we have said, it affirms us and tells us we are valued. This often creates a fundamental shift in the way a couple interacts and feels about each other. This shift has important repercussions throughout the relationship. The majority of couples I've worked with report that many problems spontaneously disappear when they take the time to actively listen and paraphrase to their partner what they hear him or her saying.

This process of communicating may seem awkward at first, but with practice it can easily be incorporated into daily conversation. It is very versatile and works successfully with all types of inter-actions.

"Hello, this is Judy Martin," said the woman on the telephone. "I'd like to speak to Frank Morton, please."

"I'm sorry. Mr. Morton isn't in right now," replied the secre-tary. "Would you like to leave a message?"

"Yes, I would. I wanted to tell Frank that I'll need his report by Tuesday. He doesn't have to call me back. I'll be hard to reach. However, if he has questions, he can reach my voice mail and I'll return the call."

"Let's see, Ms. Martin. You wanted Mr. Morton to know that you need his report by Tuesday. You don't need him to call you back, but if he has a question, he can reach your voice mail. Is that correct?"

"Yes, it is."

With children, this way of communicating is very valuable for two reasons. First, by actively listening and paraphrasing what children say to you, you validate and affirm their efforts to express themselves. As an adult, your attention is important to them. When they hear what they have said repeated, it makes them and their needs important. Second, it will serve as a model to children of basic communication skills they can use throughout their lives.

This direct communication approach disciplines us to communi-cate clearly and to get in touch with our thoughts, needs, and feelings. The more you practice direct communication in your re-lationship, the better you and your partner will be able to address the day-to-day situations that arise. More important, this process may help you and your partner begin to interact in a new, healthier way that will lay a foundation of mutual trust and respect.

If there are major problems in the relationship, you will find them reflected in any communication between you and your partner, no matter how simple. Realize that if you and your partner continually experience problems with circular communication, or become emotionally overreactive about relatively simple issues, there may be deep underlying issues you are not addressing. These issues will contaminate all your efforts to communicate. Before you can improve the situation, you will need to discover what these issues are, where they come from, and then work to resolve them. This requires an understanding of the need to resolve and how to practice a couple's dialogue.

THE NEED TO RESOLVE

It is a common scenario: You have something important to discuss with your partner. You begin by saying, "I want to share these important issues with you." The next thing you know you and your partner are yelling at each other. What is going on?

Something about communicating with this person is bringing up the same overwhelming emotions you experienced with your primary caregivers. Your partner may not be doing it intentionally— it may be just the tone of his/her voice, the look in his/her eye. It may be the way your partner corrects you when you make a mistake. Whatever it is, it sets off exaggerated reactions in you that have nothing to do with your partner, but with your own unfinished business. What's more, the closer your relationship becomes, the more emotional triggers you will encounter.

The need to resolve is a powerful force; it hooks us into a relationship with someone who will cause us to experience emotions from previous adult relationships, other adult experiences (such as work issues), and from our childhood. In fact, the most serious issues are almost always the result of unfinished childhood trauma. The more unresolved issues you have to work through, the stronger your attraction to someone who resembles your primary caregivers in significant ways, and the more often you will find yourself responding to strong emotions that have little to do with the present context.

To deal with these situations successfully, we must be aware that communication takes place on two levels: the practical level and the interpersonal process level. The practical level involves the specific issues couples encounter as they live together on a day-to-day basis. "We need to find reliable child care." "He spends too much time away from me," or "She expects me to give up my hobbies." "Who will prepare the taxes?" It involves our figuring out the who, what, when, where, and how answers to an objective problem. When we discuss practical issues that carry no emotional charge for us, we can talk about them with our partner and reach a straightforward solution based on basic problem-solving skills. Often, however, we have difficulty discussing the practical issues because our emotions get in the way.

Underneath the practical issue is the process level—the ways in which we process our thoughts, feelings, and action urges about an issue. Practical issues are distinct from process issues; each requires entirely different methods of resolution.

For example, if an elderly father has a stroke and requires nursing-home care, there are the practical questions of the type of care he needs, which is the best facility, who will be in charge of administering his affairs, and so on. These are issues to be dealt with on the practical level. How his daughter responds emotionally to her thoughts, feelings, and urges to action about his condition or about the need to find a facility to care for him represents the process level, which is also important. The daughter may be successful in finding her father a good home and taking care of his affairs but have difficulty resolving her feelings, thoughts, and actions about her father's illness. Or she may be able to work through the process level and resolve her feelings about the situation but still have trouble resolving the practical issues at stake. The fact that she has solved the process issues does not help solve practical problems and vice versa.

Levels of Communication
- Practical Level
- Interpersonal Level

Often when we have a strong emotional reaction to a seemingly straightforward situation, it means we have encountered a process-level issue. We may believe we are reacting to the present situation when, in fact, the situation has stirred up unresolved issues. When we try to solve the problem on a practical level, we get nowhere. We must learn to look below the surface to the motivations of our thoughts, feelings, and actions before we can resolve a process-level problem.

"I can't stand it!" Patty told the therapist. "Phil is always cleaning up my things and either throws them away or puts them where I can't find them. He has no respect for me or what's mine. I'm fed up!"

Then it was Phil's turn.

"Patty never cleans up anything. She's a total slob. I ask her and ask her to clean up after herself, put her papers away, help with the kitchen, take care of her clothes. When I get tired of nagging, I do it myself. And I resent that. She's not carrying her weight. Then she gets angry at me because I've done it. This is impossible!"

"You know I can't help it, Phil. My mother was a clutterer. She totally cluttered and messed up the house. We could never get anything clean because she'd never let us throw anything away. Everything was always a mess. I guess I'm no better. I'm sorry, Phil. I'm just a mess."

Thinking about it, Patty realized that one of the qualities that attracted her to Phil was that he was a neatnik. She married his capacity for neatness, hoping that he could organize her on a day-to-day basis. Instead, they ended up in an ongoing struggle. With a therapist, the couple began to negotiate how to live together more peaceably. More importantly, Patty began to confront the issue of her sloppiness and what it was that made her continually reluctant to take responsibility for her share of the housework.

Phil and Patty agreed that she could have one room that would be her own to keep however she wanted; Phil would not attempt to clean it. In the common living areas, however, Patty had to take responsibility for cleaning up her own messes.

At first Patty absolutely hated it. For her, housework was painful. But she was committed to the relationship and honestly understood the fairness of Phil's point of view. As she continued to fulfill her part of the bargain and experience all the resentments and negative emotions, she began to have an idea of what was going on. What she discovered was that in challenging her tendency to let things go she was challenging her deep-seated belief that she couldn't have an orderly, controllable life. Her life had to be a mess because she was a mess, like her mother. With the recognition of that, Patty discovered that the process of cleaning not only became easier, it became enjoyable. She discovered that it was nice to have the kitchen neat. Her clutter tolerance changed, and her willingness to perform housework changed.

The problem confronting Patty and Phil involved the practical issue of each person doing his or her share in the upkeep of the house. Underlying the practical issue, however, was the larger problem of Patty's unresolved feelings about herself and the way she lived her life. Phil couldn't change Patty, but he was responsible for creating the motivational crisis that forced Patty to change. She wanted the marriage to work, and she realized she didn't want to threaten the relationship because she didn't like to do the dishes. She had to be willing to recognize, experience, and work through her emotional reaction until it was finally resolved.

Our thoughts and feelings are closely related, like the two sides of a coin. Any time we have a thought, it generates a feeling, and every time we have a feeling, it generates a thought. Healthy people learn to search for both.

This is what Patty did. She asked herself, "Why is it so painful to keep my things orderly? It is no more trouble to put my clothes in the hamper than on the floor next to the hamper. I have to put them somewhere. Why do I feel at ease throwing them in a corner and so reluctant to throw them in a hamper?" When she discovered the answer to this question, it caused a shift on the process level and she was then more able to address the practical issue of doing her share of the cleanup.

Since we are drawn to our partner because of our need to resolve past issues, we find that interactions with our partner frequently bring up painful, sometimes overwhelming emotions. People lacking good communication skills encounter particular difficulty in these situations. The closer they become to someone, the more they are going to confront painful, unresolved issues. This problem is compounded by the fact that the more intimate they become, the more they automatically begin to reenact the communication skills they learned in their family of origin. Now there is a double problem—because the more dysfunctional the family of origin is, the greater the need to resolve, but the more dysfunctional the family, usually the poorer the communication skills the person has to do so.

To avoid the spontaneous expression of anger and other dysfunctional communication habits, both partners can learn to communicate in a manner that allows them to deal effectively with process issues and the intense emotions generated by them.

THE COUPLE'S DIALOGUE

Steve was thrilled to have his first new car. A few days after he brought it home, he noticed a scratch and a small dent on the driver's side. He took one look and knew immediately what had happened. Joyce was in the habit of loading and unloading groceries from the passenger side of her car, which faced the door on the driver's side of his car.

"She dented and scratched my car," Steve thought. "Why didn't she tell me about it?" Steve felt an intense rage building within him. He wanted to scream. For a minute he had the irrational urge to scratch Joyce's car with his keys, for revenge, but he restrained himself and tried to calm down.

"She deliberately scratched and dented my car door because she doesn't want me to have anything nice," Steve thought to himself. His gut was knotted and he felt he had to do something with his anger. He stormed into the house and confronted Joyce, who was putting files in her briefcase and getting ready to go to work.

"Joyce, you scratched my car and I don't know why you did it!" Steve said, his voice full of accusation and barely contained rage. "I can't stand it when you do things like this. Why didn't you tell me?"

Joyce was shocked and confused. "What do you mean, Steve?" she asked. "I don't know what you're talking about."

"Don't give me that," Steve snarled angrily. "You know you scratched my car, and you know that you're trying to cover it up. My car is ruined and we can't afford to get it fixed."

"What are you talking about?" asked Joyce. She was concerned, but she also needed to get to an important meeting at work.

"You know damned well what happened. When you were getting the groceries out of the car yesterday, you opened the passenger door, slammed it into my car, and dented and scratched the door. Then you didn't have the courtesy to tell me about it."

"Steve, you're overreacting. Calm down!"

"Don't tell me to calm down," Steve screamed. "I have a right to be angry. I have a right to express my anger. And if you can't handle it, that's not my problem."

"Steve, I don't have time to talk now. I've got to get to work. Can we talk about this later? After all it's just a scratch on your car. We can get it fixed and . . ."

"That's just like you," shouted Steve. "Whenever I have something important to talk about you don't have time. You're always ignoring me. My needs don't mean anything to you."

"Steve, you know that's not true. Stop being so childish. I've got to get to work. You know this is a bad time," Joyce said. "I get so angry with you. You always try to talk with me at the worst possible times, and then you accuse me of being selfish when I don't drop everything to accommodate your anger. I'm just not going to listen to this anymore. If your car is more important than I am, you can sleep with your car tonight." Joyce picked up her briefcase, stormed out the door, and slammed it behind her.

All the way to work she fumed at Steve. "How can he be so insensitive? Why do I stay married to him? I don't need this abuse. He accuses me of denting his car and I didn't do it. And he won't even listen to me. What an insensitive louse!"

Steve left the house and got into his car. As he calmed down, an intense sense of guilt and frustration overwhelmed him. "We did it again," he thought. "I knew I couldn't communicate with her. I knew I couldn't resolve this." As he drove to work, Steve felt hopeless, not only about the car but about his marriage.

When Steve discovered his car was damaged, he experienced a strong trigger from his childhood that had little to do with the immediate situation. On the practical level, the new car had been marred. A trip to the body shop and a call to the insurance company would have solved the problem. On the process level, however, the problem was much more important. It had to do with Steve's unfinished feelings at the treatment he suffered as a child. They carried over into his adult relationships, where he felt other people would treat him as poorly as his parents did.

Joyce, too, had a process-level problem that was triggered by this situation. When Joyce was a child she was always blamed for what her brothers did. She had carried her resentment of this treatment into her current relationship.

When Steve and Joyce entered marital counseling, they told their counselor about the argument they'd had about the damaged car door and that it was typical of the circular arguments they always had.

"The focus of the argument may be different," said Steve, "but the outcome is always the same. We just can't get anywhere. We end the argument feeling worse than we did before we began."

The practical issues were different each time, but the process-level issues stayed the same. Until the couple learns how to discuss these process level issues, and work them through, nothing will get better.

Creating Safety: Playing by the Rules

After discovering the dent, Steve confronted Joyce when he was overwhelmed by his emotions and unable to address Joyce rationally. Joyce was completely unprepared for his anger. She immediately felt attacked and on the defensive. Her emotions took over and she felt unjustly blamed, as she had been as a child. Neither was capable of rational communication.

The first priority in working through process issues must be to create a safe environment in which each partner can listen and be heard. This is the goal of the couple's dialogue.*

---

* Communication exercises have traditionally been part of marriage and family counseling. I first learned a four-step procedure in 1969 which consisted of one partner self-disclosing, the second partner paraphrasing, and then both partners reversing their roles. Harvelle Hendrix, author of *Getting the Love You Want,* developed a more elaborate intimate dialogue. This procedure is modified from that.

Making an Appointment

The first step in a couple's dialogue is to make an appointment. In healthy relationships, in-depth communication occurs by contract only, especially if it involves the expression of negative feelings, anger, and criticism. To make an appointment, tell your partner you have something to discuss, briefly explain what the issue is and its relative importance, and then set a mutually convenient time to discuss it. Making an appointment gives both partners an opportunity to clear their schedules so they can devote their time and energy to dealing with the issue.

Keep your statement short. "I want to talk to you about how I feel about the workshop I attended in San Diego yesterday. It's not urgent."

"What I want to talk to you about is the conflict I got into as a result of the argument I had with my best friend. I'm feeling unsettled about it and it's pretty important to me."

"What I want to talk to you about is the negative feelings I had about how you dealt with me yesterday. This is very important."

Then ask, "Is this a good time to discuss it? If not, then when?" When both partners are committed to the process of resolving conflicts, they choose to deal with important issues as soon as possible.

Using the couple's dialogue when Steve saw the scratch, he said to Joyce, "I have something serious to talk to you about. It's important and I'm very upset about it. Is this a good time or can we make an appointment to talk sometime today?"

"Now is not a good time, Steve," Joyce responded. "I'm getting ready for work and I have an important meeting in fifteen minutes. Can it wait until this evening? If not, perhaps we can meet for lunch. Which would be better for you?"

"Well, I guess waiting until this evening would be the best thing," said Steve. "I'll be home by six thirty. Would that be a good time for you?"

"Well, I'm supposed to work late tonight. Seven would be more convenient," said Joyce. "But if it's really important to you, I can get off earlier and meet you at six thirty." Steve and Joyce decided that seven would be fine. Making an appointment gave Steve a chance to think about what he wanted to communicate to Joyce, and gave Joyce a chance to set aside some time so she could listen to what Steve wanted to say.

Prepare to Self-disclose

One of Steve's major mistakes was that he got upset when he saw the scratched car door and did not prepare himself to talk to Joyce. As a result he overreacted.

To communicate effectively, you need to think through what it is you want to say and what you want to accomplish with this communication.

Identify the issue you want to communicate about. Ask yourself: What's going on? What's happening that I want to share with my partner?

Examine your feelings. Ask yourself: How do I feel about this issue? Acknowledge the feelings and validate them. Take a deep breath and affirm what's going on. "I am feeling the urge to overreact right now." Then you decide whether you're going to overreact or not. Adults use their intellect to control their emotion. They choose consciously what they're going to do about their feelings. You can make a choice. Then ask: Are my feelings so intense that I need to ventilate them before I can talk rationally about this issue?

Sort out your thoughts. Ask yourself: What do I think about this issue or problem? Do I have an inner conflict? Am I having an argument with myself about what I want to say or am I clear in my position? I recommend that couples using this technique carry a piece of paper in a wallet or purse. When a strong feeling comes up, take out the piece of paper and use it to write down your thoughts, feelings, and action urges. This will help you clarify your thoughts about the issue so you can eliminate distortions and confusion.

Know what you're doing and what you have an urge to do. Sometimes we do things, nonverbally, that create problems. For example, Steve was so angry when he was talking to Joyce that he looked hostile and his fists were clenched. Joyce responded to this by feeling nervous and fearful and becoming defensive. If Steve had relaxed physically Joyce might have been relaxed enough to hear what he was saying. Steve also wanted to punish Joyce for what he believed she had done. This urge to punish her created the anger and hostility that Steve indicated nonverbally. Whether you consciously acknowledge your urges or not, you will communicate them with your body language.

Sort out your motivations. Ask yourself: What is the current issue and does it warrant the reaction I am having? Often we experience a reaction that is entirely appropriate to the situation. Jeff was angry when the waitress dumped a chocolate milkshake in his lap at the drive-in. His reaction was perfectly understandable. He was angry, but he didn't overreact. Instead, he accepted their offer of a free meal and payment for the cleaning bill.

Other times, particularly in intimate communication with our partner, our reactions may not be appropriate to the situation. If so, some other motivations are probably driving the response. Ask yourself: How is my reaction related to unfinished relationship issues? Has anything like this ever happened to me before in other relationships? Are there any feelings that I didn't express to other partners that I am now attempting to take out on my current partner? Am I bringing home frustrations and anger resulting from what happened to me at work? Have I had any arguments with friends or relatives which might be causing me to respond in this way? Is there some other past, adult experience that is affecting my reactions?

And, finally, is the current situation triggering any unresolved childhood experiences? Since your most serious intimate communication problems will stem from unfinished childhood experiences, it's important to get a clear understanding of the types of issues you're sensitive to. Practicing the couple's dialogue will show you what these issues are. Over time, you will begin to see a pattern to the situations that set you off.

Since Steve had learned the couple's dialogue, he walked out of the house and noticed the dent and scratch on the car. He felt angry but then stopped himself and asked, "What's going on?"

He consciously asked himself, "What am I thinking about this?"

He noticed he was upset because his car was dented and he was blaming his wife for it. He also noticed that he was feeling rage and the immature desire to scratch her car.

He then stopped to examine his feelings and asked himself, "How am I feeling about this?" He noticed very intense anger and a sense of sadness. He then asked himself, "What do I have the urge to do about it?" He noticed an irrational urge to scratch Joyce's car and run into the house and yell at her. The intensity of his reaction gave him clues that he was reacting to something more than just the dent and the scratch on his car. He asked himself, "What are my motivations?"

In sorting out his motivations, he remembered that, when he was a child, he usually received secondhand toys and secondhand clothes. Whenever he got anything new and nice, his older brother would take it and play with it until it broke, then give it back to him. His mother and father never protected Steve from his older brother. Steve's reaction to the scratched door was an echo of the feelings he used to have when his brother broke his toys.

Sorting out his feelings and reactions helped Steve put the situation in perspective.

Preparing to Listen

Listening is a skill that takes time and practice to develop. This is why it is a good idea to practice active listening on a regular basis, even on mundane topics. An effective listener is able to hear what the other person is saying without getting defensive or interrupting with his or her own thoughts. This takes preparation.

Joyce told me that before she learned the couple's dialogue she had a hard time listening to Steve because she felt he was trying to attack her. So, while Steve was talking, instead of listening to what he was saying, Joyce was busy preparing her defense. Consequently, when it was Joyce's turn to talk, she wouldn't respond to what Steve had just said, she would present her defense.

There are several things you can do to prepare yourself to listen to your partner in a couple's dialogue:

Stay calm. Tell yourself, "I don't have to overreact to what is being said. It may have little or nothing to do with me."

Detach yourself from your own needs. Say to yourself, "I am not here to meet my needs right now. I am here to focus on my partner and my partner's needs."

Actively engage your partner. Say to yourself, "It is my job at this moment to listen to, understand, take seriously, and affirm my partner and what he or she is saying."

Joyce now went through a private ritual in her own mind. She thought, "I know Steve has something serious to talk to me about. I'm scared and nervous, but I don't have to overreact to what he says. No matter how bad it is, I can listen to him without getting so angry or hurt that I walk out of the room. I'm not here to meet my own needs right now. No matter what the issue is, Steve and I can resolve it, if I can just listen to him and understand what's going on. For the next few minutes it's going to be my job to be here for Steve. I am here to listen to him, and try to understand what he's saying, and to take his point of view seriously. I don't have to prove I'm right or prove him wrong. If I can see the situation from his frame of reference and affirm his position, we can resolve this issue."

Some people describe this preparation as putting up a psychic shield. Many call it detaching from their partner. Whatever you call it, once you have gone through this preparation, you will be ready to listen.

Self-disclosure

When you are self-disclosing a personal problem, it's important to tell your partner about four things: the issue that you are concerned with, your thoughts and feelings about that issue, the actions you want to take to resolve the issue, and the motivations that are causing you to think, feel, and act that way.

Here's how Steve disclosed the problem to Joyce: "Joyce, I was very upset this morning when I saw a big dent and scratch in my car door you made when you took the groceries out. I couldn't understand how you could be so careless and then not have told me about it.

"I think it was really insensitive and dishonest of you not to tell me. I began to think that you might have done it deliberately. I felt so angry that I wanted to scratch your car, to get even. I even had an urge to yell and scream at you, but I realized that wouldn't have resolved the issue.

"When I stopped to sort things out, I realized that I was reacting to this situation the way I used to react when my brother broke my new toys. When I was a child, I often felt like I could never have anything nice. When I saw the dent in my new car, after only a few days, I felt it had been ruined. I think this whole incident is triggering feelings I have about some things from my childhood that I still haven't resolved."

Notice how complete this communication is. Steve told Joyce exactly what the issue was. He clearly described what he was thinking and feeling. He also described what he wanted to do about it and identified that urge as irrational. And, finally, he acknowledged that some of his feelings stemmed from unfinished childhood business.

Self-disclosing in this manner provides your partner with information relevant to the issue you want to talk about. It also gives your partner an opportunity to listen, without feeling threatened or feeling the need to defend himself or herself. You know that you have a receptive listener.

Active Listening

In the active-listening phase, we listen to our partner, paraphrase in our own words what we heard, and then confirm it with our partner.

While Steve is talking, it's Joyce's job to try to understand what he is saying. As Joyce listens to Steve, she focuses on answering several questions: What is Steven thinking? What is he feeling? What is he telling me he wants to do about this issue? What are Steve's motivations? Is his response consistent with the situation? Are there inconsistencies between the way he is acting and what he is saying? How much of this is related to the actual incident, and how much of it is related to unfinished business stemming from something else?

If at any time Joyce is confused by what Steve is saying, she asks clarifying questions. For example, a typical conversation may go like this.

Steve: "Joyce, I was really upset about what happened this morning. I was angry and thought you did it deliberately."

"Joyce: "Excuse me, Steve, but I don't know what you're talking about. What do you think I did?"

Steve: "There's a dent and scratch on my car that you put there yesterday when you were taking the groceries out of your car. I was angry and upset that you didn't tell me about it. I was so mad that I wanted to scratch your car and yell at you."

Joyce: "What I hear you saying is that there is a dent and a scratch on your car and you think I did it. Is that what you're saying?"

Steve: "That's right."

Joyce: "I also hear you saying that you're very angry with me because of this."

Steve: "That's correct."

Finally, we validate our partner by telling him or her that we understand what he or she is thinking and feeling. In order to do this, we have to get into our partner's frame of reference and see the truth as he or she sees it so that we can understand the situation from their point of view. Hearing our partner's thoughts, feelings, and urges to action gives us the frame of reference that enables us to do this. This is the crux of the couple's dialogue.

Joyce said, "You know, Steve, it makes sense to me that you'd be angry. If I thought you deliberately damaged my car and then lied to me about it, or refused to tell me about it, I'd be angry, too. I understand that you feel this way."

Reversing the Roles

When Steve had finished, Joyce said, "Steve, after listening to you and hearing what you've had to say, I've got something I need to communicate to you. Is this a good time for you to listen to me?"

Steve said, "Yes, it is," and they reversed roles. Each one took a moment to consciously shift gears: Joyce shifted from listener to speaker and prepared to self-disclose; Steve prepared to listen and put up his psychic shield. He was still quite upset about the situation, but he realized his job was to listen, understand, take seriously, and affirm Joyce's point of view. If he could do that, he believed they could work this through.

Joyce: "Steve, what I'm thinking is that I didn't dent your car. I didn't even know it was dented until you told me about it. I didn't even go grocery shopping yesterday, so I didn't open that car door. If I had noticed that your car was scratched or dented, I would have told you about it, but I didn't see it.

"What I'm feeling is anger and hurt that you'd think that I would do such a thing! Why would you have married me if you thought I was a liar? Why would you want to be with me if you thought that I was so immature that I would damage your car and not tell you?

"Steve, I know you had a hard time with your family. I know you've never had anything nice and that this car is very important to you. But I'm not your brother, I am not your mother, I am not your father. I don't act that way.

"What I have an urge to do is just push you away and walk out of here. But I don't want to do that because I understand how you could overreact with this. And I realize that what is motivating this response is that when I was a child, my brothers would always set me up to take the blame for anything that went wrong, and then my parents would punish me for what they did. That's what's getting hooked in me right now. I'm tired of being blamed for what I didn't do. You're doing the same thing that my father did to me, and that's what really upsets me about this. It's not so much the dent in the car, because I could understand how it could look like I dented your car, but boy, I don't feel it's okay the way you're treating me."

Now it's Steve's job to paraphrase what he heard. "What I'm hearing you say is that you didn't dent my car. You think that I judged you unfairly and that there is something wrong with me for assuming you did it, am I right?"

Joyce said, "Yes, Steve, you are." If she had said, "No," Steve would have said, "Well, tell me again; I misunderstood. Explain that to me. I don't understand that.

"What you're feeling is that you're angry and hurt, and you realize that the anger is out of proportion to the situation. What you have the urge to do is to push me away and even end the marriage because you are so angry and disappointed in me. What's motivating your reaction is that you feel blamed and scapegoated just the way you did by your father and brothers in your family. Is this right?"

Joyce replied, "Yes, you got it."

Steve then validated Joyce's frame of reference. "You know, it's making sense to me that you would feel that way because if I were on the receiving end of what I just said to you, I would feel that way, too."

At this point, each partner had the chance to self-disclose about the situation and each had been an active listener for the other. Many times this is enough to allow both partners to see the situation differently and develop a better understanding of their own feelings, thoughts, actions, and motivations and their partner's. Each has had a chance to see the situation from the other's point of view. If so, the couple is ready to bring closure to the dialogue. Other times, the partners will have gained new information, but still hold widely different viewpoints. They may require more turns self-disclosing and listening before they are ready to bring closure.

Closure

Steve began first. "Because of this dialogue, Joyce, I realize that you didn't damage my car. I was overreacting because of some unfinished business left over from when I was a kid. But I would like to request something from you. I'd like you to assure me that if you ever do damage anything of mine, you will tell me about it first because this is a sensitive issue for me." Then Steve asked, "What did you hear me ask for?"

Joyce said, "I heard you request that if I ever break anything of yours, that I tell you about it first."

"Are you willing to do it?"

"Yes, Steve, I am."

Then it is Joyce's turn. "What I'm aware of as a result of this dialogue is that I'm really sensitive to being blamed. I want to request a change in you, Steve. I want you to not blame me for things I didn't do. If you think I did something before you blame me for them, I want you to ask me, did you do this? And if I didn't do it, I don't want to take the rap for that. Now, what did you hear me say?"

"Well, Joyce, I heard you say you want me to stop blaming you and if I think that you did something to me, you want me to ask you if you did it before I accuse you of doing it. Yeah, I agree with that. That sounds reasonable."

Many people think the procedures are difficult. One of my patients told me, "I think I should be able to say what I want, when I want, to my partner. This procedure forces me to think it through first and channel my thoughts and feelings and I don't like it."

My response was, "You don't have to like it, you just have to do it." The truth is that every behavior has consequences. If we dump emotionally charged issues on our partner, without any thought about what we are doing, it will injure the relationship. If we do it over and over again, it will eventually destroy the relationship.

When you begin to practice a procedure such as the couple's dialogue consistently, you may be amazed to see that seemingly irreconcilable problems are solved. This is because most of the time, the surface problem is not the core issue. The core issue is that one or both partners don't feel heard by his or her partner. In the process of truly listening to each other and responding to each other, both partners are heard. The core issue is resolved and the surface problem works out spontaneously.

LEARNING HOW TO VENTILATE

In a perfect world, we would all be masters of our emotions and not overreact to emotionally charged situations. But it is not a perfect world and we are imperfect people. There are times when we overreact and have a need to vent the strong feelings and thoughts that well up inside us before we can begin to talk rationally about them. It is possible to vent your feelings in such a way that you don't traumatize your partner. Again, you do this by following the rules, but different rules, because ventilating your feelings is not communicating.

Again, you prepare your partner by telling him or her what is happening to you. Say simply, "I'm really upset and I have to vent these feelings before I get anywhere. So let me tell you exactly how I feel. This may just be emotional craziness, but I've got to get it out. Would you prepare yourself to listen to this? Take it with a grain of salt because I'm just really upset. Is that okay?"

Your partner then knows to put up a psychic shield and detach from your emotion. Unlike in the couple's dialogue, your partner does not have to focus on understanding or trying to find logic in your words. Your partner's job is to simply receive your words. It is very important that he or she not take your emotions personally and that he or she affirm your feeling that way. "I can understand that you're feeling that way; that's not crazy." Your partner may not understand why you are experiencing those feelings, or agree with them, but he or she acknowledges that given your frame of reference, you are not crazy for thinking or feeling that way.

There will be times when your partner is so angry that he or she will not be willing to sit and hear you out. Your partner may say to you, "No, I'm too upset myself right now to be here for you. I need a time-out." It's important that you honor his or her right to do that.

This ventilating procedure allows you to take responsibility for your actions and the way you choose to express your feelings. Just because you are enraged is not license to victimize your partner. You have an alternative. Warning your partner and giving him or her the choice of whether or not to hear you creates further safety and trust in your relationship. It also helps both of you realize that communication is a separate and very different process from ventilating.

ADDRESSING CONTENT ISSUES:
THE BETTER SOLUTION

The couple's dialogue helps us to express and resolve problems on the process level of our relationship—the interpersonal issues that are difficult to talk about due to the strong emotions they evoke. There are other times, however, when you and your partner need to solve a practical problem: "How do we earn the income we need to buy a house?" "Where can we go on vacation?" "What kind of car should we buy to meet our needs?" These problems require a different process; I call it finding the better solution.

Seven-Step Problem-Solving Process
• Identify the problem
• Clarify the problem
• Identify all the available options
• Project the consequences of each
• Make a decision
• Implement that decision
• Evaluate the decision

Many people misunderstand the idea of compromise. They think that when people compromise, both get less than he or she originally wanted. I want to go to the beach on our vacation and you want to go to the mountains. So we compromise and go to the desert where neither one of us wants to be. That's not a compromise; it's a default. A compromise enables us to discover a solution that is better than either partner's individual options. To do this, I recommend a seven-part procedure.

• Identify the problem. You state simply, "The problem is . . ."

• Clarify the problem, breaking it down into its components. "What is my role in it? What's your role? How do we participate in it together as a couple? What's my thinking on it? What's your thinking on it?"

• Identify all the available options. The goal is to uncover alternatives neither partner could have come up with alone.

• Project the consequences of each alternative, identifying the benefits and disadvantages of each one. What is the best thing that could happen if we did this? What is the worst thing that could happen if we did it? And what is the most likely thing that probably will happen if we do it? Sometimes we find we don't have all the information we need to make a decision. In that case we have to do some research to get that information.

• Make a decision. On the basis of our thinking about the problem and the options we have available, what are we going to do?

• Implement that decision. Put it into action for a trial period.

• Evaluate the decision. What was the result of implementing that alternative? Did it solve the problem? If not, go back to step one and start again, choosing another option.

Connie and Pete had two sons, ages seven and ten. Connie was going back to work full time and the couple needed to figure out how to get their children to and from school and taken care of when not in school.

Connie and Pete sat down with paper and pen, ready to work on the problem. First, they identified the problem in general terms. Pete wrote, "Connie is going back to work and will be gone from 8:30 to 5:30 and will no longer be available to drop the kids off at school or pick them up afterward. How can we get the children to school and taken care of until either parent comes home?" They recognized that both parents were equally responsible for solving the problem; therefore, it was "our problem."

Then they were ready for Step 2. In clarifying the problem, they discovered there were actually several problems.

Problem 1: Getting the kids to school

How are we going to get the kids picked up at home and taken to school now that Connie has to leave at 8:30 and can no longer take them?

Problem 2: Afterschool care

How are we going to get the kids picked up after school and cared for until 5:30?

Problem 3: Sick-day care

Who's going to take care of them when they get sick and both parents are working?

Problem 4: Vacation day care

What arrangement can we make for school holidays when both parents work?

Connie and Pete then went through each of the four problems one by one. They considered the first one: getting the children to school. They considered the alternatives:

Getting kids to school—options

1. Have a neighbor take them to school.
2. Hire a high school child to come to the house when we leave and walk the kids to school.
3. Drop them off at school early and have them wait around until school opens.
4. Have them take the school bus.
5. Have a taxi take them to school.

"All right," said Pete, "what are the benefits and disadvantages of each of these options?" As he and Connie brainstormed together, he wrote the following:

Benefits/Disadvantages of Problem 1 Options:

Getting the children to school

Option 1. Ask Neighbor

Benefits: Children in the care of a responsible, trustworthy person.

Disadvantages: Too much to ask on a day-in and day-out basis. It would strain our friendship with the neighbor.

Option 2. Hire Teenager

Benefits: An easy solution since it would not cost much and there are many high school kids in the neighborhood.

Disadvantages: Not practical in very cold or wet weather; we don't know any teenagers well enough to know who is trustworthy. Since high school starts at the same time as the grammar school, there may not be a high school kid able to do it.

Option 3. Drop Off at School Early

Benefits: It would get the kids to school and allow Connie to get to work on time.

Disadvantages: It would leave the children unsupervised in a public place.

Option 4. School Bus

Benefits: Responsible driver who would pick them up at the bus stop right down the block. The kids can leave the house and walk down to the corner to catch the bus.

Disadvantages: We don't know when the bus leaves; will need to call the school and find out.

Option 5. Taxi

Benefits: Responsible driver who would pick kids up at the door and take them to school.

Disadvantages: Cost is prohibitive.

Pete and Connie looked over their list and saw that having the children take the school bus seemed to be the best option, but they didn't know what the schedule was. Connie made a call to the school and found out it left at 8:25, five minutes before she had to leave. The timing was perfect.

The couple did the same problem solving for each of the problems created as a result of Connie's going back to work.

They then agreed to put their options into practice for a week and evaluate the results at the end of that time. It turned out that the children loved it and all went off without a hitch.

Other times when Pete and Connie tried to use this technique, they found themselves back in a circular argument. Using the couple's dialogue to explore the issues involved, they realized that there were a lot of process-level issues being brought into their problem solving that needed to be resolved before they could address the practical issues. They recognized that the two processes were distinct and learned to use both appropriately.

Any practical issue can be dealt with using this seven-part process. The issue can be basic household tasks. "We both work full time and neither of us likes doing the housework. What are the options?" It can be communication around sexual issues. "I like this particular sexual activity, and you don't. How can we work this out?" It can be around children's friends, "How often and how long should friends be allowed to stay?"

Problem solving is an important part of a healthy relationship. No relationship is problem free. When we are unable to resolve problems, frustration and dissatisfaction result. When we can work productively with our partner to solve the problems that occur, we gain confidence and trust in ourselves and each other.

INTIMACY—A DANGEROUS POTENTIAL

Intimacy, the true sharing of ourselves with another human being, is scary. When we are honest with ourselves and our partner, we will experience a whole range of feelings and thoughts that bring up old issues, old hurts and disappointments, even severe trauma. We may be tempted to push away these feelings and not face them. If we ignore them, we hope, they will go away. But they don't. In fact, they intensify. They flare up and subside, only to flare up again, this time more vehemently.

When we become intimate with our partner, we do so with the expectation that our partner is willing and capable of meeting our needs. One of our primary needs is to be heard and acknowledged. When our partner listens to our communication, affirms our feelings and our point of view, we know we are seen and valued. At times, circumstances and our own unfinished conflicts bring out our worst side. If our partner can listen to and affirm us even at these times, affirming our right to feel even our strongest emotions, we develop a deep sense of safety and trust. It contributes to the cycle of increasing contentment and safety that characterizes healthy relationships.

If you and your partner practice healthy communication, your relationship will get better, but you will have to confront your own growth issues. You will not have the luxury of blindly acting out your own pathology. You will not have the luxury of acting out your family-of-origin issues and then blaming it on somebody else. You'll have to grow up and take responsibility for what you do in your relationships with others.

In its purest form, intimacy is simply the ability to communicate your most important inner experiences to your partner honestly in a safe and supportive environment. Without safety, without the ability to be honest, you cannot have true intimacy.

When you truly love your partner, you are willing to go through the effort to communicate well. Basic communication strategies can clear the way to having profoundly in-depth and beautiful feelings of love and intimacy about your partner.

Self-assessments

Completing the following questionnaire will enable you to become more aware of your present communication skills and those of your partner.

If you are not presently in a relationship, complete the answers on the basis of past relationships. If you have a partner, set up a meeting and compare your answers with your partner's. Whether you complete this exercise alone or with a partner, it can show you which communication skills you feel you practice effectively in your relationship and which tend to create problems for you.

Basic Communication Skills

Do you and your partner have healthy communication skills?
When my partner talks I
    ____**a.** don't really listen.
    ____**b.** listen without responding.
    ____**c.** actively listen and paraphrase what I heard.

When I talk my partner
    ____**a.** doesn't really listen.
    ____**b.** listens without responding.
    ____**c.** actively listens and paraphrases what he/she heard.

When my partner and I talk about important subjects
    ____**a.** we usually get into an argument.
    ____**b.** we sometimes get into an argument over certain issues.
    ____**c.** we usually have a good discussion.

When I talk to my partner
    ____**a.** I always feel heard.
    ____**b.** I sometimes feel heard.
    ____**c.** I never really feel heard.

When my partner talks to me
    ____**a.** I am always able to make him/her feel heard.
    ____**b.** I am sometimes able to make him/her feel heard.
    ____**c.** I don't make my partner feel heard.

Handling Strong Emotions

When I feel a strong emotion about my partner
____a. I usually try to repress it.
____b. I usually overreact.
____c. I am usually able to think it through and discuss it with him/her.

When my partner feels a strong emotion about me
____a. he/she usually hides it from me.
____b. he/she usually overreacts.
____c. he/she is usually able to think it through and discuss it with me.

Problem Solving

When there is a problem
____a. we usually try to ignore it.
____b. we usually solve it.
____c. we usually get into an argument about how to solve it.

When there is a *me* problem
____a. I usually try to solve it alone.
____b. I ask my partner to solve it for me.
____c. I talk it out with my partner and gain his/her support.

When there is a *you* problem
____a. I usually try to solve it for my partner.
____b. my partner usually tries to solve it alone.
____c. my partner talks it out with me and I try to be supportive.

When there is an *us* problem
____a. I usually try to solve it alone.
____b. my partner usually tries to solve it alone.
____c. we both talk it out and try to find a solution.

Chapter 11

RELATIONSHIP TRANSFORMATION: EVALUATION, RENEGOTIATION, AND TERMINATION

PRINCIPAL CHOICES
- To remain true to *me, you,* and *us* in the context of the relationship.
- To consciously identify your rights and expectations within the relationship.
- To monitor changes in your life that may affect your relationship.
- To renegotiate your relationship with your partner honestly and in good faith as your needs or life circumstances change.

Many people feel the ultimate goal in life is to have a healthy, committed relationship. They believe that once they find a compatible partner, their search for happiness will be over.

People who think this way regard relationships as static, unchanging entities. Once we establish a good relationship, it is supposed to stay the same. Unfortunately, a relationship doesn't operate that way. Rather, it is a dynamic process that unfolds between two human beings. This process continually undergoes changes as the individuals involved grow and change.

As healthy partners, we engage in this process to enrich our lives and to experience more than we could without it. The *us* enhances the *me* and the *you* without diminishing or detracting from either. Our life together supports and facilitates our personal goals, both on a day-to-day basis and in the larger context of our lives.

When we enter into a long-term relationship, our commitment takes into account all three relationship components. My first commitment is to *me*, to stay true to myself by getting my own needs met within the context of the relationship. My job is to assertively let my partner know what my needs are, and to teach my partner how he or she can successfully meet them. At first, this may sound selfish, but the rationale is clear. If I do not love *me* in a healthy way, I cannot love *you* in a healthy way. First the self, then the possibility of healthy intimacy.

My second commitment is to *you*, to stay true to my partner by helping him or her meet his/her needs within the context of the relationship. When my partner presents a need, I'm willing to do my level best to see that he or she feels fulfilled in this relationship, as long as it doesn't violate my first responsibility to myself.

My third responsibility is to *us:* to do what is necessary to maintain the relationship itself. This involves spending time together communicating, problem solving, and sharing our lives at each relationship level: as casual acquaintances, companions, friends, and lovers.

To fulfill this three-way responsibility, I must possess the skills required to build and maintain a healthy relationship. Before my needs can be met, I need to know what I am thinking, feeling, have the urge to do, and what is motivating that urge. I need to know who I am and what I want in the relationship and in my life generally. I also have to take responsibility for my sexual drives and preferences. Then I need to have the communication skills necessary to convey this information to my partner. My partner, too, must possess these skills.

My partner and I must share a balance of interdependent personality traits, so that neither is extremely codependent or counterdependent. A codependent abdicates his or her relationship commitment by being extremely other-focused, and failing to honor the needs of *me* and *us*. A counterdependent abdicates his or her relationship commitment by being extremely self-focused and failing to honor the needs of *you* and *us*.

In the long run, how well and how enduring our relationships will be depends on whether we find a quality, compatible partner. The criteria we use to determine compatibility go beyond the immediate here and now to include issues of larger magnitude. What do I want for my life in the long run? Are my partner and I going in the same direction? Do we have compatible goals and values? Do we roughly agree on the priorities we want to assign certain aspects of our lives? Do we enjoy the same life-style? Couples who can answer "Yes" to most or all of these questions tend to create the most enduring relationships.

To answer these questions I need to take the time to identify my primary purpose in life. What do I find meaningful? What role in life gives me a sense of purpose that enhances my identity? It might be a high-powered career as a politician or performing public service work; it might be a life spent in scholarly research or a life based around home and family.

From his earliest years, Bill wanted to go into politics, just as his grandfather had. When he was in college he married Madelyn, a bright, ambitious woman who wanted to become a lawyer. They shared the same outlook on life and both hoped to do well in their career. After college and law school, Bill began to run for local elections. Madelyn found that while she could encourage Bill in his career, she couldn't leave her practice to actively support him in his campaigning. She refused to sacrifice her professional responsibilities to his career. After several years of conflict, they ended their marriage.

Sharon was very different from Madelyn. She wanted to be a politician's wife. She enjoyed campaigning with Bill, enjoyed centering her life around it, enjoyed the duties and all the responsibilities of an elected official's wife. As a result, Bill and Sharon had a fulfilling and satisfying relationship.

People who are able to find their basic life role and then integrate their relationships into the context of that role usually succeed in building healthy, satisfying relationships. Those who do not find such a role tend to have problems in relationships. Such people find partners who are not compatible with who they really are. Their relationships become a constant struggle because their partner expects them to do things that they don't want to do, to be things they aren't, and to act in ways they don't want to act. They cannot be true to themselves, their partner, or the relationship. No matter what their partner does, no matter what their relationship is, they can't feel fulfilled or happy.

THE CONSCIOUS COMMITMENT

Intimate relationships represent an agreement between two people. We agree to think in certain ways, to act in certain ways, to have certain feelings and not others. We want and expect certain things from our partner and from our relationship, and take our partner's commitment to the relationship to mean that he or she will provide them. When the terms of the agreement are kept and our needs, wants, and expectations are met, we perceive the relationship as going well. If not, we feel dissatisfied, even cheated.

Many couples enter into committed relationships without discussing their agreement in concrete terms. They assume their partner understands the relationship as they do. As time goes on, they are surprised to discover this is not true. Many problems can develop when expectations are held but not communicated. The situation is made worse by the fact that many of these expectations are in the form of mandates and injunctions, which the partners unconsciously bring into the relationship as a result of their programming in their family of origin. This situation can exist between partners for years, resulting in increasing frustration and resentment as needs and expectations go unmet.

Partners can overcome this problem by consciously identifying and then discussing these issues with their partner. A good place to start is with a Relationship Bill of Rights.

As human beings, all of us have certain inalienable rights. We have other rights as mature adults within a healthy relationship. Here is a list of these basic rights to get you started. If you like, you can reword the following statements to fit your personal style.

RELATIONSHIP BILL OF RIGHTS

1. I have the right to be treated with dignity and respect.

2. I have the right to be free from psychological or physical abuse.

3. I have the right to proper notice and negotiation prior to the relationship being terminated.

4. I have the right to experience my own thoughts and feelings.

5. I have the right to tell my partner honestly and responsibly what I am thinking and feeling—even if my partner does not agree—without being condemned for it.

6. I have the right to have my own life outside of the relationship.

7. I have the right to continue to learn and grow.

8. I have the right to talk openly about and seek to resolve relationship problems.

9. I have the right to end the relationship if it is not meeting my needs.

10. I recognize that my partner has the same rights I do.

In addition to basic rights, you and your partner should take time to identify those rights that are personally important to you within your relationship. Someone who values his/her independence might say, "I have the right not to be questioned about where I am when I am not with you." Another person might say, "I have the right to keep my correspondence private," or "Over and above my share of what is required for living expenses, I have the right to spend my money in any way I choose."

Your Bill of Rights should detail what you believe you have a right to expect from your partner, what you believe your partner has a right to expect from you, and what each of you has a right to expect from the relationship. You might also want to discuss it with your therapist, who can help you determine if your attitude and orientation toward these rights are realistic.

At the outset of a long-term, committed relationship, it is important to sit down together and go over your list of rights point by point. Ask your partner, "Do you agree that I have these rights?" If there is disagreement, you will need to use the couple's dialogue to explore the issue and come to an agreement.

In some cases one of the rights you claim may not be acceptable to your partner. You then have a choice between defending your right and satisfying your partner. Neal wrote, "I have the right to be as messy as I want to be in my own house." His wife, Jackie, replied, "I agree you have a right to be as messy as you want, but I'm not going to live with that. If you want to be a slob, I'm going to end the relationship." Neal had to decide which was more important to him: his right to do as he pleased or his relationship with Jackie.

A Bill of Rights outlines the general terms and agreements of a relationship, but many of our expectations are more specific. As long as these expectations remain unspoken and unacknowledged, neither of us can take responsibility for meeting them. We may begin to feel dissatisfied but not know what is wrong, what to change, or the alternatives we might choose.

Barbara was devastated when Justin lost his temper and told her, "You never support me in my career. What I do for a living is of no importance to you whatsoever!"

"What do you mean?" said Barbara. "I do everything I can. I never object to your business dinners or out-of-town conferences. You're free to do whatever you need to advance your career."

"But you never come with me! Other people's spouses attend the conferences, but my work is so unimportant to you that you don't even consider it!"

"Justin, I never knew you wanted me to come. I always thought I was doing you a favor by staying home. I thought I was helping you most by allowing you the freedom to take care of your business without worrying about me."

Justin had never verbalized his expectations and as a result had misinterpreted Barbara's actions and intentions.

It is our responsibility to make our expectations known to our partner. This may be difficult for us to do because many times the expectations we hold are unconscious. As children we internalized an idea of what a man or a woman should be, what a wife or a husband does, what a parent is, but never thought to identify these ideas for what they are. Instead, these ideas often lie buried in unconscious mandates and injunctions and cause problems in our relationship without our even realizing it. It is important to examine these expectations and communicate about them with our partner. An excellent exercise to accomplish this is the Partner Job Description.

If you were to advertise for a person to fill the position of your partner, what would you write? If your partner is going to do his/her "job" up to your standards—i.e., be the ideal partner for you

—what does he/she have to do? The questions at the end of this chapter will guide you in writing your own Partner Job Description.

Once both partners have compiled their descriptions, they can discuss their expectations with one another and negotiate an agreement. They can see what is realistic and what is unrealistic in the context of their life together. They can then use their problem-solving skills to reach an agreement on these issues.

Some of the items Justin wrote were, "I expect you to support my career by accompanying me to important conferences and professional dinners; to meet and socialize with my coworkers and their spouses; to occasionally host a dinner party for my colleagues.

"I'm not very neat and clean, so I expect you to run the household and keep the house neat. I also expect you to be intimate with me, to enjoy our sex life, to make love when I want to, at least two or three times a week, and when we have sex I want you to be very committed, very intense, and make those very intense and gratifying experiences. I want you to spend time with me, sharing in my interests and sharing your interests with me."

They sat down and discussed Justin's description point by point. After a period of discussion, Barbara and Justin were able to reach a general agreement on how these aspects of the relationship would be handled.

Then Barbara filled out a job description for Justin and they went through the process again. "Well, I'm not very good at being social, so I expect you to bring in friends and help structure our social life. Since I also work full time, I want you to carry your own weight around the house and share housekeeping responsibilities. I expect you to provide the majority of our income so that I don't have to worry about salary considerations when I take a job."

The exercise was very revealing for both Justin and Barbara for two reasons. They learned for the first time what the other expected of them in concrete terms. More revealing, however, were the discoveries they made about their own expectations of their partner.

"As Barbara and I went through the whole list," said Justin, "it suddenly dawned on me that practically all of my expectations for

Barbara were exactly what my father expected of my mother. I realized that unconsciously I was saying, 'This is what a wife does for a husband.' The wife manages the money; the wife supports the husband's professional responsibilities; the wife takes care of the house. It was simply uncanny."

After you complete your Partner Job Description at the end of this chapter, go back to your answers in the mandate and injunctions self-assessment in chapter 5. How many of your expectations reflect those mandates and injunctions?

Both the Partner Job Description and the Relationship Bill of Rights can serve as effective ways to identify and communicate about our relationship needs. The more open and willing you are to discuss these essential aspects of your partnership, the more likely you and your partner are to successfully fulfill your responsibilities toward *me, you,* and *us.*

RELATIONSHIP AS PROCESS

It is said that no two people ever stay in the same relationship longer than seven years. I agree. Even those who stay together in lifelong monogamous relationships must actually adapt and renegotiate their relationship periodically as each one either enters a new life stage or undergoes significant psychological growth as a result of his or her life experiences. In some cases, it is possible for a couple to change and develop in complementary ways and continue to meet one another's needs, even as those needs change. For many people, however, this is not the case. Census statistics reveal that the average long-term committed relationship today lasts between seven and eleven years. Then people disconnect and move onto another committed relationship with another partner.

Given the complexity of our society and the world today, and the amount of education and psychological growth available, it is understandable that we change and grow. As healthy, proactive individuals we encounter many influences, both internal and external, that contribute to our ongoing development.

One reason for significant change in a person's life may be the undertaking of a program of personal development, whether it is recovery from addictive disorders or entering individual psychotherapy, or another regimen that helps an individual shift from dysfunctional behaviors to a healthier life-style. As a result of reading this book, for example, and working through the self-assessments, you may find that your relationship preferences and needs are undergoing a change. If you had many codependent traits and have worked to embrace your counterdependent shadow traits, you may already be seeing a change in the dynamic of your relationship as you no longer respond to your counterdependent partner in the same way. Or, as you practice the couple's dialogue, your perspective on various issues may change as you confront and resolve past experiences. All these changes in *me* will cause important changes in the relationship. Of course, your partner's personal growth and change will result in important changes in the relationship also.

Another primary reason for renegotiation is personal psychological growth as a result of significant life experiences. This might include the loss of a job or injury in an accident, the birth of a child, the death of a friend or loved one.

A third reason for change is the normal, even predictable development we undergo as we grow older and experience different stages of life. Daniel J. Levinson, in his book *The Seasons of a Man's Life,* divides normal adult development into four life-stages of approximately twenty-five years each: childhood and adolescence (ages 0 to 22); early adulthood (ages 17 to 45); middle adult era (ages 40 to 65); and late adulthood (age 60 until the time of death).

Each of these stages is preceded by a life transition, during which a shift occurs in a person's whole way of thinking about self, other people, and the world. Such periods are a time of rapid and profound internal change. Many people find that their relationships do not survive these transitional periods because one partner changes his/her values and develops a new set of needs and wants to such an extent that the other partner is unwilling or unable to meet them.

This is often seen in relationships between partners of different ages, such as a woman in her late twenties who marries a man in his mid-thirties; it is the woman's first marriage, but the man has been married before and has two children who live with their mother. For several years, this couple's goals and values might be in sync as they both pursue their careers and enjoy their vacations together traveling. As times goes on, however, the woman may want to start a family. Her husband, who has already experienced fatherhood, may be seeking greater independence and a desire to pursue his career more aggressively. If the woman is unwilling to forgo having children and the man is unwilling to be tied down with a family, the conflict in goals may cause the relationship to end.

When the changes are significant enough, they will begin to affect our ability to have our needs met within the context of the relationship. Our values and life goals may no longer be reinforced or supported by our partner or the life-style that we have created. We may begin to feel at odds with our partner, rather than in sync. The relationship will begin to feel constraining or inadequate.

Joni and Kevin built their life around an active social life and many outdoor activities. After their children were born, Joni joined a strict fundamentalist church and became active in church activities. She began to change many of her habits and requested Kevin to follow her example for the sake of the children. Kevin, however, was unable to embrace her religious beliefs. Over time, this shift in personal values caused increasing dissatisfaction in the relationship and Joni and Kevin separated.

Changes affecting the relationship may occur in *me* or *you* as individuals, as in the case of a career move, or in *us,* as in the birth of a child or a significant change in income and life-style. Sometimes these significant changes are sudden. More often, however, these changes occur gradually, an inch at a time, so that we don't notice that we are different, or that we have been slowly changing the rules on our partner. My new job may be taking more of my time, so that I am no longer as available to my partner as I once was. Or, as a parent, I have different expectations of my spouse than I had before we became parents.

It is important to be aware that changes will occur and to have a way of monitoring these changes. One way to do this is to complete a personal inventory on a regular basis, for example, once a year on New Year's Eve. Ask yourself: "How have I changed in the course of the year? How has my spouse changed in the course of the year? What about my close personal friends, my employer," and so on. This will allow you to see the changes more clearly and to anticipate the need for renegotiation. It will enable you to stay current with your relationship so that you and your partner can more easily work together to resolve problems and conflicts as they arise.

An annual inventory can be a time of sharing with your partner and even with children in the family. You can frame it as a story and play the role of storyteller. Together you can reminisce about the past year. "What were the outstanding experiences? What were the good things that happened? What were the bad things? Remember when this happened?" This ritual can become part of the family heritage. You can record it and save the tape of each year as a keepsake.

RELATIONSHIP RENEGOTIATION

When you discover that a fundamental change has occurred—that you have a new need or a change in needs; or find that an essential need is no longer being met—it is important that you realize it and accept the fact that it will influence the relationship. You must take responsibility to discover what is wrong and what needs to be done. Then you need to take that information and communicate it to your partner and discuss it openly.

Often when people confront a major change or difficulty in a committed relationship, they make one of two mistakes. One, they break their commitment too soon. They simply bail out when the relationship starts to get tough. In essence they say, "I'm only committed as long as the relationship is fun and easy. I'm not willing to stay with you through the tough decisions or the hard stages of relationship transforming or periods of unpleasant emotions while we work things through."

Some people leave the relationship prematurely because they assume their partner will be unwilling to make the changes necessary to reestablish a productive partnership. The tendency in troubled relationships is for each partner to blame the other for the problems and see the partner as unwilling to change. This may not be the case. You may find your partner is just as unhappy as you are with the relationship for the same reasons. He or she may be just as anxious to change but view you as resistant or unwilling.

Or, they make the mistake of staying in a relationship when they should leave. They or their partner have changed to such an extent that the relationship fails to meet their basic needs, but they stay on, out of misplaced loyalty or because they feel trapped and unable to get out. Commitments are not unconditional. When the relationship becomes unhealthy or unfulfilling, it is time to renegotiate that relationship, to work out a satisfactory solution, or, if that fails, to end it.

Some couples choose to undergo relationship renegotiation on a regular basis. They evaluate what is working well in the relationship and what needs to be changed. They determine the core issues and use their problem-solving skills to negotiate the necessary adjustments. If you find you need to enter into a renegotiation with your partner, here are some guidelines to keep in mind.

• Take some time to identify what needs to be discussed and worked out. A common problem in renegotiating occurs when the couple is not negotiating the core issues of the conflict. It is rare for couples to confront the issue directly: "Do you want to be connected with me? Do you want to bond with me?" Instead, issues such as time availability, income, or other petty matters get in the way. Using the couple's dialogue to explore motivations can help.

• When you know what you have to say, make an appointment with your partner. Explain that you are going to need to renegotiate the relationship and ask your partner if he or she is willing to do that with you.

• Come to the process in good faith and trust in your partner's good faith. True renegotiation ends with a win-win situation. At the outset, both partners have to assume that together they can come up with a solution that is better than what either currently has or can develop on his or her own.

• Explain to your partner the changes you are going through. Talk about the ways in which you would like your partner to respond or adapt to those changes, addressing each component of the relationship: "This is the new set of needs I have now and this is how I want to restructure my life around the new person that I'm becoming. I want to help you to understand these changes and to be a part of them. I am inviting you to change and grow with me. Out of this, I want us to talk about how we can structure a life together that can accommodate these changes."

• Realize that your partner may also have issues to renegotiate. This is what brings balance to the relationship. When I seek to have my needs met with a partner who actively seeks to get his or her needs met, we are prepared to interact in the type of negotiation that keeps a relationship alive. When one or the other partner abdicates his or her responsibility to be true to self, the relationship becomes unbalanced and suffers as a result.

• Use your communication and dialogue skills to listen to and hear your partner's reaction. It is normal for your partner to feel angry and cheated because you are changing the rules. Change is always difficult. You need to be prepared to listen to, understand, take seriously, and affirm your partner's feelings and emotions but also to hold firm that these are the changes that need to be made because you have changed to the extent that you can no longer be happy with the relationship as it was.

• Don't threaten your partner: "Change or I leave." Relationships cannot thrive on threats. Healthy relationships are about shared power, not control. You need to exercise your compassion and understanding. You need to communicate to your partner that you're willing to try and work it through.

• Be warned: when you undergo a fundamental renegotiation, there is never any guarantee of the outcome. When you begin the renegotiation process, one of two things will happen. You will either successfully develop a new relationship based upon a different set of rights and expectations or the relationship will end.

DISCONNECTING

No matter how just the cause, no matter how hard you fight, sometimes the dragon wins.

Many people want to find a lifelong relationship, and that is an admirable goal. It is important to realize, however, that not all relationships can survive. Even healthy partners who have had a good relationship together for many years may find they need to disconnect. They may have fit very well together in one stage of their life and personal development, but as they've grown, they can no longer comfortably or meaningfully connect with one another.

If it becomes apparent that your partner cannot or will not change in the ways that you desire, or vice versa, you will need to end the relationship and disconnect from your partner. Ending a committed relationship, especially a long-term relationship, is a complex process. I strongly recommend that couples seek marital counseling for help in terminating their relationship, whether they are actually married or not. Many people say this is an expensive proposition, but the time, energy, and money that you will save in the long run make counseling a worthwhile investment.

The primary goal for both partners at this time should be to end the relationship in a way that affords both partners dignity and respect. You don't have to be angry or enraged to end a relationship. You don't have to hurt or damage your partner. It is possible to disconnect with love, if you can recognize that this separation is in the best interest of both because either you or your partner can no longer be true to yourselves: you can no longer be what your partner needs you to be and your partner can no longer be what you need him or her to be. The relationship can no longer be what you both need it to be. It is time to end it and move on to the next.

Many people believe that they have failed if their relationship ends. Ending a relationship is sad and painful, but it is not bad or wrong. You have been taught to believe that the only healthy relationship is a lifelong marriage, and that any relationship that falls short of that is wrong. That is not true. In today's society, with so much growth and change available in people's lives, we need to judge ourselves by a different yardstick. Today people are choosing to engage in healthy, productive relationships and to end unhealthy and unsatisfactory relationships. We expect more of ourselves and our partners; we seek more in our relationships. As healthy choice makers, we refuse to be trapped in relationships that can't meet the needs of *me, you,* and *us.*

When we have connected with someone in a genuine and meaningful way, we have created something for ourselves that retains its value no matter what happens afterward. If you and your partner have shared such experiences, they are no less valuable because the relationship later ended. Take some time to appreciate your relationship for what it was, what it gave you, and what you learned from it, even while you recognize the necessity of moving on.

IN THE END...

There is no one way to get love right. You must discover your own way on the basis of your own self-knowledge. Some people find a lifelong companion early in their lives and that one relationship lasts their entire life. Other people are happy to live their lives enjoying a series of shorter relationships and never building one major committed relationship. Still others have a series of relationships, each of which enriches them and allows them to grow in unique and positive ways, until they are ready to make a lasting commitment in a lifelong relationship.

The majority of people find that their first committed relationships do not last for the rest of their lives. This is not surprising if we consider that, in many ways, our relationships are assignments to help us grow and develop. We invite a particular relationship into our life at a given time to help us identify and move beyond certain personal growth and development issues. When we stay long enough and remain open enough to learn those lessons of personal growth and development, we move on as a better person to a healthier relationship in the future.

When we heed the lessons, we grow and become more worthy of healthy intimacy. When we are honest about our relationship needs, and make our commitments to our partner consciously, we can realize the potential that relationship holds for us. We can enrich our life and the life of our partner.

If we want to build a lasting worthwhile relationship, we need to practice healthy intimacy. This means beginning by working on ourselves and recognizing how our early life experiences affect our relationships. It means taking the time to select a healthy, compatible partner, and working together to build a relationship on a foundation of communication, caring, and commitment. It means accepting the challenge to remain true to the *me, you,* and *us,* and working with our partner to confront the problems and understand the changes in our relationship.

Self-assessments

I. Relationship Bill of Rights

Look over the following Bill of Rights. Which rights are operating in your present relationship (if you are currently in a relationship)? Which were operating in your last relationship? Do you agree that you have each of these rights? Do you agree that your partner has each of these rights?

1. I have the right to be treated with dignity and respect.

2. I have the right to be free from psychological or physical abuse.

3. I have the right to proper notice and negotiation prior to the relationship being terminated.

4. I have the right to experience my own thoughts and feelings.

5. I have the right to tell my partner honestly and responsibly what I am thinking and feeling, even if my partner does not agree, without being condemned for it.

6. I have the right to have my own life outside of the relationship.

7. I have the right to continue to learn and grow.

8. I have the right to openly talk about and seek to resolve relationship problems.

9. I have the right to end the relationship if it is not meeting my needs.

10. I recognize that my partner has the same rights I do.

Besides the ten basic rights listed above, what rights are important to you in your current relationship, or have been important to you in past relationships? Write the five personal rights that you want to establish in your relationship. (e.g., "I have the right to travel up to ten days out of every month on business.")

II. My Personal Bill of Rights
11.

12.

13.

14.

15.

Partner Job Description

Imagine you are writing a job description for your partner. Answer the following questions.

1. What general duties and responsibilities do you expect your partner to fulfill?

2. What are your partner's responsibilities in terms of superficial communication in casual contact?

3. What do you expect of your partner at the companionship level in terms of planning and executing a social life, sharing enjoyable activities?

4. What do you expect of your partner at the friendship level in terms of trust and loyalty, in respecting your feelings, and taking an interest in you as a person?

5. What do you expect of him/her at the romantic level in terms of keeping the romance alive, physical affection and sensuality, sexuality, seduction?

6. What do you expect of your partner in terms of family, children, parenting?

7. What do you expect of your partner in terms of routine home maintenance, money management, housekeeping?
Other:

Personal Inventory

As you conduct your annual personal inventory to identify the major changes and transitions in your life, ask yourself the following questions. Don't be afraid to identify other questions you feel are important.

In the past year,

1. how have I changed as a person?
2. what positive growth experiences have I had?
3. what negative experiences or adversities have I gone through that have tested me?
4. what types of negative changes have I gone through?
5. what has happened in my life that I'm not pleased with or happy about?
6. Basically, what are the milestones of the last year?

When you have completed these answers for yourself, answer the above questions for each of the following people: partner, boss, children, close friends, coworkers, other family, other significant people.

A FINAL WORD

Getting love right is not a matter of luck or chance. It's a matter of choice. We can choose to learn the skills and information we need to bring about the consequences we want, or we can choose to accept less than we want and less than we could have.

We all make choices in our lives on a daily basis. We may not realize it, however, because these choices are too often unconscious and passive. We choose to accept the legacy of a dysfunctional upbringing and the confused understanding of intimacy we learned from our parents. We may choose to be victims of our emotions and sexual drives; and we may choose to remain trapped by self-defeating relationship styles and behaviors, even though these styles and behaviors don't get us what we want.

Getting love right is deciding to become a conscious choice maker capable of building intimate, fulfilling relationships that meet your needs. It is choosing to become a person capable of loving yourself and knowing that you are worthy of the love of others. If you are from a dysfunctional family or have had relationship problems in the past, you can choose to live in the problem or make the changes you need to find the solution.

Getting love right goes beyond here-and-now relationships to the larger choice to take charge of ourselves and our lives, to be responsible for who we are, what we do, and the consequences of our actions. Healthy intimate relationships are an important part of this growth process.

It is said that until we confront ourselves in the minds and hearts of our fellows, we cannot be free. Through healthy, intimate relationships we can choose to confront ourselves through our partner and discover the strengths that we have that are truly lovable and worthwhile; we can learn that we have a right to be here, that we are really enough. And we can discover the ability and capacity within ourselves to stretch in ways we never believed we could, to challenge the injunctions from our childhood that say *don't think, don't feel, don't be, don't do, don't succeed.* In a healthy relationship, our partner is going to make us stretch, saying, "You can do it. Just because you're scared, do it anyway. You've got it in you to resolve the unfinished, painful issues of the past, get free of them, and move on."

When we think back to the myth of the perfect partner, that impossible someone who can make us feel whole and complete once and for all, we realize the imperfect reality goes one step further. Our real-life, fallible partner will challenge us to grow and reach beyond where we are now, to fulfill a greater potential. In the end, we will be more than we were when we entered the relationship.

We can choose to become a worthy partner and then to strive to continue our growth and development, just as we can support our partner as he or she continues to grow and develop. This is possible in a quality relationship. Healthy change is possible. You don't have to do it alone, but no one can do it for you. Only you can make the commitment to change and then follow through on that commitment.

In this book I have given you the essential tools to become a healthy choice maker. This information is based on my many years of professional training and experience. I have given you information to understand how your early experiences in your family of origin have affected your adult relationships, and information on how to find a healthy partner and to go about building a relationship; I have shown you how to communicate and problem-solve in that relationship and, finally, how to renegotiate the relationship and weather the changes all long-term relationships experience. In short, I have taught you what you should have learned in your family of origin but probably never did.

I know this information has helped many people achieve healthier relationships, but only you can decide what is right for you. After you read this book and work through the self-assessments, I suggest that you talk them over with your partner. Share them with your support group or therapist. Think about the ideas and information here and how they fit into your life. Don't accept them whole. It is your job—and no one else's—to choose the information that can effect the changes you want in your life.

CRISIS IN INTIMACY

Many people ask me, "Why be concerned about intimacy? Aren't we done with 'the me-first generation'? Isn't this being kind of selfish? Let's get down to some more important issues."

I reply, "What can be more important than trying to figure out how to live successfully with other human beings? How to treat other human beings in such a way that we can live and grow and prosper together?"

The basic foundation for the transmission of human values occurs in the intimate relationship. It occurs in the close, day-to-day living relationship of two adults with an infant who develops according to his or her learning and environment throughout childhood and adolescence. When his or her parents lack a practical knowledge of healthy intimacy, the cycle of dysfunctional families continues, generation after generation.

This is the present situation in our country today—a crisis in intimacy. The fundamental ways in which our society fosters its families and communities don't work to promote essential human values that enhance its citizens rather than diminish them.

There is hope. I believe that the personal growth and healthy development of thousands, even hundreds of thousands, of people herald a new revolution in this country. Family by family, we can begin to live and transmit healthy values that can end the crisis in intimacy. Through our growth and change, we can choose to break the cycle of dysfunctional families, and learn healthier ways to live together. Perhaps one day it will be the exception to come from a dysfunctional family, instead of the other way around.

It all begins with you. You can choose to become a healthy choice maker. First the self; then the possibility of intimacy. The possibility of getting love right.

BIBLIOGRAPHY

Ackerman, R. J. *Children of Alcoholics*. New York: Simon & Schuster, 2d ed., 1987.

Ackerman, R. J. *Children of Alcoholics: A Guide for Parents, Educators, and Therapists*. New York: Simon & Schuster, 2d ed., 1983.

Ackerman, R. J. *Growing in the Shadow*. Pompano Beach, FL: Health Communications, Inc., 1986.

Ackerman, R. J. *Let Go and Grow*. Pompano Beach, FL: Health Communications, Inc., 1987.

Ackerman, R. J. *Same House, Different Homes*. Pompano Beach, FL: Health Communications, Inc., 1987.

Augustine Fellowship, The. *Sex and Love Addicts Anonymous*. Boston: Fellowship-Wide Services, Inc., 1986.

Bader, Ellyn and Peter T. Pearson. *In Quest of the Mythical Mate: A Developmental Approach to Diagnosis and Treatment in Couples Therapy*. New York: Brunner/Mazel, Inc., 1988.

Black, Claudia. *Double Duty*. New York: Ballantine Books, 1990.

Black, Claudia. *It Will Never Happen to Me*. Denver: M.A.C., 1982.

Black, Claudia. *My Dad Loves Me, My Dad Has a Disease*. Denver: M.A.C., 1979.

Black, Claudia. *Repeat After Me*. Denver: M.A.C., 1985.

Booth, L. *Meditations for Compulsive People*. Pompano Beach, FL: Health Communications, Inc., 1987.

Bowden, Julie and Herbert Gravitz. *Genesis: Spirituality in Recovery from Childhood Traumas*. Pompano Beach, FL: Health Communications, Inc., 1988.

Bradshaw, John E. *Bradshaw on the Family: A Revolutionary Way of Self-*

Discovery. Deerfield Beach, FL: Health Communications, Inc., 1988.

Bradshaw, John E. *Healing the Shame that Binds You.* Deerfield Beach, FL: Health Communications, Inc., 1988.

Bradshaw, John E. *Homecoming: Reclaiming and Championing your Inner Child.* New York: Bantam, 1990.

Brown, S. *Treating Adult Children of Alcoholics: A Developmental Perspective.* New York: John Wiley & Sons, Inc., 1988.

Carnes, P. *Out of the Shadows: Treating Sexual Addiction.* Comp-Care Publications, 1987.

Castine, J. *Recovery from Rescuing.* Deerfield Beach, FL: Health Communications, Inc., 1989.

Cermak, T. *A Time to Heal.* Los Angeles: Jeremy P. Tarcher, Inc., 1988.

Cermak, T. *Diagnosing and Treating Co-Dependence: A Guide for Professionals Who Work with Chemical Dependents, Their Spouses and Children.* Minneapolis: Johnson Institute Books, 1986.

Changes (bimonthly magazine devoted to ACOA issues). Health Communications, Inc., Enterprise Center, 3201, S.W. 15th Street, Deerfield Beach, FL 33442.

Clarke, J. I. *Self-Esteem: A Family Affair.* New York: Harper & Row, 1978.

Cowan, Connell and M. Kinder. *Smart Women—Foolish Choices.* New York: Clarkson N. Potter, Inc., 1985.

Curran, Dolores. *Traits of a Healthy Family.* Minneapolis: Winston Press, 1983.

Dowling, C. *The Cinderella Complex.* New York: Summit Books, 1981.

Ellis, D. *Growing Up Stoned.* Pompano Beach, FL: Health Communications, Inc., 1987.

Forward, S. *Men Who Hate Women and the Women Who Love Them.* New York: Bantam, 1986.

Fossum, M. A. and M. J. Mason. *Facing Shame: Families in Recovery.* New York: W. W. Norton and Co., 1986.

Friedman, E. *Generation to Generation.* New York: Guilford Press, 1985.

Friedman, E. *Men Are Just Desserts.* New York: Warner Books, Inc., 1983.

Glenn, H. Stephen and Jane Nelson. *Raising Children for Success: Blueprints and Building Blocks for Developing Capable People.* Fair Oaks, CA: Sunrise Press, 1987.

Gordon, Sol. *Why Love Is Not Enough.* Boston: Bob Adams, Inc., 1988.

Gravitz, H. L. *Handbook for Children of Alcoholics.* South Laguna, CA: The National Association for Children of Alcoholics, 1985.

Gravitz, H. L. and J. Bowden. *Guide to Recovery: A Book for Adult Children of Alcoholics.* Holmes Beach, FL: Learning Publications, 1985.

Halas, C. and R. Matteson. *I've Done So Well—Why Do I Feel So Bad?* New York: Macmillan Publishing Co., Inc., 1978.

Kritsberg, W. *The Adult Children of Alcoholics Syndrome: From Discovery to Recovery.* Pompano Beach, FL: Health Communications, Inc., 1985.

Larson, E. *Stage II Relationships: Love Beyond Addiction.* New York: Harper & Row, 1987.

Lee, J. *The Flying Boy: Healing the Wounded Man.* Deerfield Beach, FL: Health Communications, Inc., 1989.

Leman, K. *The Pleasers: Women Who Can't Say No—And The Men Who Control Them.* New York: Dell Publishing, 1987.

Lerner, H. G. *The Dance of Anger: A Woman's Guide to Changing the Patterns of Intimate Relationships.* New York: Harper & Row, 1985.

Lerner, R. *Daily Affirmations.* Pompano Beach, FL: Health Communications, Inc., 1985.

Lewis, D. and C. Williams. *Providing Care for Children of Alcoholics.* Pompano Beach, FL: Health Communications, Inc., 1986.

McGill, Michael E. *The McGill Report on Male Intimacy.* New York: Holt, Rinehart and Winston, 1985.

Mellody, Pia, Andrea Wells Miller, and J. Keith Miller. *Facing Codependence.* New York: Harper & Row, 1989.

Miller, A. *The Drama of the Gifted Child.* New York: New American Library, 1983.

Miller, A. *Thou Shalt Not Be Aware: Society's Betrayal of the Child.* New York: New American Library, 1984.

Naireh, S. and G. Smith. *Why Can't Men Open Up?* New York: Warner Books, 1983.

Norwood, R. *Women Who Love Too Much.* New York: Simon & Schuster, 1985.

Peck, M. S. *The Road Less Traveled.* New York: Simon & Schuster, 1978.

Peele, Stanton and Archie Brodsky. *Love and Addiction.* New York: Signet Books, 1975.

Satir, V. *Peoplemaking.* Palo Alto, CA: Science & Behavior Books, Inc., 1972.

Schaef, Anne Wilson. *Codependence: Misunderstood—Mistreated.* Minneapolis: Winston Press, Inc., 1986.

Schaeffer, B. *Is It Love or Is It Addiction?* Center City, MN: Hazelden, 1987.

Smith, A. *Grandchildren of Alcoholics.* Pompano Beach, FL: Health Communications, Inc., 1988.

Solomon, Robert C. *Love: Emotion, Myth & Metaphor.* Buffalo, NY: Prometheus Books, 1990.

Subby, R. *Lost in the Shuffle: The Co-Dependent Reality.* Pompano Beach, FL: Health Communications, Inc., 1987.

Tiebout, Harry M. *The Ego Factors in Surrender in Alcoholism.* New Brunswick, NJ: Hazelden, 1954. Reprint (vol. 15, pp. 610–621).

Twerski, A. J. *Like Yourself and Others Will, Too.* New York: Prentice Hall, 1978.

Wegscheider, S. *Another Chance: Hope and Health for the Alcoholic Family.* Palo Alto, CA: Science and Behavior Books, 1980.

Wegscheider, S. *Choice-Making for Co-Dependents, Adult Children and Spirituality Seekers.* Pompano Beach, FL: Health Communications, Inc., 1985.

Whitfield, C. *Healing the Child Within.* Pompano Beach, FL: Health Communications, Inc., 1987.

Woititz, J. *Adult Children of Alcoholics.* Pompano Beach, FL: Health Communications, Inc., 1983.

Woititz, J. *Home Away From Home: Adult Children in the Workplace.* Pompano Beach, FL: Health Communications, Inc., 1987.

Woititz, J. *Struggle for Intimacy.* Pompano Beach, FL: Health Communications, Inc., 1985.

INDEX